An Introduction to the Microsoft Bot Framework

*Create Facebook and Skype™ Chatbots
using Microsoft Visual Studio and C#*

(This book covers the Microsoft Bot Framework Preview Edition)

Michael Washington

An Introduction to the Microsoft Bot Framework

Create Facebook and Skype Chatbots using Microsoft Visual Studio and C#

(This book covers the Microsoft Bot Framework Preview Edition)

Copyright 2016
Published By
The Ai Help Website
http://AiHelpWebsite.com

Copyright

Copyright © 2016 by Michael Washington

Cover and internal design © Michael Washington

Editing by Andrea Dickinson (www.QualityBookServices.com)

All rights reserved. No part of this book may be reproduced in any form or by any electronic or mechanical means including information storage and retrieval systems – except in the case of brief quotations in articles or reviews – without the permission in writing from its publisher, AiHelpWebsite.com.

All brand names and product names used in this book are trademarks, registered trademarks, or trade names of their respective holders. We are not associated with any product or vendor in this book.

Microsoft Visual Studio is a registered trademark of Microsoft Corporation.

Skype is a registered trademark of Microsoft Corporation.

Facebook is a registered trademark of Facebook Inc.

Table of Contents

Copyright 3

Table of Contents 4

Dedication 7

    Michael Washington 7

Thank You 8

    Microsoft 8

    Community 8

Preface 9

    Requirements 9

Chapter 1: Understanding the Microsoft Bot Framework 10

    What Is the Microsoft Bot Framework? 10

Chapter 2: Create a Hello World! Bot 13

    Creating A Hello World! Bot 13

    Using The Bot Emulator 17

    Saving User Data 18

    Publishing The Bot 23

    Registering The Bot With The Microsoft Bot Framework Developer Portal ...28

Chapter 3: Using FormFlow 34

    A Walk Through 35

    Creating The Project 37

    Test The Application 43

    Saving The Data 45

Chapter 4: Using Dialogs 50

    Walk Through 51

    Creating The Application 52

    Test The Application 61

    Dialog Prompts 63

Chapter 5: Using Images, Cards, Carousels, and Buttons 69

    Hero Card 71

    Carousel 78

    Rich Card Attachments In Dialogs 82

    Create The Hero Card In The Dialog Class 86

    Creating A Re-Usable Hero Card 90

Chapter 6: Implementing A SQL Server Database With Your Bot 95

    Create The SQL Server Database 96

    Create An ADO.NET Entity Data Model 106

    Log To The Database 113

    Log Messages In The Dialog Class 116

    Test The Database Logging Code 118

    View The Data 121

    Logging High Scores 123

    Update ADO.NET Entity Data Model 126

    Alter Code To Log High Scores 128

    Display The High Scores 130

    Test The Code 133

    Publishing A Microsoft Bot Framework Application That Uses a Database .. 134

Chapter 7: Implementing Language Understanding Intelligent Service (LUIS) . 145

    Create The LUIS Application 147

    Update The Bot Application 156

    Implement High Scores 165

Chapter 8: Calling The Microsoft Bot Framework Using The Direct Line API.170
    Configuring The Direct Line Connector 174
    Create The Web Application 178
    Complete The Web Application 187
    Run The Application 193

Chapter 9: Using Application Insights To Monitor Your Bot 198
    Enable Application Insights 201
    Debug The Application 206
    Using The Bot Emulator 207
    Custom Telemetry 215
    Application Insights API summary 217
    Application Insights Portal 221
    Monitoring A Published Application 223

Chapter 10: Creating a Skype Bot 226
    Publishing The Bot 228
    Registering The Bot With The Bot Connector 233
    Configure Skype 240

Chapter 11: Creating A Facebook Messenger Bot 243
    Set-Up Facebook 245
    Create A Facebook Developer Account 247
    Create A Facebook App 248
    Get Page Token 253
    Configure The Callback URL and Verify Token 254
    Configure The Microsoft Bot Connector 259
    Talking To Your Bot 260

About The Author...265

Dedication

<u>Michael Washington</u>

As always, for Valerie and Zachary

Thank You

Microsoft

Dan Driscoll

Jim Lewallen

Simon Michael

Anna Roth

Rebecca Duffy

Daniel Egan

Community

Ezequiel Jadib

Joe Mayo

Robin Osborne

Gary Pretty

Mahesh Chand

Johnathan Lightfoot

Preface

Requirements

You must have a computer running Microsoft Windows with **Microsoft Visual Studio 2015** (or higher) with **Update 3** (or higher) to create the applications described in this book.

You can download the free **Visual Studio Community Edition** from https://www.visualstudio.com/vs/community/

You will also need to download and install the **Visual Studio 2015 Bot** template from http://aka.ms/bf-bc-vstemplate

Chapter 1: Understanding the Microsoft Bot Framework

This book covers using **Visual Studio 2015** to create **Chatbots** using the **Microsoft Bot Framework**. The purpose of this book is to demonstrate, provide examples of, and to explain important concepts of the technology.

What Is the Microsoft Bot Framework?

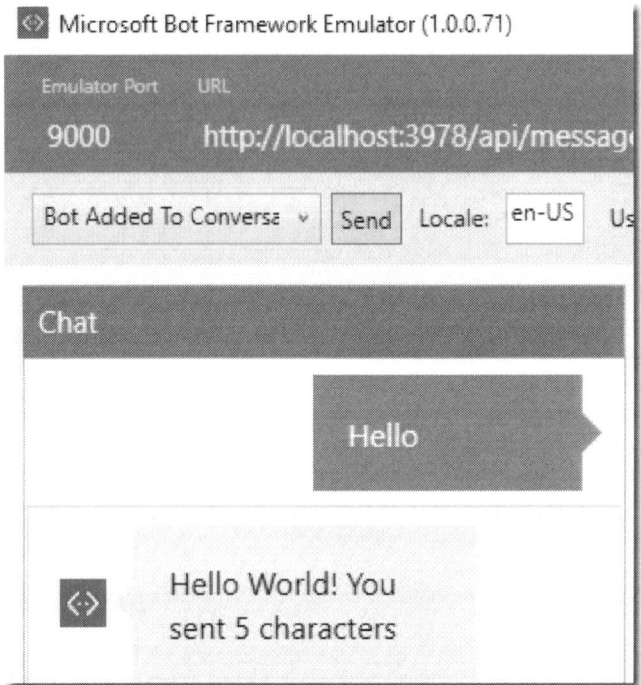

The **Microsoft Bot Framework** allows you to easily create **Bots**.

An Introduction to the Microsoft Bot Framework

You can create bots that interact with your users naturally wherever they are, including **Facebook**, **text**, **Skype**, **Office 365 email**, and other popular services.

An Introduction to the Microsoft Bot Framework

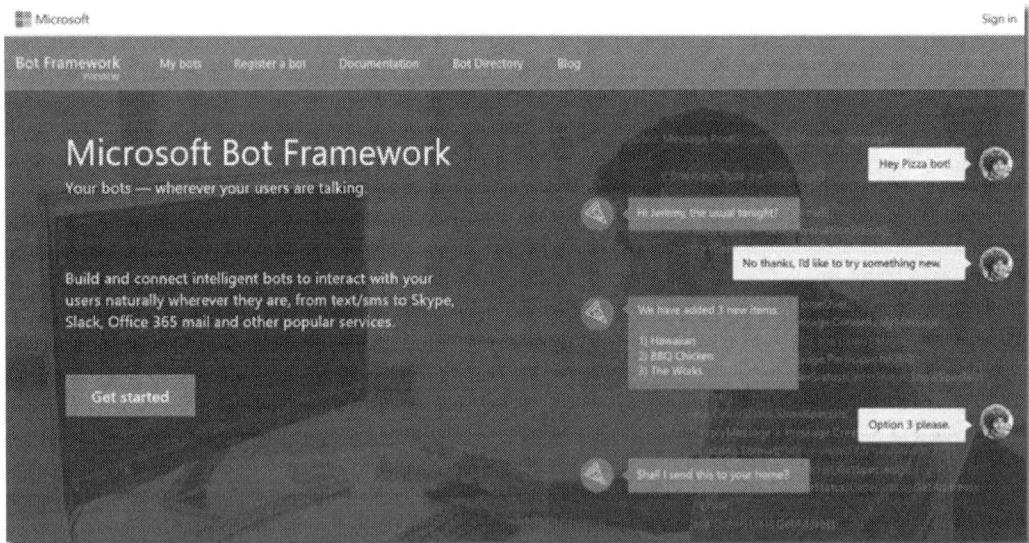

The **Microsoft Bot Framework** contains the following components:

- **Bot Framework Developer Portal** – A service that connects your Bot to communication channels such as Facebook, Skype, and email.
- **Bot Builder SDK** – A C# and Node.js library that provides a powerful framework for constructing bots that can handle freeform and guided interactions.
- **Bot Directory** – A directory of Bots that you can connect to.

The **Bot Framework Developer Portal** helps you connect your **Bot** to communication channels. You can write a **Bot** and expose the **Microsoft Bot Framework**-compatible API on the Internet. The **Bot Framework Developer Portal** will forward messages to users, and will send the user messages back to your **Bot**.

The **Bot Builder SDK** is an open source SDK *hosted on GitHub* (https://github.com/Microsoft/BotBuilder-Samples) that provides everything you need to build dialogs. Bot developers at Microsoft created this library to encapsulate functionality required for conversational bots.

The **Bot Directory** (located at https://bots.botframework.com/) features **Bots** that you can communicate with through channels exposed through the **Bot Connector**.

12

Chapter 2: Create a Hello World! Bot

The sample code for this chapter can be obtained at the link "Creating a Hello World! Bot Using The Microsoft Bot Framework" at http://AiHelpWebsite.com/Downloads

The purpose of this chapter is to demonstrate how to get started using the **Microsoft Bot Framework**, how to create a simple **Bot**, and how to publish it to the **Microsoft Bot Framework Developer Portal**.

Creating A Hello World! Bot

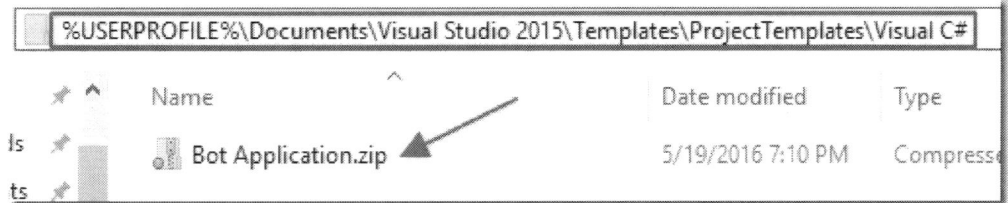

Download the **Visual Studio 2015** template from http://aka.ms/bf-bc-vstemplate

Save the **.zip** file in the templates directory of your windows computer located at %USERPROFILE%\Documents\Visual Studio 2015\Templates\ProjectTemplates\Visual C#

This creates a template that you can use in **Visual Studio** to create **Bot** projects.

Open **Visual Studio**.

An Introduction to the Microsoft Bot Framework

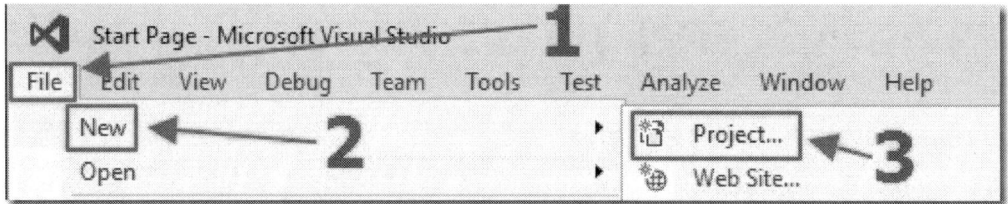

Create a new **Project**.

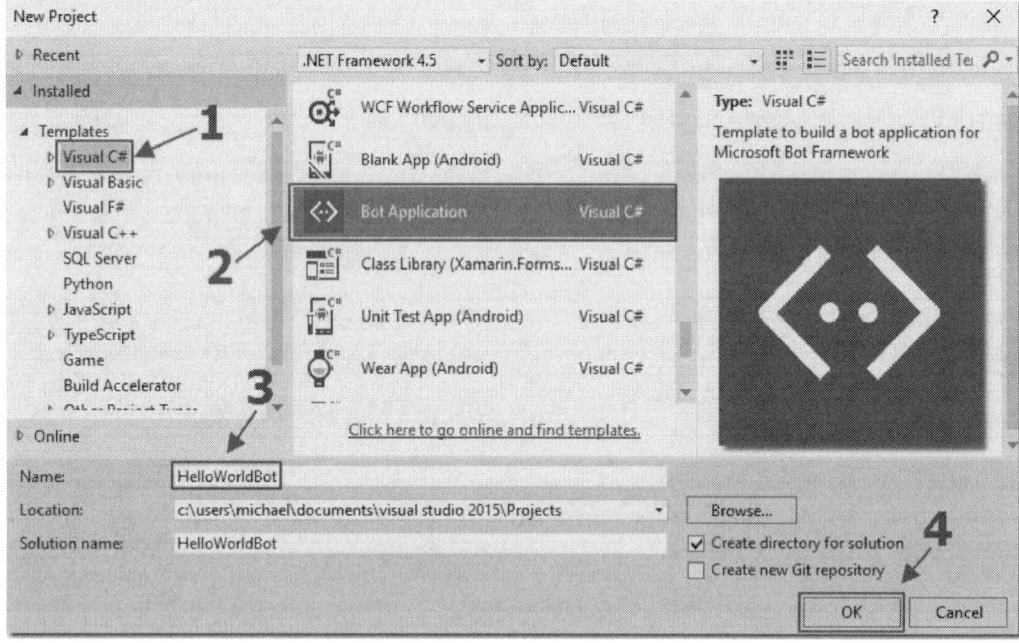

Select the **Bot Application** template and name the project **HelloWorldBot**.

An Introduction to the Microsoft Bot Framework

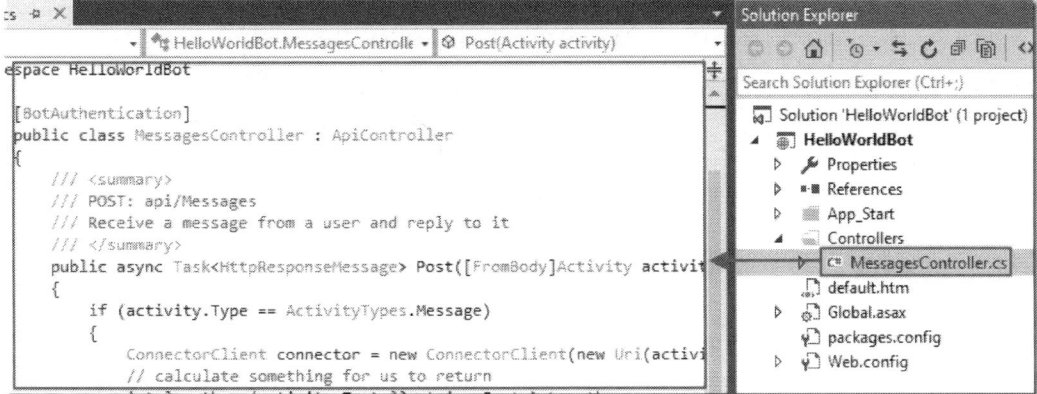

Open the **MessagesController.cs** file in the **Controllers** folder.

Change the **Post** method to the following:

```csharp
public async Task<HttpResponseMessage> Post([FromBody]Activity activity)
{
    if (activity.Type == ActivityTypes.Message)
    {
        ConnectorClient connector = new ConnectorClient(new Uri(activity.ServiceUrl));
        // calculate something for us to return
        int length = (activity.Text ?? string.Empty).Length;
        // return our reply to the user
        Activity reply = activity.CreateReply($"Hello World! You sent {length} characters");
        await connector.Conversations.ReplyToActivityAsync(reply);
    }
    else
    {
        HandleSystemMessage(activity);
    }
    var response = Request.CreateResponse(HttpStatusCode.OK);
    return response;
}
```

An Introduction to the Microsoft Bot Framework

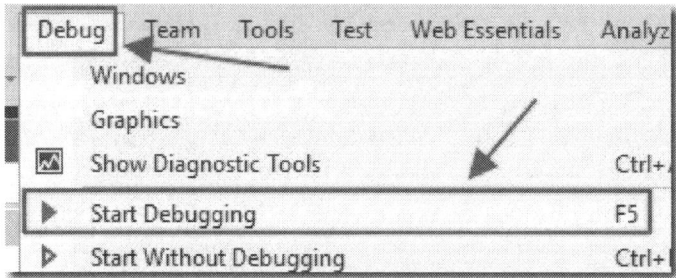

Hit **F5** to run the project.

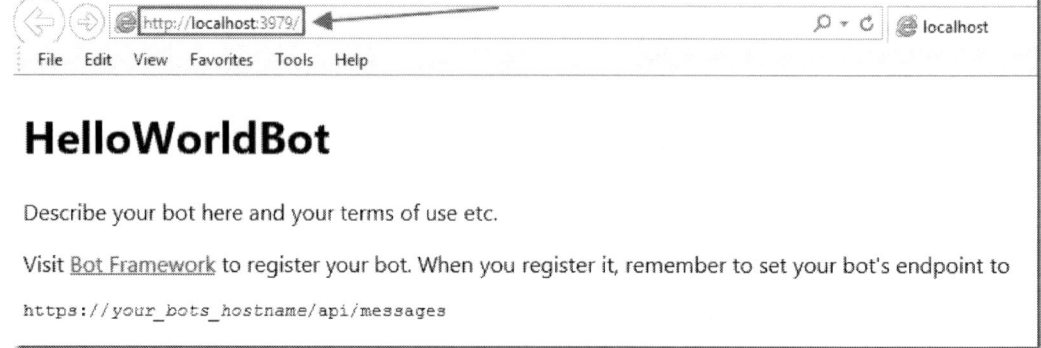

Note the web address. You will need it in the next step.

An Introduction to the Microsoft Bot Framework

Using The Bot Emulator

Download, install, and run the **Bot Framework Emulator** from https://aka.ms/bf-bc-emulator

When the emulator starts, connect to the **Bot** by setting the address to the address indicated in the web browser. However, add **/api/messages** to the end.

An Introduction to the Microsoft Bot Framework

In the **Bot Emulator**, enter **Hello** in the text box and click the send key (or press enter).

You will see the response in the **Chat** window and the **JSON** contents of the response in the **JSON** window.

Saving User Data

An important part of any conversation is remembering what a user has previously said.

We can do this using **GetPrivateConversationData** and **SetPrivateConversationData**.

To demonstrate how this is handled, add the following to the top of the **MessagesController.cs** file in the **Controllers** folder:

```
using System.Text;
```

An Introduction to the Microsoft Bot Framework

Next, change the **Post** method in the **MessagesController.cs** file to the following:

```csharp
public async Task<HttpResponseMessage> Post([FromBody]Activity activity)
{
    // Global values
    bool boolAskedForUserName = false;
    string strUserName = "";
    if (activity.Type == ActivityTypes.Message)
    {
        // Get any saved values
        StateClient sc = activity.GetStateClient();
        BotData userData = sc.BotState.GetPrivateConversationData(
            activity.ChannelId, activity.Conversation.Id, activity.From.Id);
        boolAskedForUserName = userData.GetProperty<bool>("AskedForUserName");
        strUserName = userData.GetProperty<string>("UserName") ?? "";
        // Create text for a reply message
        StringBuilder strReplyMessage = new StringBuilder();
        if (boolAskedForUserName == false) // Never asked for name
        {
            strReplyMessage.Append($"Hello, I am **AIHelpWebsite.com** Bot");
            strReplyMessage.Append($"\n");
            strReplyMessage.Append($"You can say anything");
            strReplyMessage.Append($"\n");
            strReplyMessage.Append($"to me and I will repeat it back");
            strReplyMessage.Append($"\n\n");
            strReplyMessage.Append($"What is your name?");
            // Set BotUserData
            userData.SetProperty<bool>("AskedForUserName", true);
        }
```

An Introduction to the Microsoft Bot Framework

```csharp
            else // Have asked for name
            {
                if (strUserName == "") // Name was never provided
                {
                    // If we have asked for a username but it has not been set
                    // the current response is the user name
                    strReplyMessage.Append($"Hello {activity.Text}!");
                    // Set BotUserData
                    userData.SetProperty<string>("UserName", activity.Text);
                }
                else // Name was provided
                {
                    strReplyMessage.Append($"{strUserName}, You said: {activity.Text}");
                }
            }
            // Save BotUserData
            sc.BotState.SetPrivateConversationData(
                activity.ChannelId, activity.Conversation.Id, activity.From.Id, userData);
            // Create a reply message
            ConnectorClient connector = new ConnectorClient(new Uri(activity.ServiceUrl));
            Activity replyMessage = activity.CreateReply(strReplyMessage.ToString());
            await connector.Conversations.ReplyToActivityAsync(replyMessage);
        }
        else
        {
            HandleSystemMessage(activity);
        }
        // Return response
        var response = Request.CreateResponse(HttpStatusCode.OK);
        return response;
    }
```

An Introduction to the Microsoft Bot Framework

Finally, alter the following section in the **HandleSystemMessage** method (in the **MessagesController.cs** file) to the following:

```csharp
if (message.Type == ActivityTypes.DeleteUserData)
{
    // Get BotUserData
    StateClient sc = message.GetStateClient();
    BotData userData = sc.BotState.GetPrivateConversationData(
        message.ChannelId, message.Conversation.Id, message.From.Id);
    // Set BotUserData
    userData.SetProperty<string>("UserName", "");
    userData.SetProperty<bool>("AskedForUserName", false);
    // Save BotUserData
    sc.BotState.SetPrivateConversationData(
        message.ChannelId, message.Conversation.Id, message.From.Id, userData);
    // Create a reply message
    ConnectorClient connector = new ConnectorClient(new Uri(message.ServiceUrl));
    Activity replyMessage = message.CreateReply("Personal data has been deleted.");
    return replyMessage;
}
```

An Introduction to the Microsoft Bot Framework

Now when we chat with the **Bot**, it can remember our name.

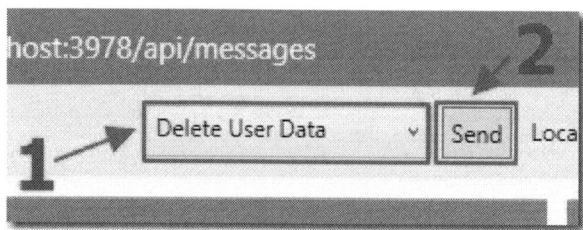

If we tell it to **Delete User Data**…

An Introduction to the Microsoft Bot Framework

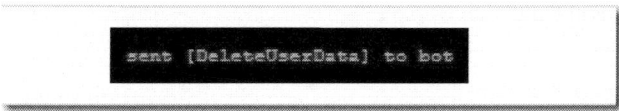

It will respect our wishes.

Publishing The Bot

To connect your Bot through channels such as **Skype** and **Facebook Messenger**, you need to configure it on the **Microsoft Bot Framework Developer Portal**. To do that, you will first need to publish it in a *publicly accessible location.*

This can be any server; however, publishing to **Azure** is recommended because publishing to it has built-in support in **Visual Studio**.

First, go to https://azure.microsoft.com and create an account and a subscription if you don't already have one.

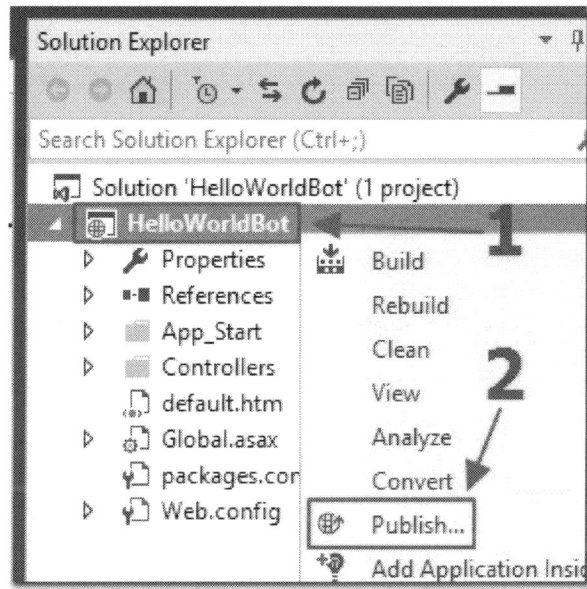

Next, *Right-click* on the **Project** node (*not* the **Solution** node) in **Visual Studio** and select **Publish**.

An Introduction to the Microsoft Bot Framework

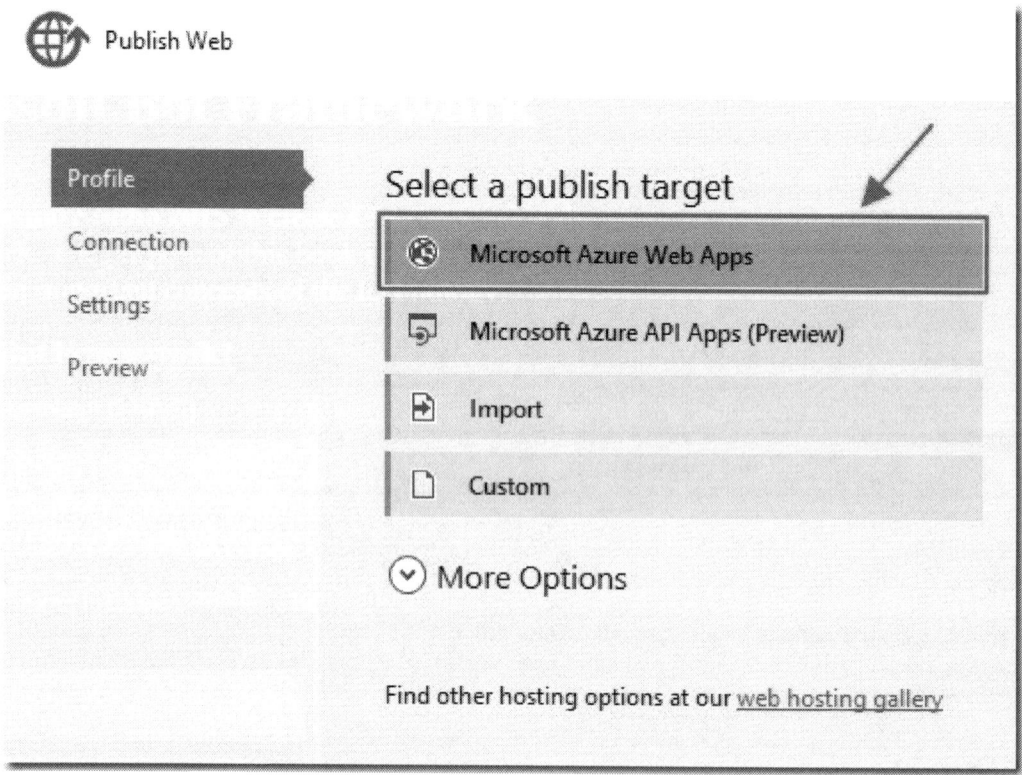

Select **Microsoft Azure Web Apps**.

An Introduction to the Microsoft Bot Framework

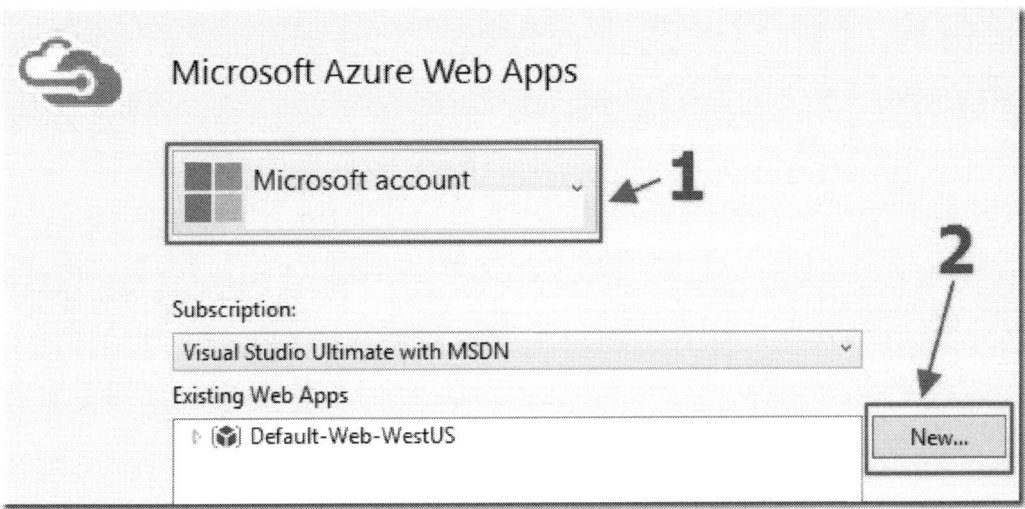

Sign into your **Azure** account.
Select a subscription.
Then click the **New** button.

An Introduction to the Microsoft Bot Framework

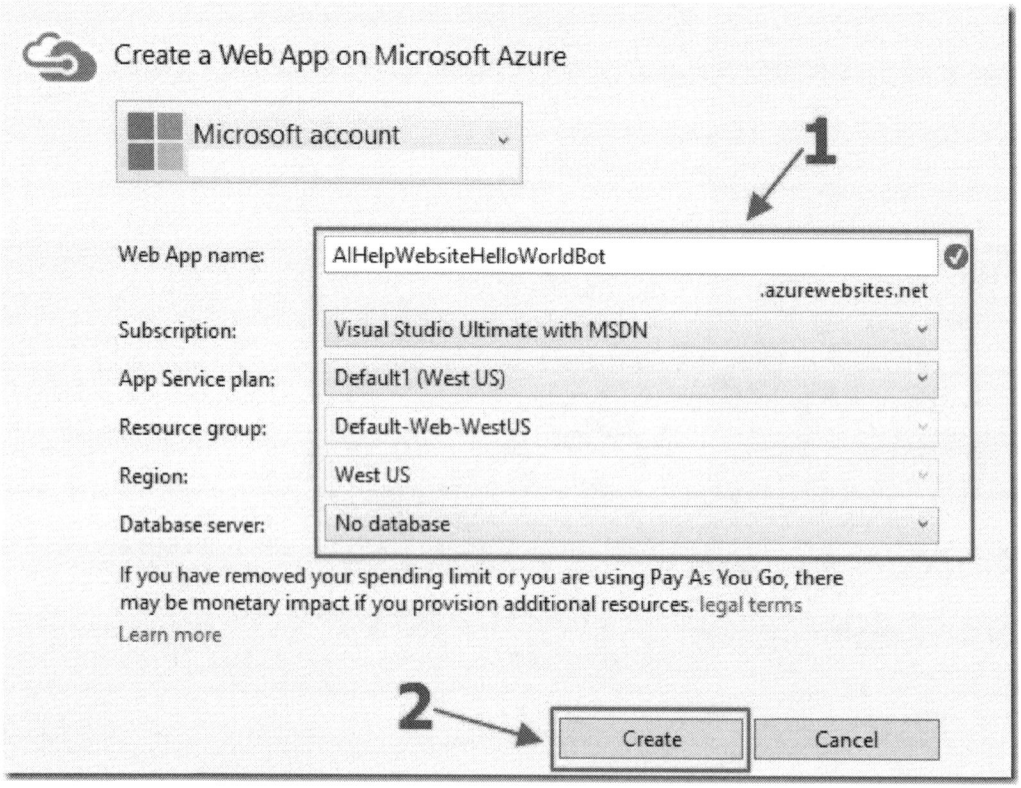

Enter a unique **Web App name**.
Select your **subscription**.
Select or create a **service plan**, **resource group** and **region**.
Then click the **Create** button.

An Introduction to the Microsoft Bot Framework

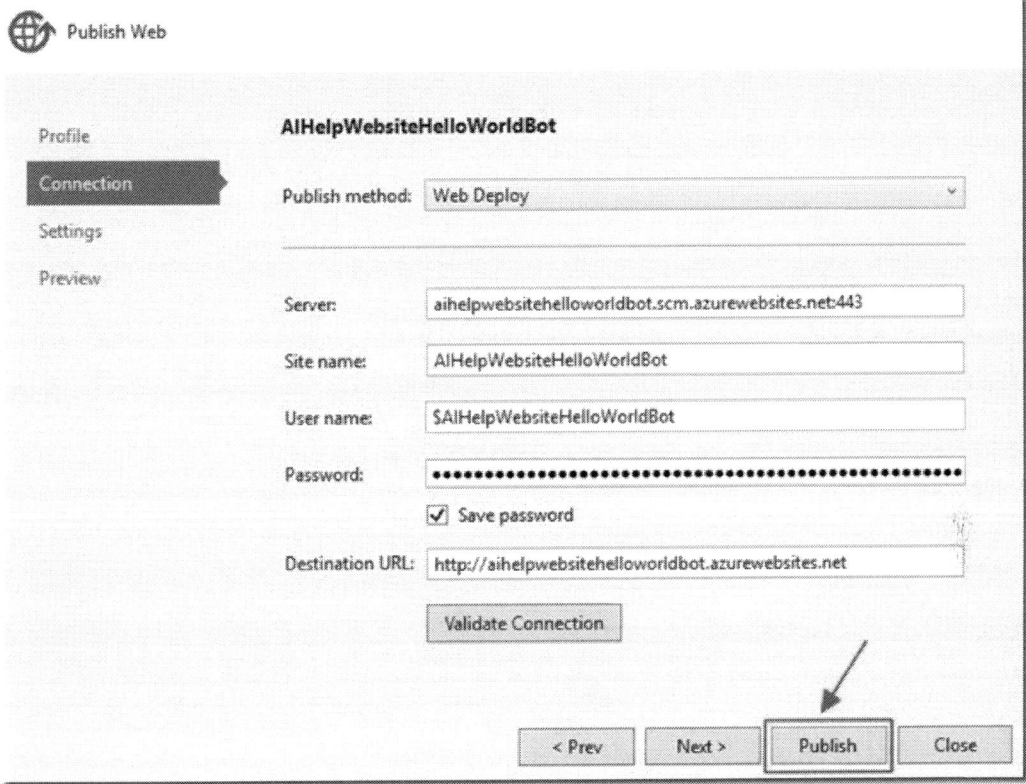

After the **web app** has been created, click the **Publish** button.

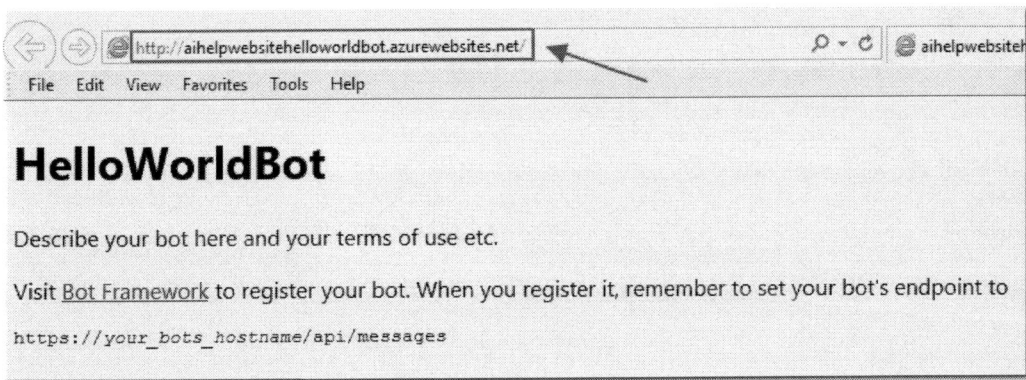

The web app will open in the web browser.

An Introduction to the Microsoft Bot Framework

Note the web address. You will need it in a later step.

Registering The Bot With The Microsoft Bot Framework Developer Portal

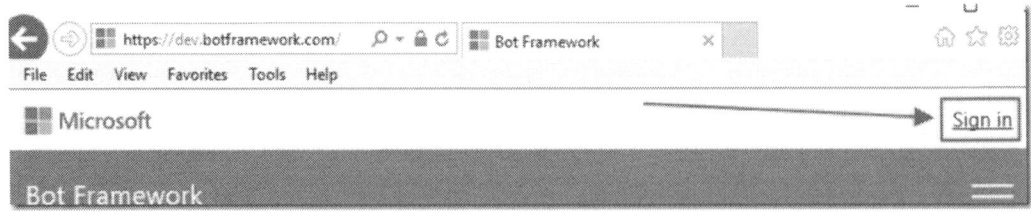

Go to the **Microsoft Bot Framework Developer Portal** at https://www.botframework.com and sign in with your **Microsoft Account**.

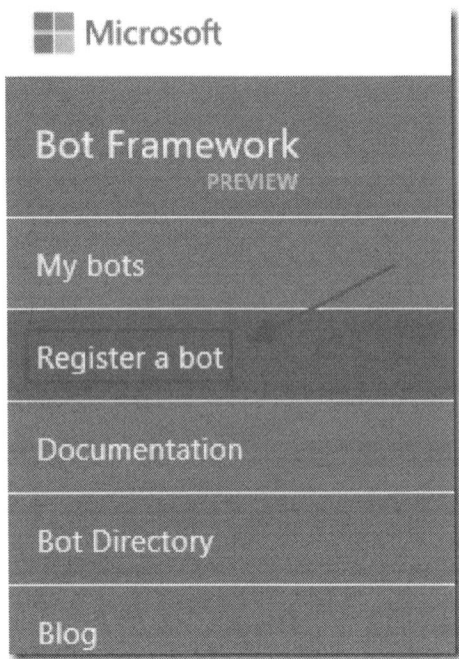

Select **Register a bot**.

28

An Introduction to the Microsoft Bot Framework

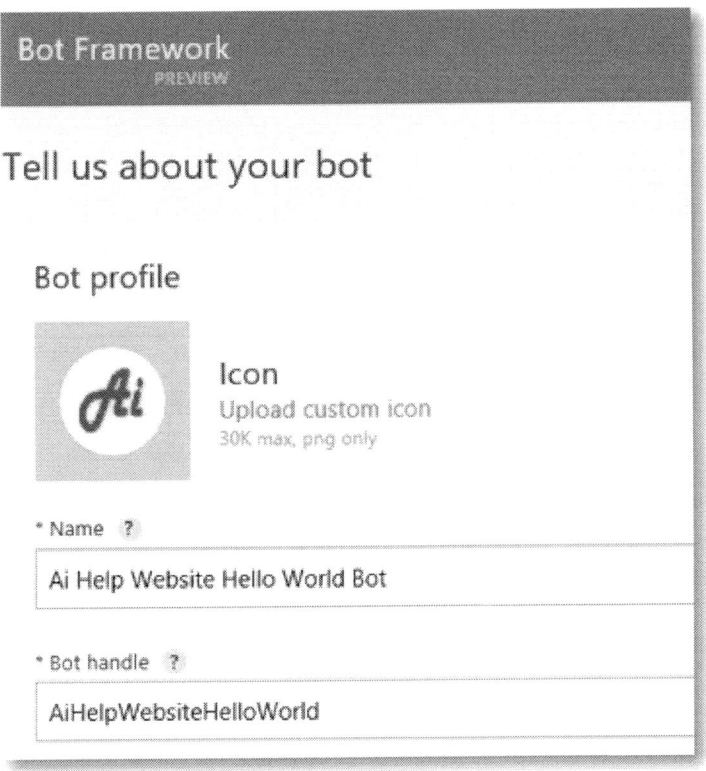

Fill in all of the fields.

*Note: The end point web address is what you saw when the web browser opened in the previous step. However, remember you have to add "/api/messages" to the end of the address and use **https://** rather than **http://**.*

During the process, you will be prompted to click a link to go to https://apps.dev.microsoft.com.

It is there that you will get an **Application ID** and a **password**.

An Introduction to the Microsoft Bot Framework

Make a note of them because you will need to use them to update the **Visual Studio** project in later step.

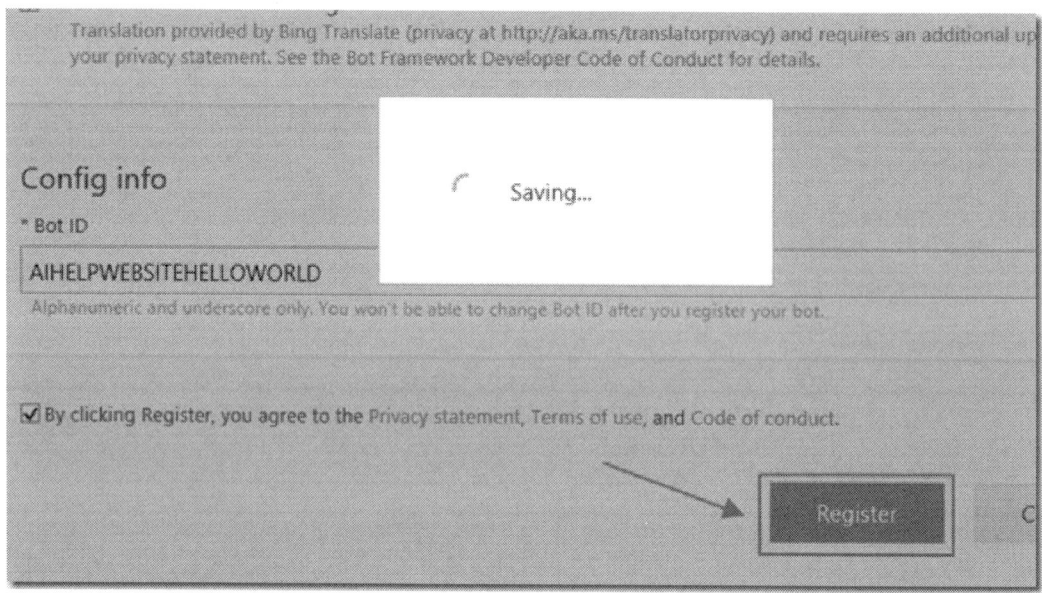

Click the **Register** button.

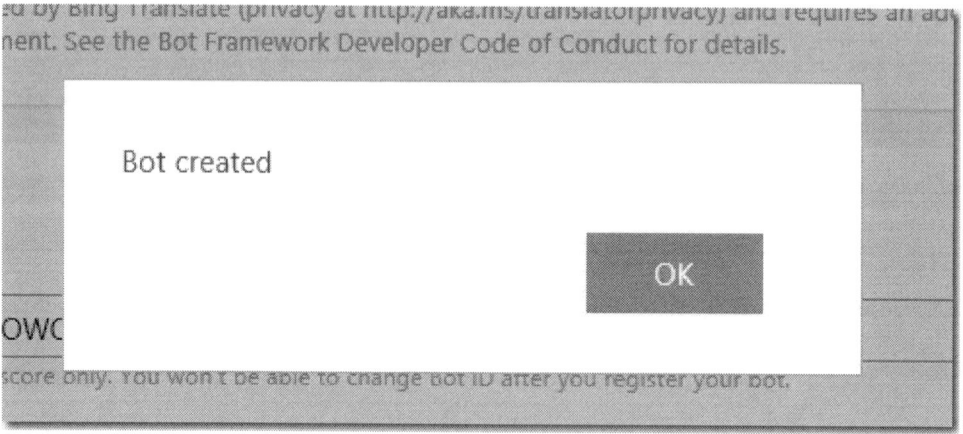

The **Bot** registration will be created.

An Introduction to the Microsoft Bot Framework

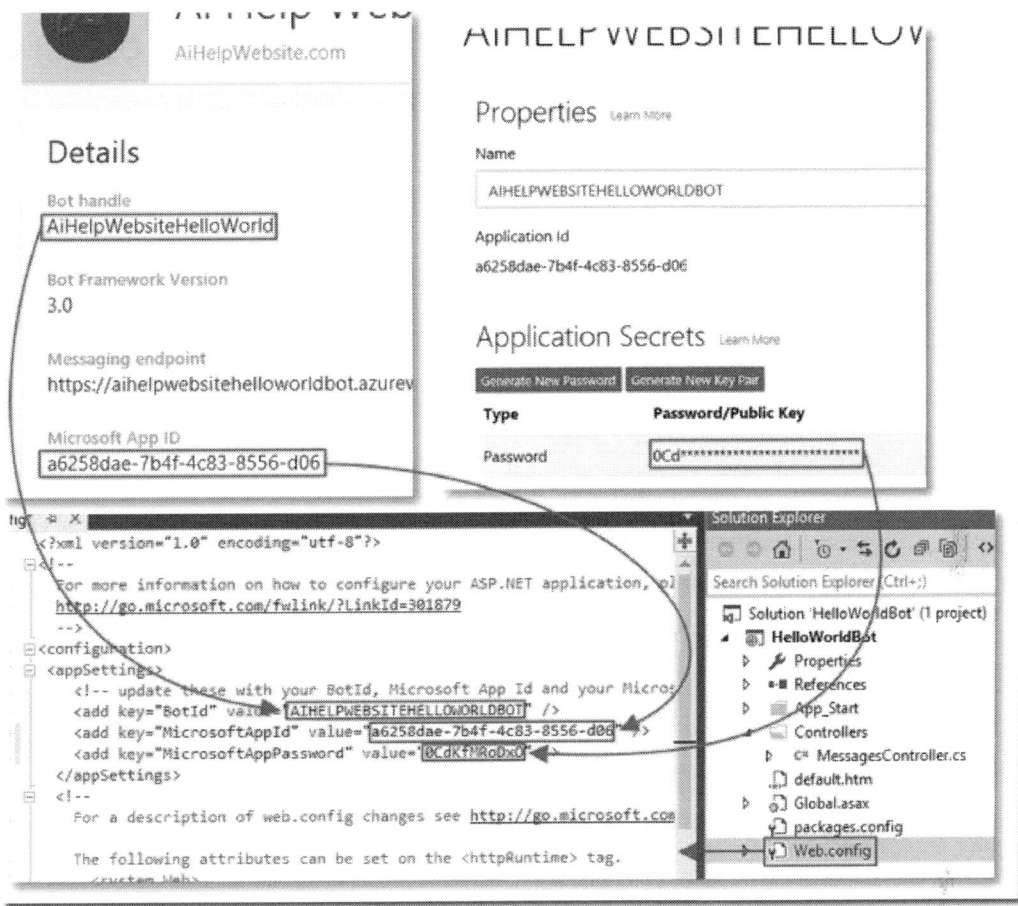

Copy the **Bot ID** and **MicrosoftAppId** from the https://dev.botframework.com site, and **MicrosoftAppPassword** from the https://apps.dev.microsoft.com site, to the **web.config** of the **Bot** in **Visual Studio**.

*Note: If you forgot to note the **MicrosoftAppPassword** in the earlier step, you can click the **Generate New Password** button to create another one.*

An Introduction to the Microsoft Bot Framework

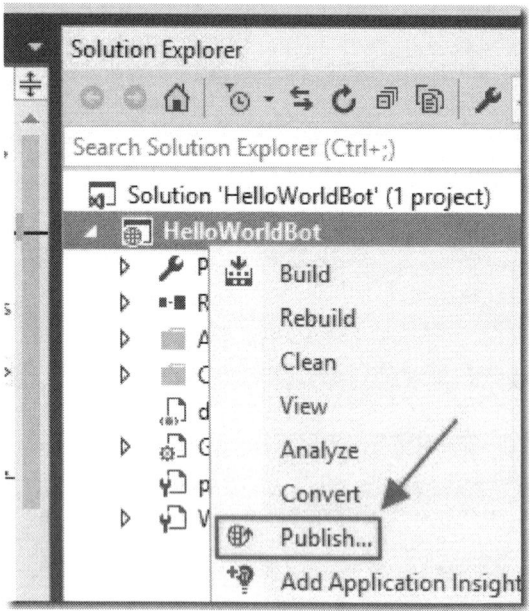

Publish the **Bot** again.

You are doing this because the **Bot Framework** will pass the **Bot ID**, **MicrosoftAppId**, and **MicrosoftAppPassword** when it communicates with it.

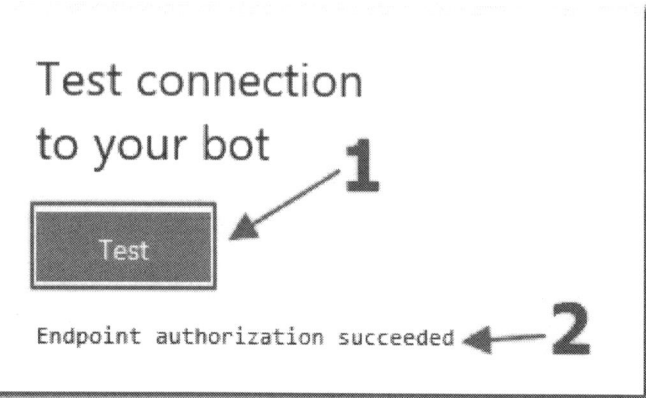

You can now test your **Bot** using the **Bot Framework Developer Portal** web page.

An Introduction to the Microsoft Bot Framework

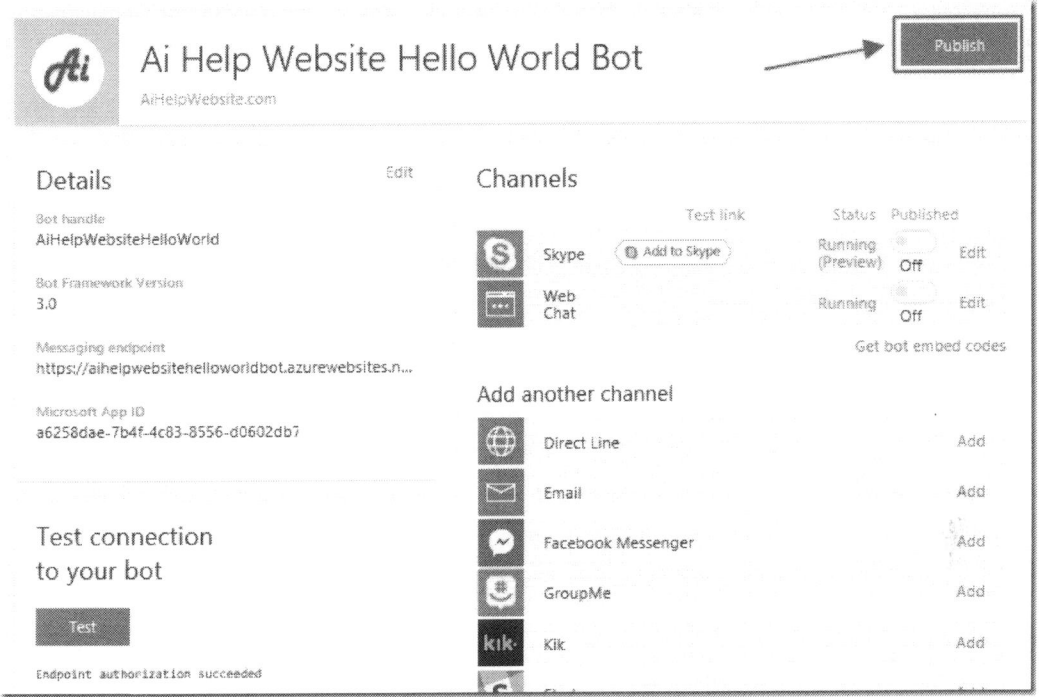

If you desire, you can click the **Publish** button to submit your **Bot** to the **Bot Directory**.

You can also configure channels for your **Bot**.

Even if you do not publish your **Bot** to the **Bot Directory**, you can still call it from your own applications and through any channels you configure.

*Note: Chapters 10 and 11 cover how to use the **Bot Framework Developer Portal** to configure the **Skype** and **Facebook Messenger** channels to deploy your **Bot** on those networks.*

Chapter 3: Using FormFlow

The sample code for this chapter can be obtained at the link "Introduction To FormFlow With The Microsoft Bot Framework" at http://AiHelpWebsite.com/Downloads

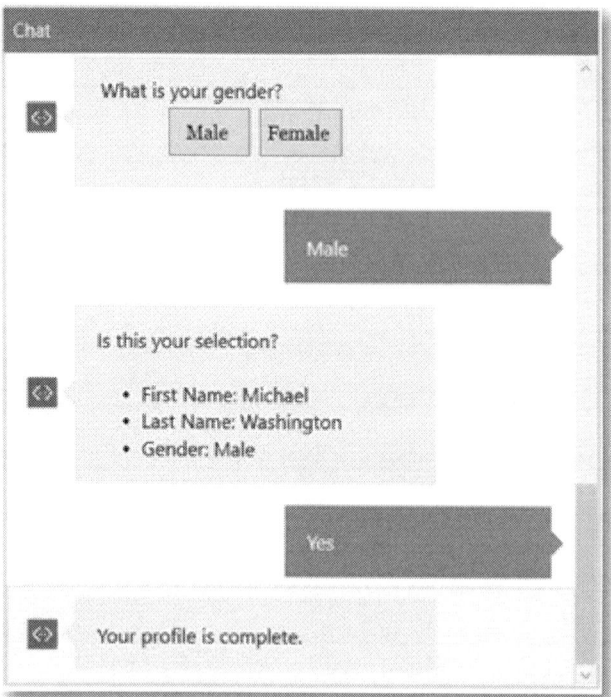

Using **FormFlow** with the **Microsoft Bot Framework** allows you to quickly create a guided conversation to gather information from a user with the least amount of code. While it is less flexible than using **Dialogs** (**Dialogs** are covered in the next chapter), it can be combined with **Dialogs** to increase its functionality.

An Introduction to the Microsoft Bot Framework

A Walk Through

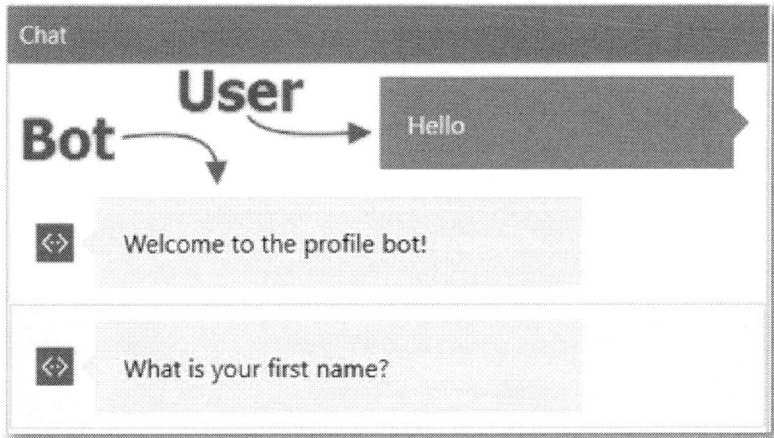

When a user begins a conversation with the **Bot**, it introduces itself and asks the user's name.

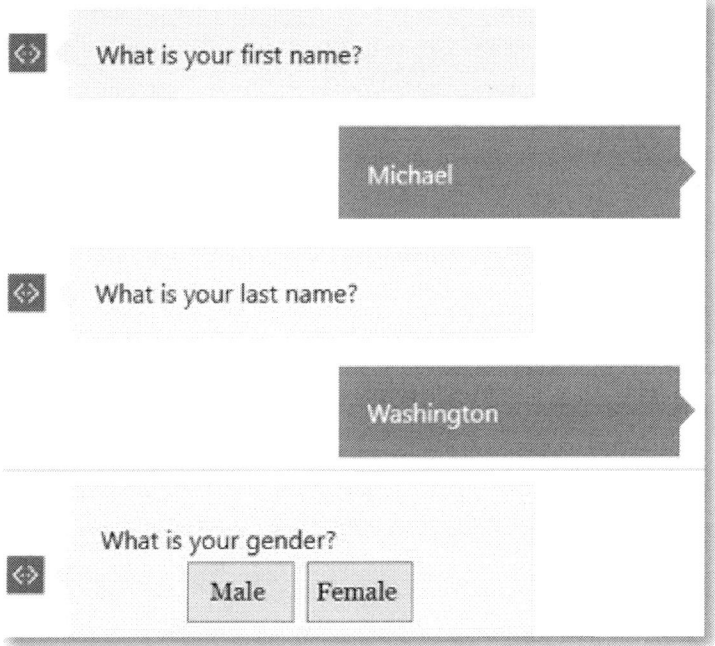

The **Bot** proceeds to ask questions and gather the responses.

An Introduction to the Microsoft Bot Framework

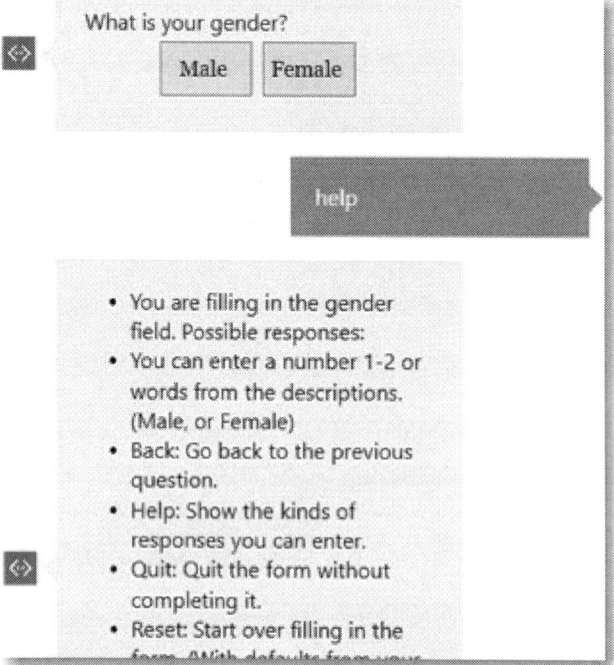

A feature of **FormFlow** is that the user can type *help* at any time to obtain assistance with any question or the **FormFlow** itself.

As a developer, you get this functionality without the need to write any additional code.

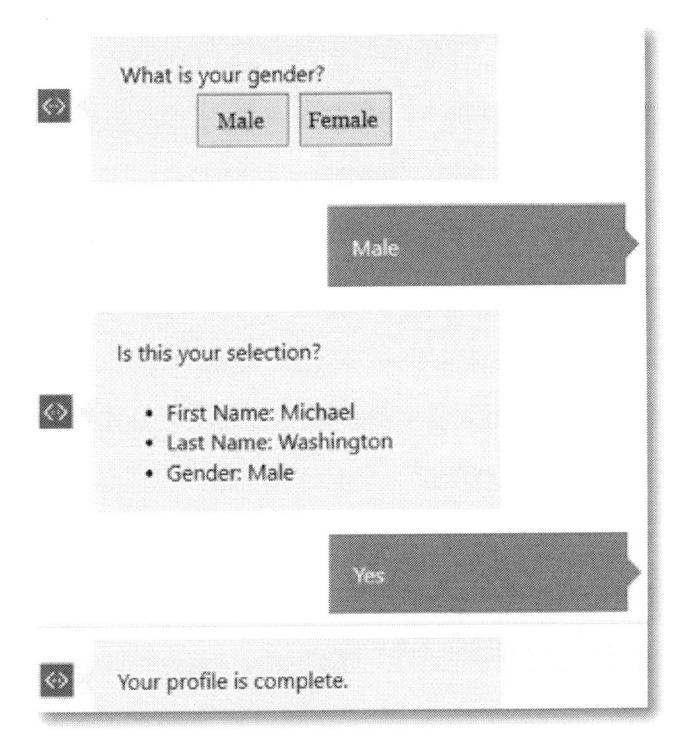

An Introduction to the Microsoft Bot Framework

The **FormFlow** continues until the form is complete.

Creating The Project

Open **Visual Studio**.

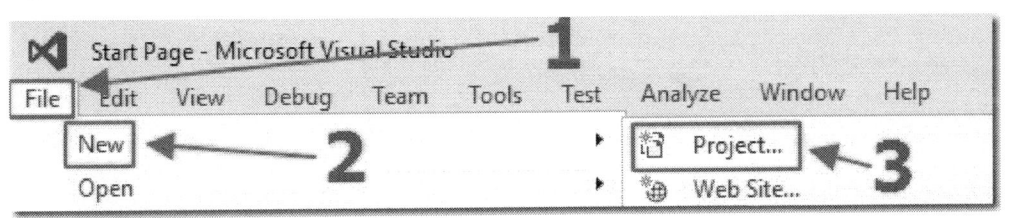

Create a new **Project**.

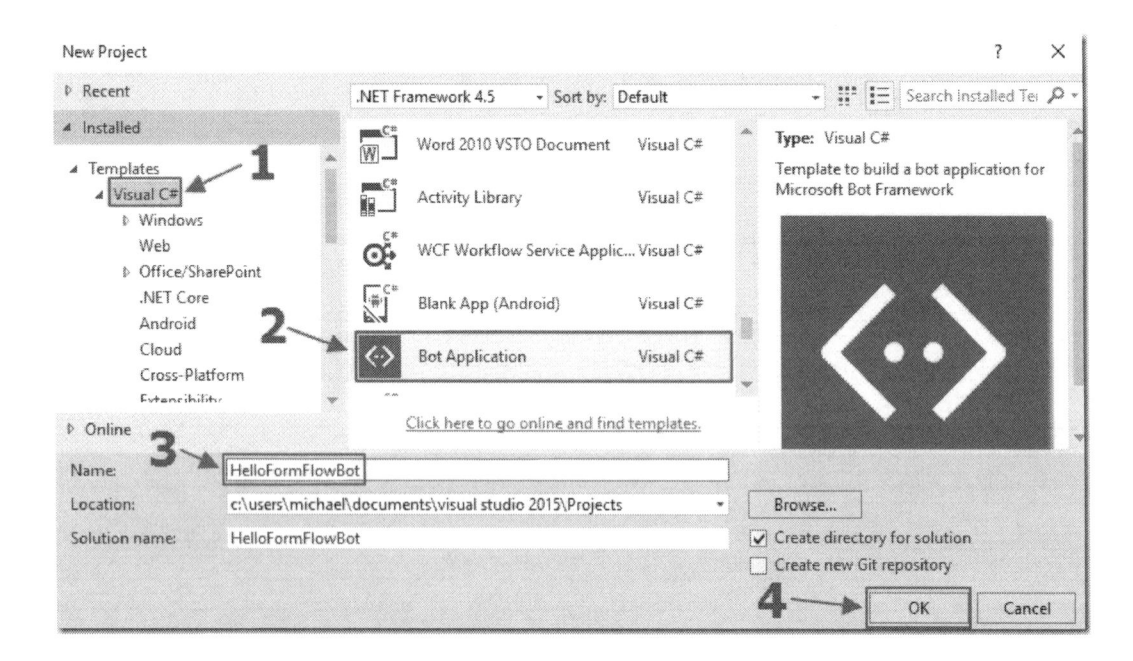

An Introduction to the Microsoft Bot Framework

Select the **Bot Application** template and name the project **HelloFormFlowBot**.

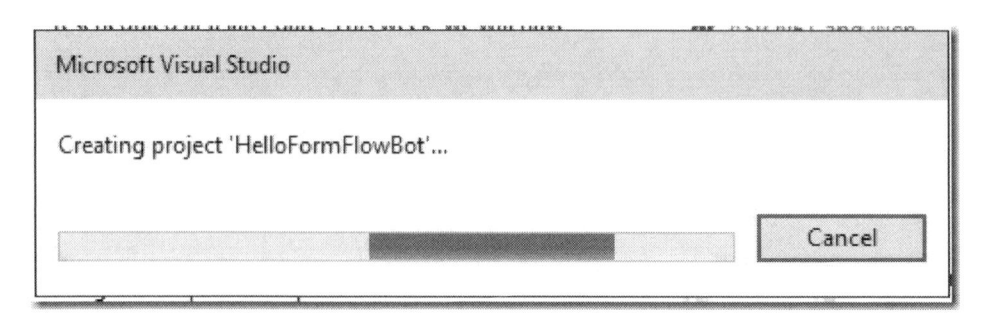

The project will be created.

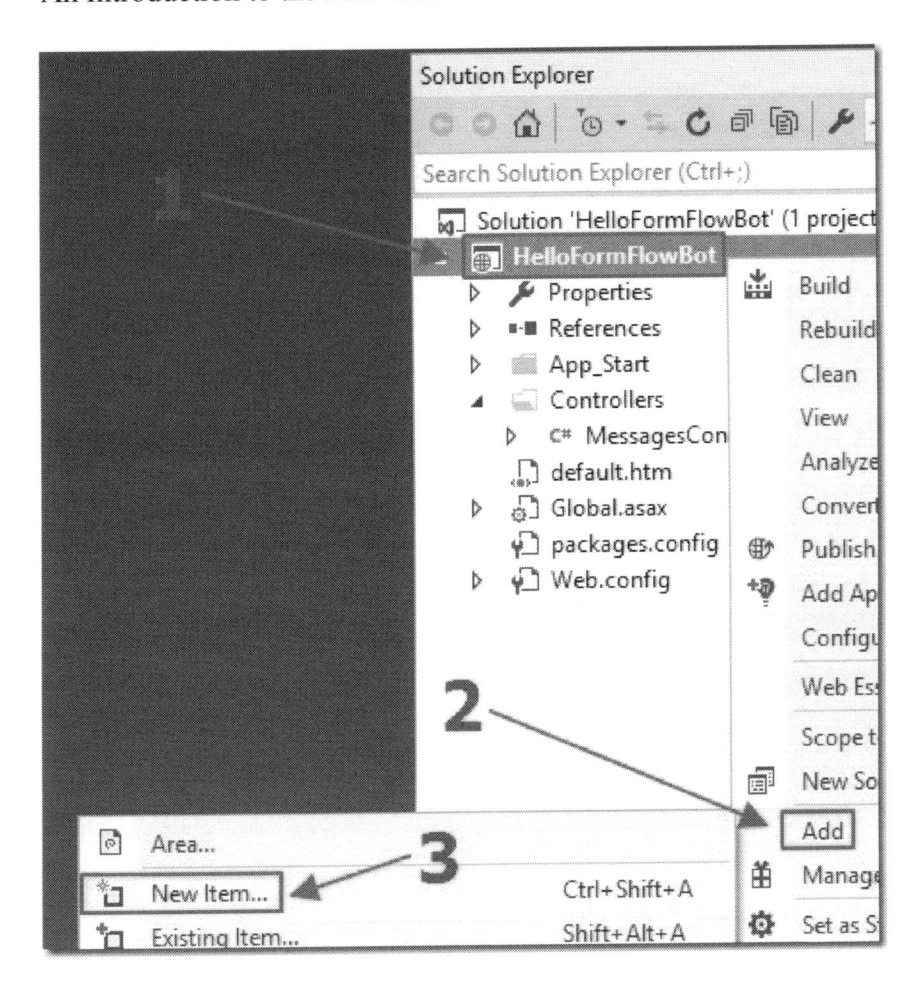

An Introduction to the Microsoft Bot Framework

Right-click on the project. Select **Add** and then **New Item**.

We will now create the class that will contain the logic for our **FormFlow**.

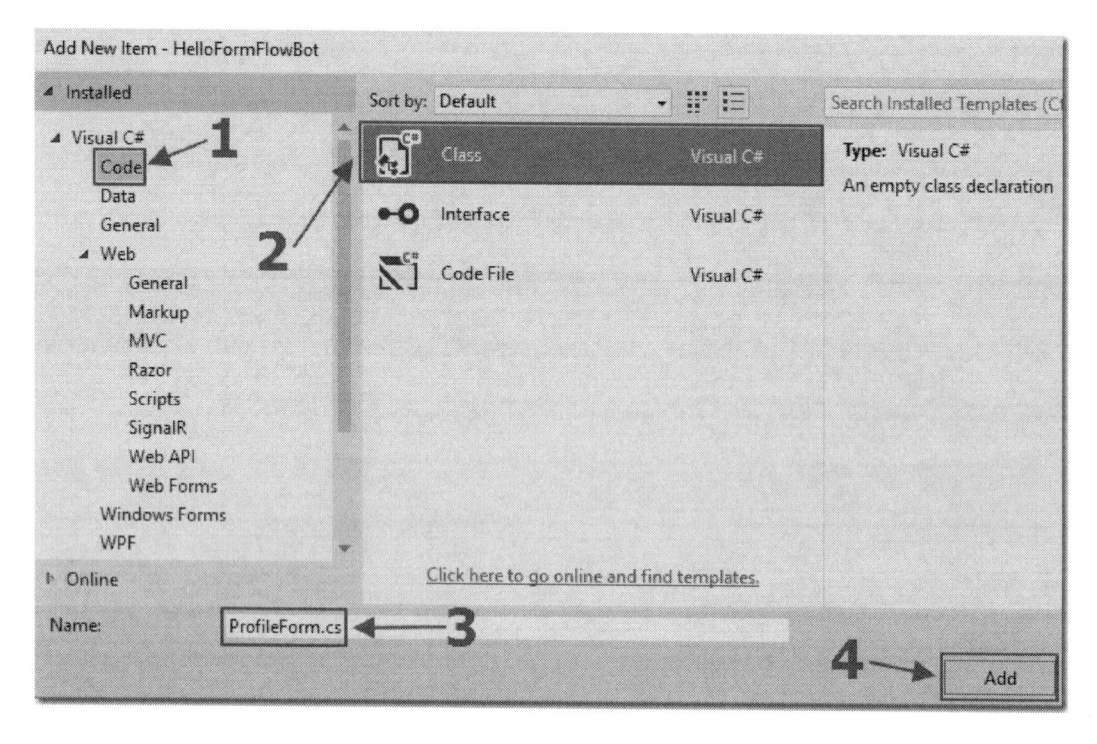

An Introduction to the Microsoft Bot Framework

Add a new **C#** class called **ProfileForm.cs**.

An Introduction to the Microsoft Bot Framework

Replace all the code with the following code:

```csharp
using System;
using Microsoft.Bot.Builder.Dialogs;
using Microsoft.Bot.Builder.FormFlow;
namespace HelloFormFlowBot
{
    [Serializable]
    public class ProfileForm
    {
        // these are the fields that will hold the data
        // we will gather with the form
        [Prompt("What is your first name? {||}")]
        public string FirstName;
        [Prompt("What is your last name? {||}")]
        public string LastName;
        [Prompt("What is your gender? {||}")]
        public Gender Gender;
        // This method 'builds' the form
        // This method will be called by code we will place
        // in the MakeRootDialog method of the MessagesControlller.cs file
        public static IForm<ProfileForm> BuildForm()
        {
            return new FormBuilder<ProfileForm>()
                    .Message("Welcome to the profile bot!")
                    .OnCompletion(async (context, profileForm) =>
                    {
                        // Tell the user that the form is complete
                        await context.PostAsync("Your profile is complete.");
                    })
                    .Build();
        }
    }
    // This enum provides the possible values for the
    // Gender property in the ProfileForm class
    // Notice we start the options at 1
    [Serializable]
    public enum Gender
    {
        Male = 1, Female = 2
    };
}
```

An Introduction to the Microsoft Bot Framework

This code indicates the fields we will gather with our **FormFlow**.

Notice that the class, as well as the **Gender** *enum* that it consumes, is marked **[Serializable]**.

The Microsoft Bot Framework requires that the classes must be *serializable*, so the **Bot** can be stateless.

Save the file.

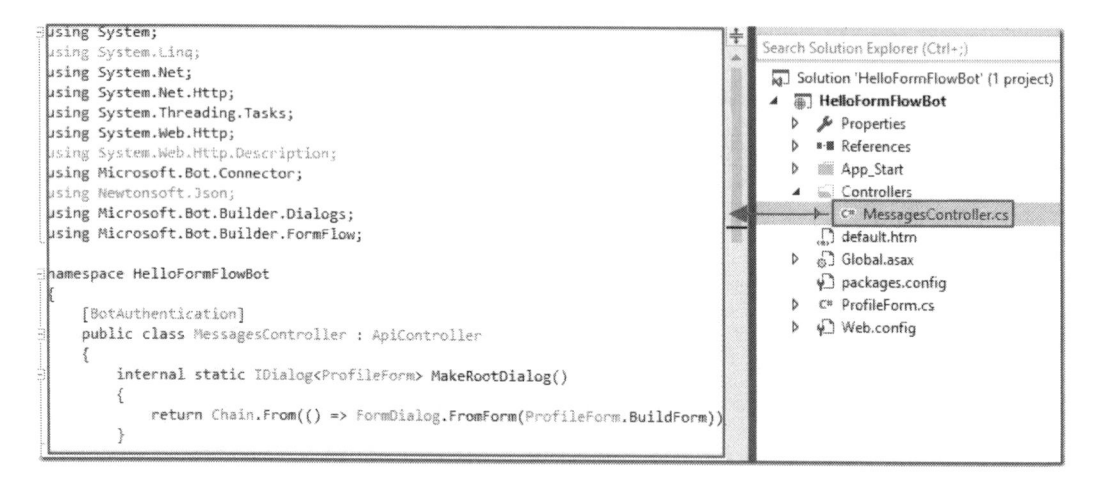

```
using System;
using System.Linq;
using System.Net;
using System.Net.Http;
using System.Threading.Tasks;
using System.Web.Http;
using System.Web.Http.Description;
using Microsoft.Bot.Connector;
using Newtonsoft.Json;
using Microsoft.Bot.Builder.Dialogs;
using Microsoft.Bot.Builder.FormFlow;

namespace HelloFormFlowBot
{
    [BotAuthentication]
    public class MessagesController : ApiController
    {
        internal static IDialog<ProfileForm> MakeRootDialog()
        {
            return Chain.From(() => FormDialog.FromForm(ProfileForm.BuildForm))
        }
```

Open the **MessagesController.cs** file.

Add the following *using* statements at the top of the file (to support the **FormFlow** code):

```
using Microsoft.Bot.Builder.Dialogs;
using Microsoft.Bot.Builder.FormFlow;
```

An Introduction to the Microsoft Bot Framework

Add the following **MakeRootDialog** method to the **MessagesController** class to call the **BuildForm** method in the **ProfileForm** class we created earlier:

```
internal static IDialog<ProfileForm> MakeRootDialog()
{
    return Chain.From(() => FormDialog.FromForm(ProfileForm.BuildForm));
}
```

Finally, alter the **Post** method in the **MessagesController** class to the following:

```
public async Task<HttpResponseMessage> Post([FromBody]Activity activity)
{
    // Detect if this is a Message activity
    if (activity.Type == ActivityTypes.Message)
    {
        // Call our FormFlow by calling MakeRootDialog
        await Conversation.SendAsync(activity, MakeRootDialog);
    }
    else
    {
        // This was not a Message activity
        HandleSystemMessage(activity);
    }
    // Return response
    var response = Request.CreateResponse(HttpStatusCode.OK);
    return response;
}
```

Save the file.

Test The Application

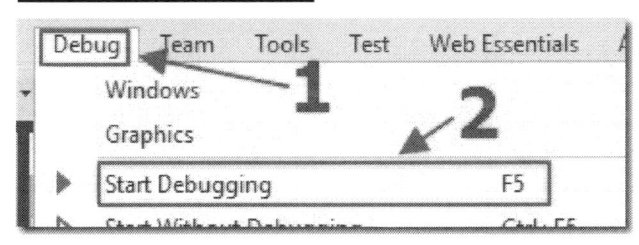

Hit **F5** to run the application.

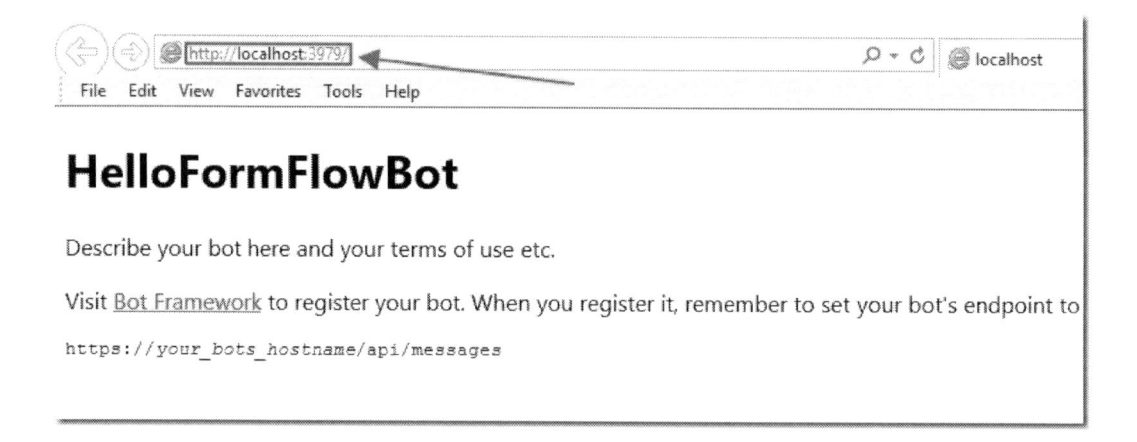

An Introduction to the Microsoft Bot Framework

HelloFormFlowBot

Describe your bot here and your terms of use etc.

Visit Bot Framework to register your bot. When you register it, remember to set your bot's endpoint to

`https://your_bots_hostname/api/messages`

The web browser will open.

Note the port number and the web address.

Open and run the **Microsoft Bot Framework Emulator**.

When the emulator starts, connect to the **Bot** by setting the address to the one indicted in the web browser; however, add **/api/messages** to the end.

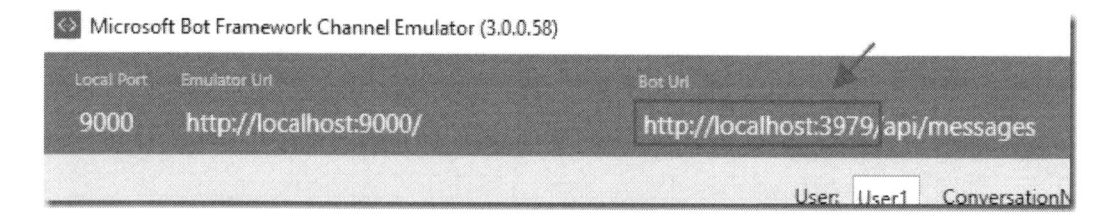

Ensure that the **Bot URL** is connecting to the correct address.

44

An Introduction to the Microsoft Bot Framework

Type a message and click the **send** key (or press **Enter**).

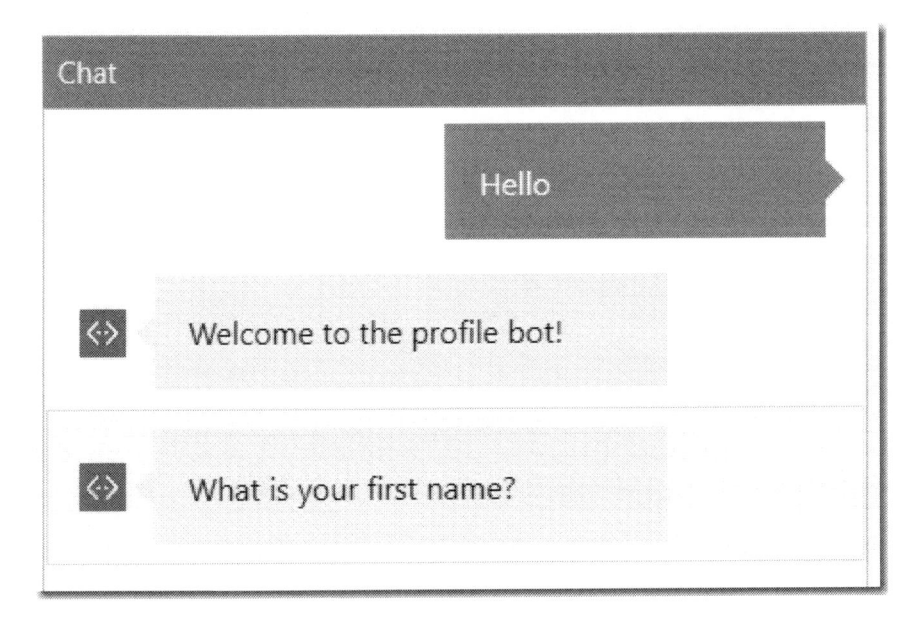

You can now converse with the **Bot** and fill out the **FormFlow**.

Saving The Data

Currently the application does not save the responses from the user. In fact, after you fill the **FormFlow** out, it will simply ask you to fill it out again.

We can use the **Bot State Service** to save and retrieve the values.

An Introduction to the Microsoft Bot Framework

Alter the **BuildForm** method in the **ProfileForm.cs** file to the following to save the values entered into the form:

```
public static IForm<ProfileForm> BuildForm()
{
    return new FormBuilder<ProfileForm>()
            .Message("Welcome to the profile bot!")
            .OnCompletion(async (context, profileForm) =>
            {
                // Set BotUserData
                context.PrivateConversationData.SetValue<bool>(
                    "ProfileComplete", true);
                context.PrivateConversationData.SetValue<string>(
                    "FirstName", profileForm.FirstName);
                context.PrivateConversationData.SetValue<string>(
                    "LastName", profileForm.LastName);
                context.PrivateConversationData.SetValue<string>(
                    "Gender", profileForm.Gender.ToString());
                // Tell the user that the form is complete
                await context.PostAsync("Your profile is complete.");
            })
            .Build();
}
```

We are not only storing the values provided by the user, but we are also setting a flag (*ProfileComplete*), so we don't ask the user to fill out the form again.

An Introduction to the Microsoft Bot Framework

Finally, alter the **Post** method in the **MessagesController** class to the following:

```csharp
public async Task<HttpResponseMessage> Post([FromBody]Activity activity)
{
    // Detect if this is a Message activity
    if (activity.Type == ActivityTypes.Message)
    {
        // Get any saved values
        StateClient sc = activity.GetStateClient();
        BotData userData = sc.BotState.GetPrivateConversationData(
            activity.ChannelId, activity.Conversation.Id, activity.From.Id);
        var boolProfileComplete = userData.GetProperty<bool>("ProfileComplete");
        if (!boolProfileComplete)
        {
            // Call our FormFlow by calling MakeRootDialog
            await Conversation.SendAsync(activity, MakeRootDialog);
        }
        else
        {
            // Get the saved profile values
            var FirstName = userData.GetProperty<string>("FirstName");
            var LastName = userData.GetProperty<string>("LastName");
            var Gender = userData.GetProperty<string>("Gender");
            // Tell the user their profile is complete
            System.Text.StringBuilder sb = new System.Text.StringBuilder();
            sb.Append("Your profile is complete.\n\n");
            sb.Append(String.Format("FirstName = {0}\n\n", FirstName));
            sb.Append(String.Format("LastName = {0}\n\n", LastName));
            sb.Append(String.Format("Gender = {0}", Gender));
            // Create final reply
            ConnectorClient connector = new ConnectorClient(new Uri(activity.ServiceUrl));
            Activity replyMessage = activity.CreateReply(sb.ToString());
            await connector.Conversations.ReplyToActivityAsync(replyMessage);
        }
    }
    else
    {
        // This was not a Message activity
        HandleSystemMessage(activity);
    }
    // Send response
    var response = Request.CreateResponse(HttpStatusCode.OK);
    return response;
}
```

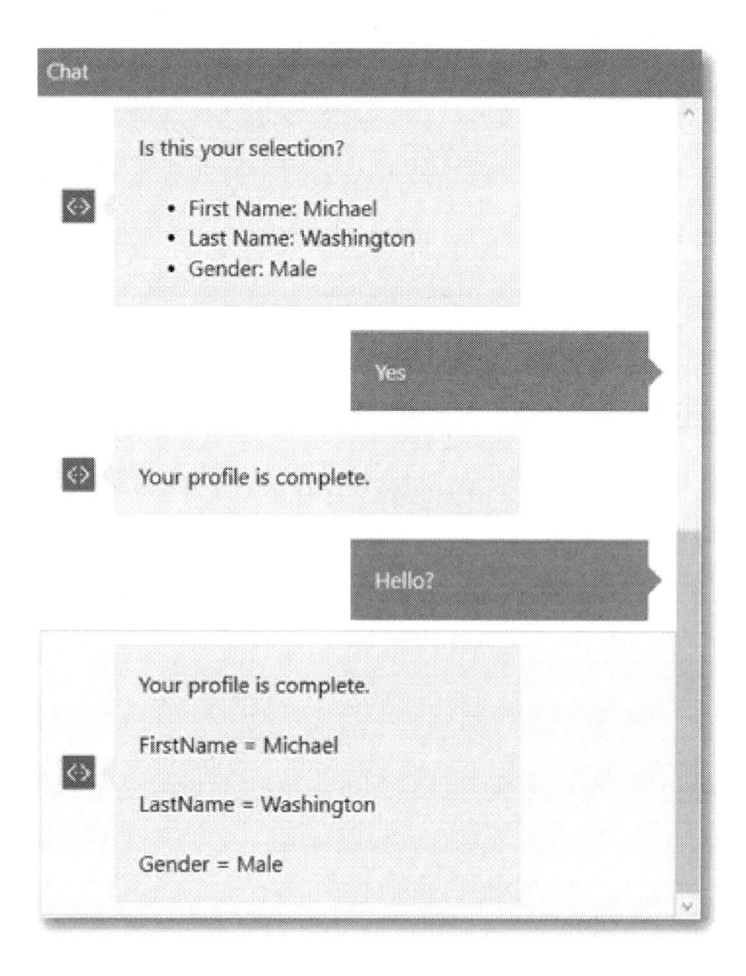

An Introduction to the Microsoft Bot Framework

![Chat window showing: "Is this your selection? First Name: Michael, Last Name: Washington, Gender: Male" - User: "Yes" - Bot: "Your profile is complete." - User: "Hello?" - Bot: "Your profile is complete. FirstName = Michael, LastName = Washington, Gender = Male"]

Now the application will only ask the user to fill in the form one time and display the values received using the **Bot State Service**.

The values will be persisted by the **Microsoft Bot Framework** keyed to that user in that conversation.

An Introduction to the Microsoft Bot Framework

In our example, we used **PrivateConversationData**, but the **Bot State Service** exposes the following methods, each with a different scope:

Method	Scoped	Description
SetUserData()	User	Remembering context object with a user
SetConversationData()	Conversation	Remembering context object with a conversation
SetPrivateConversationData()	User & Conversation	Remembering context object with a person in a conversation

An Introduction to the Microsoft Bot Framework

Chapter 4: Using Dialogs

The sample code for this chapter can be obtained at the link "Introduction To Using Dialogs With The Microsoft Bot Framework" at http://AiHelpWebsite.com/Downloads

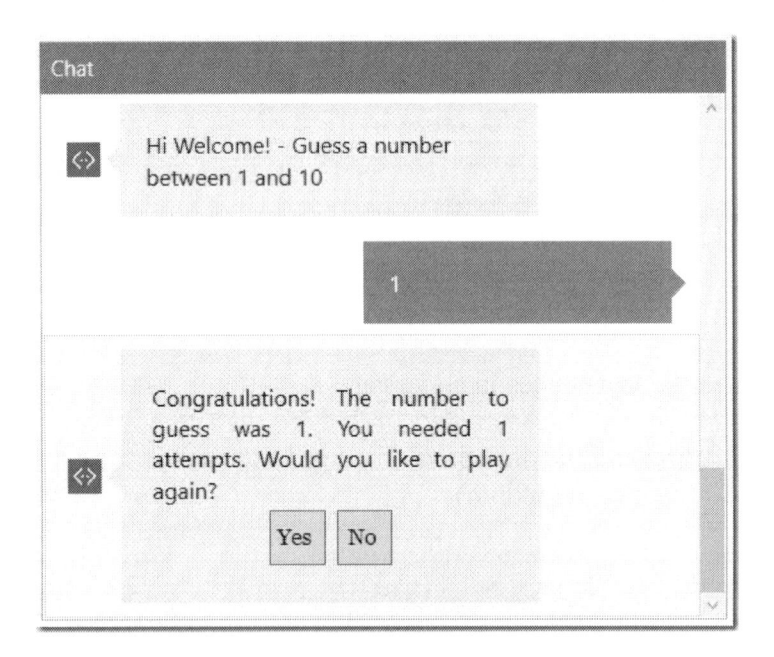

Using **Dialogs** with the **Microsoft Bot Framework** allows you to model a conversation with a user. While they are more flexible than using a **FormFlow** (covered in the preceding chapter), **Dialogs** require more code.

A **Dialog** is a class that implements the *IDialog* interface. **Dialogs** can be composed with other dialogs to maximize reuse.

A **Dialog** has a context that contains a stack of dialogs active in a conversation and will maintain the state of the conversation. A **Dialog** sends messages to a user and is suspended when it is waiting for a response from a user.

An Introduction to the Microsoft Bot Framework

A **Dialog** uses a *state* stored in its *context* to resume a conversation. This *state* is stored in the state service provided by the **Microsoft Bot Framework** service.

Walk Through

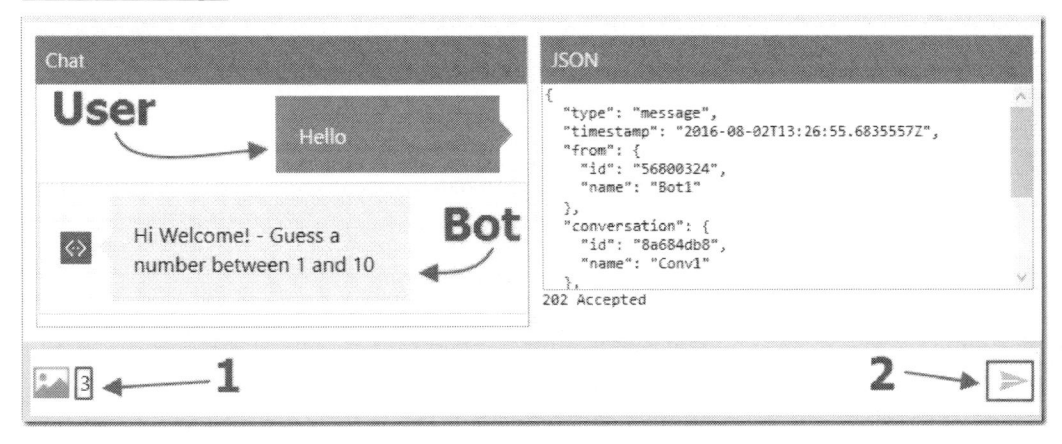

The conversation starts when the **User** types in a message.

The **Bot** responds with a greeting and the directions of the game, which is to guess a number from 1 to 10 (chosen at random).

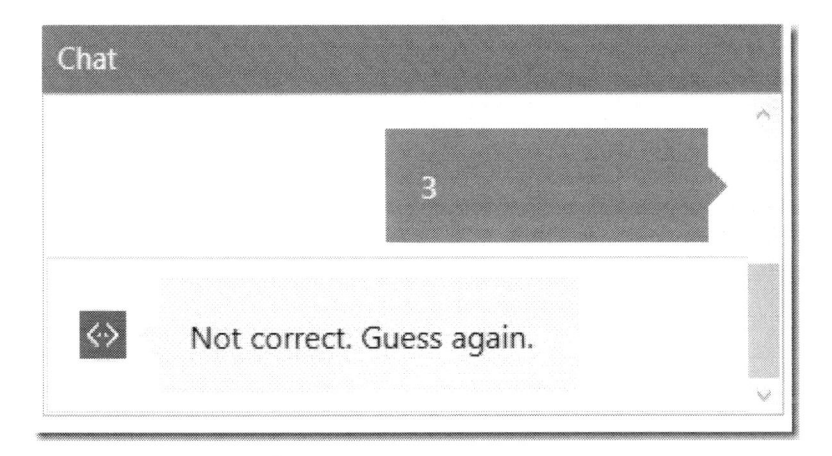

The **User** guesses a number, and the **Bot** informs the **User** if they are correct or not.

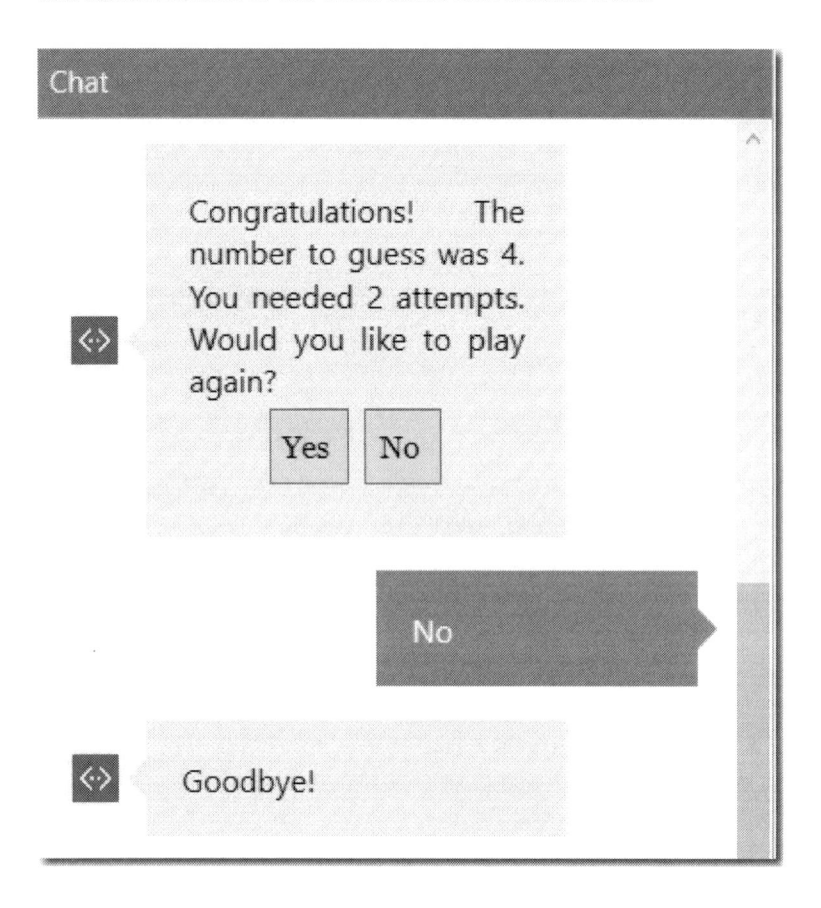

An Introduction to the Microsoft Bot Framework

When the **User** guesses the number correctly, they are offered a chance to play the game again.

If the **User** chooses not to play the game again, the **Bot** tells them goodbye.

Creating The Application

Open **Visual Studio**.

An Introduction to the Microsoft Bot Framework

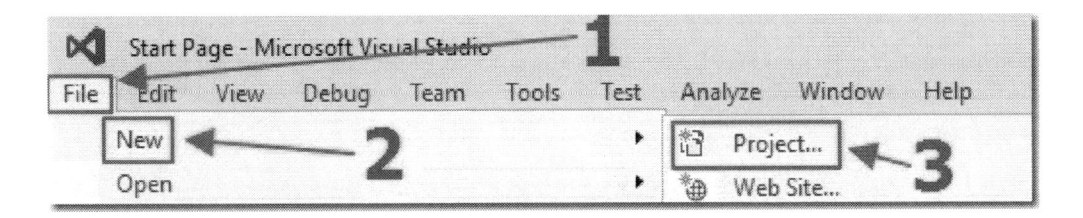

Create a new **Project**.

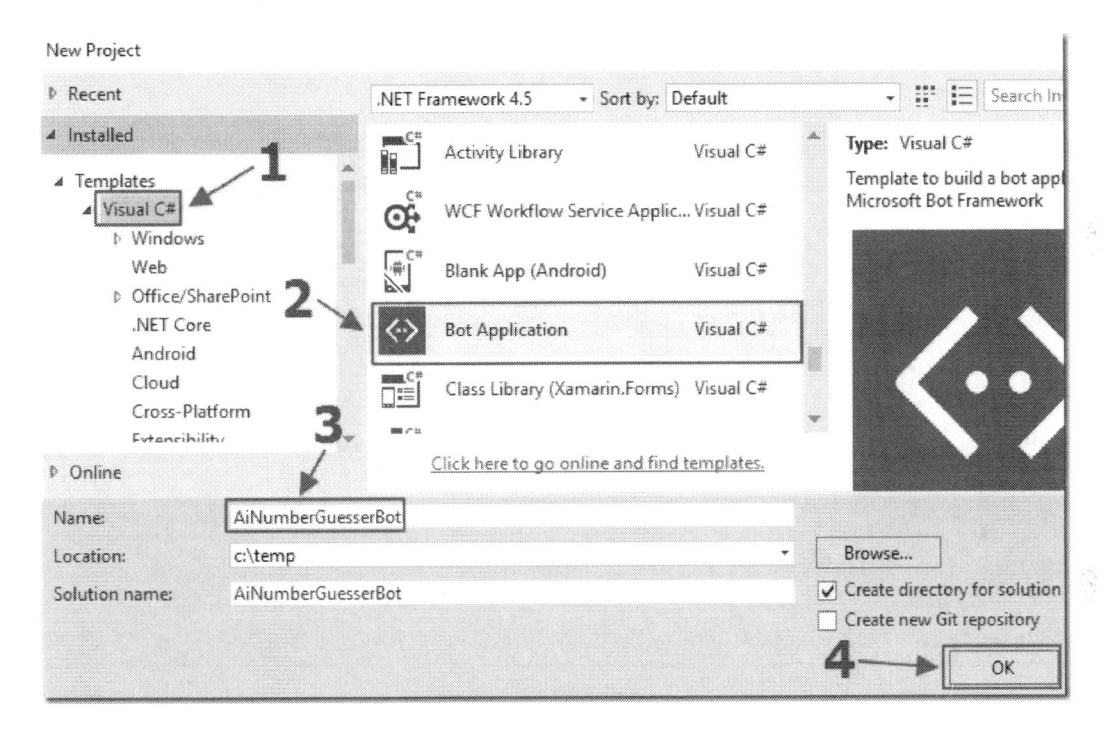

Select the **Bot Application** template and name the project **AiNumberGuesserBot**.

An Introduction to the Microsoft Bot Framework

The project will be created.

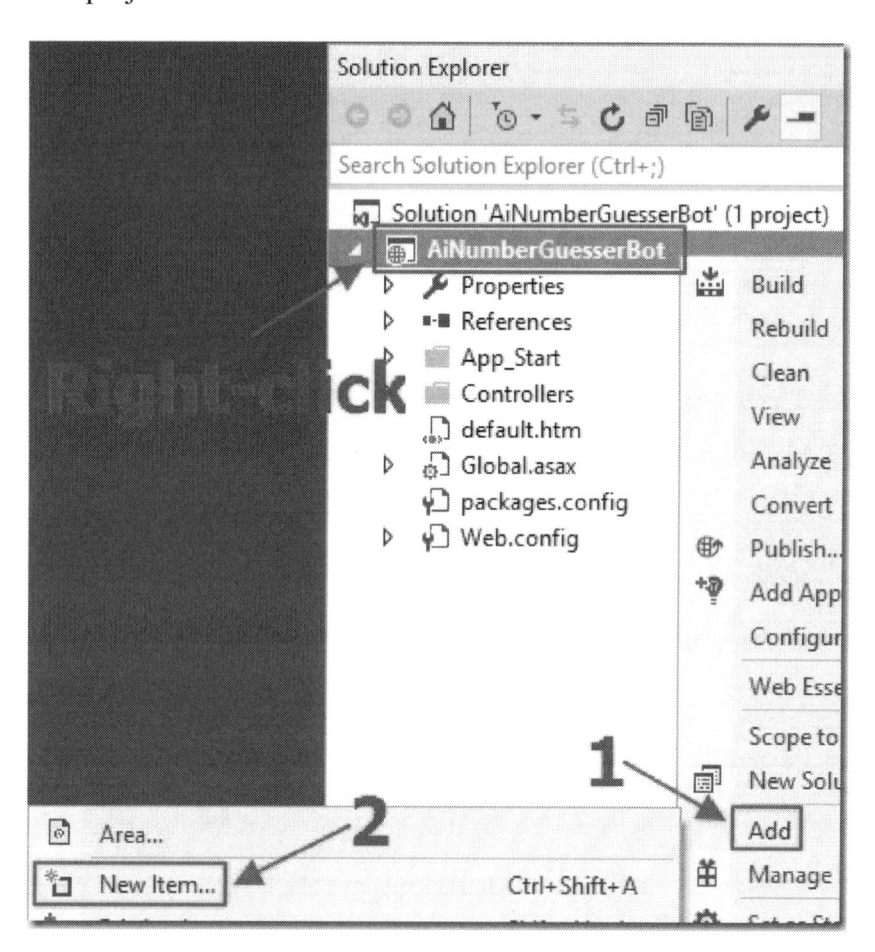

Right-click on the project. Select **Add** and then **New Item**.

An Introduction to the Microsoft Bot Framework

We will now create the class that will contain the logic for the **Dialog**.

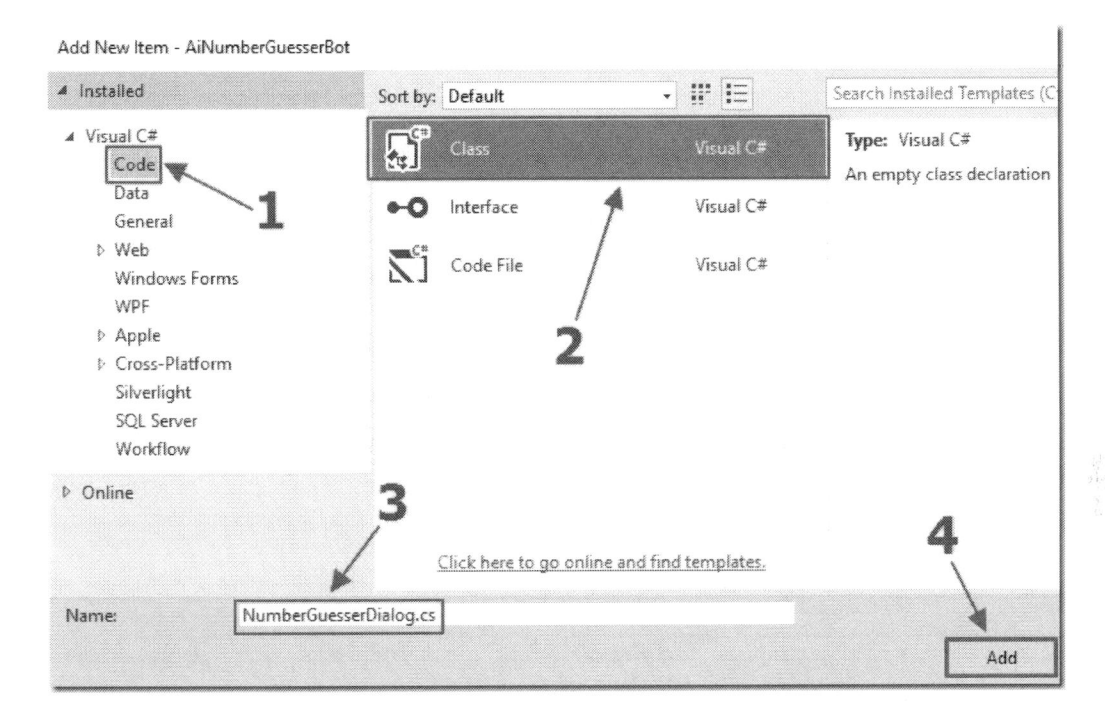

Add a new **C#** class called **NumberGuesserDialog.cs**.

An Introduction to the Microsoft Bot Framework

Replace all the code with the following code:

```
using System;
using System.Threading.Tasks;
using Microsoft.Bot.Builder.Dialogs;
using Microsoft.Bot.Connector;
using System.Text;
namespace AiNumberGuesserBot
{
    [Serializable]
    public class NumberGuesserDialog : IDialog<object>
    {
        protected int intNumberToGuess;
        protected int intAttempts;
    }
}
```

A **Dialog** is a class that inherits from **IDialog**.

Note that we must decorate this class as **[Serializable]**.

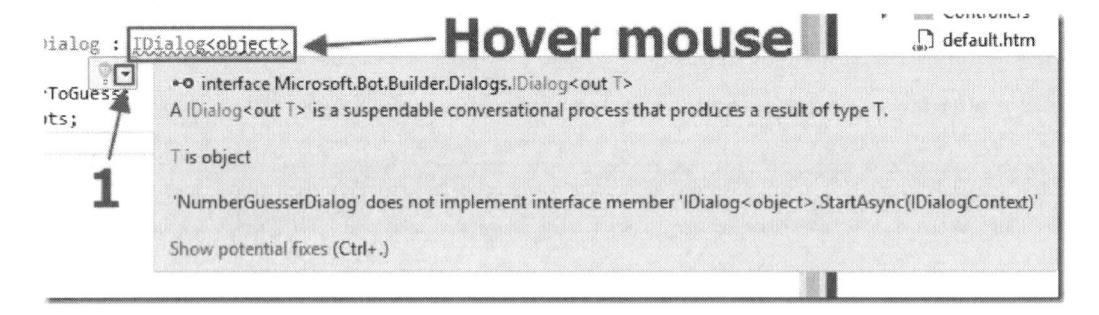

![Hover mouse screenshot showing IDialog<object> tooltip with interface Microsoft.Bot.Builder.Dialogs.IDialog<out T>, "A IDialog<out T> is a suspendable conversational process that produces a result of type T.", "T is object", and "'NumberGuesserDialog' does not implement interface member 'IDialog<object>.StartAsync(IDialogContext)'"]

This requires you to implement a **StartAsync** method.

To implement this, hover the mouse over **IDialog<object>**, wait a few seconds, and the interface option window will appear.

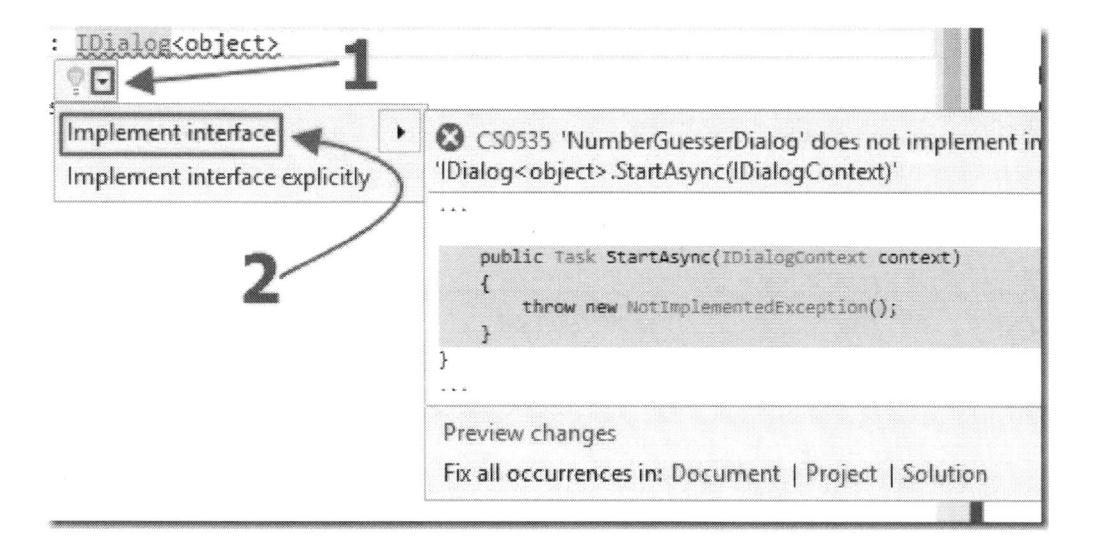

An Introduction to the Microsoft Bot Framework

Click the black arrow next to the light bulb and select **Implement interface**.

The **StartAsync** method will be created.
This will be called when the **Dialog** is first instantiated.

We want the code to run *asynchronously*, so add **async** to the method signature.

An Introduction to the Microsoft Bot Framework

Now, change the code inside the method, so the complete method is coded as follows:

```
public async Task StartAsync(IDialogContext context)
{
    // Generate a random number
    Random random = new Random();
    this.intNumberToGuess = random.Next(1, 10);
    // Set Attempts
    this.intAttempts = 1;
    // Start the Game
    context.Wait(MessageReceivedAsync);
}
```

The last line in the method is **context.Wait**. This suspends the current **Dialog** until the user has sent a message to the **Bot**.

The **Wait** method takes a method as a parameter (in this case **MessageReceivedAsync**) to be called to *resume* the conversation when the *response* has been received.

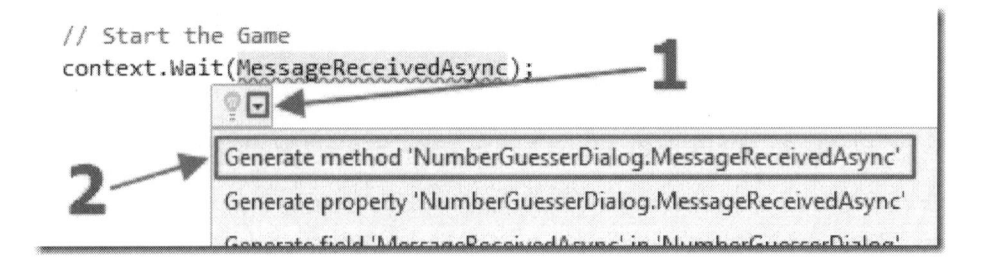

```
// Start the Game
context.Wait(MessageReceivedAsync);
```

1 →
2 →
Generate method 'NumberGuesserDialog.MessageReceivedAsync'
Generate property 'NumberGuesserDialog.MessageReceivedAsync'

To implement it, hover the mouse over **MessageReceivedAsync**, wait a few seconds, and the interface option window will appear.

Click the black arrow next to the light bulb and select **Generate method 'NumberGuesserDialog.MessageReceivedAsync**.

An Introduction to the Microsoft Bot Framework

```
private Task MessageReceivedAsync(IDialogContext context, IAwaitable<object> result)
{
    throw new NotImplementedException();
}
```

The **MessageReceivedAsync** method will be created.

Notice it takes the *context* of the **Dialog** and an argument (*result*).

```
public virtual async Task MessageReceivedAsync(IDialogContext context,
    IAwaitable<IMessageActivity> argument)
{
    throw new NotImplementedException();
}
```

Change the type of the argument from *object* to **IMessageActivity** and change the name of the variable from *result* to *argument*.

Again, we want the code to run *asynchronously*, so add **async** to the method signature and mark it as *virtual*.

Alter the code in the method, so the complete method is coded as follows:

```
public virtual async Task MessageReceivedAsync(IDialogContext context,
    IAwaitable<IMessageActivity> argument)
{
    int intGuessedNumber;
    // Get the text passed
    var message = await argument;
    // See if a number was passed
    if (!int.TryParse(message.Text, out intGuessedNumber))
    {
        // A number was not passed
        await context.PostAsync("Hi Welcome! - Guess a number between 1 and 10");
        context.Wait(MessageReceivedAsync);
    }
}
```

An Introduction to the Microsoft Bot Framework

Notice the last line (**context.Wait(MessageReceivedAsync)**) simply calls the method the code is contained in again and again.

We are only doing this to make this example as simple as possible. We will explore a more realistic example in the next section when we add a **PromptDialog**.

```
/// <summary>
/// POST: api/Messages
/// Receive a message from a user and reply to it
/// </summary>
public async Task<HttpResponseMessage> Post([FromBody]Activity activity)
{
    if (activity.Type == ActivityTypes.Message)
    {
        // Call NumberGuesserDialog
        await Conversation.SendAsync(activity, () => new NumberGuesserDialog());
    }
    else
    {
        HandleSystemMessage(activity);
    }
    var response = Request.CreateResponse(HttpStatusCode.OK);
    return response;
}
```

Next, open the **MessagesController.cs** file at *...\AiNumberGuesserBot\AiNumberGuesserBot\Controllers\ MessagesController.cs*

Replace the default code in the code block that begins:

```
if (activity.Type == ActivityTypes.Message)
```

With the code:

```
// Call NumberGuesserDialog
await Conversation.SendAsync(activity, () => new NumberGuesserDialog());
```

This tells the **Bot** to direct any messages to the **NumberGuesserDialog** class.

An Introduction to the Microsoft Bot Framework

Finally, add the following *using* statement to the top of the code file:

```
using Microsoft.Bot.Builder.Dialogs;
```

Test The Application

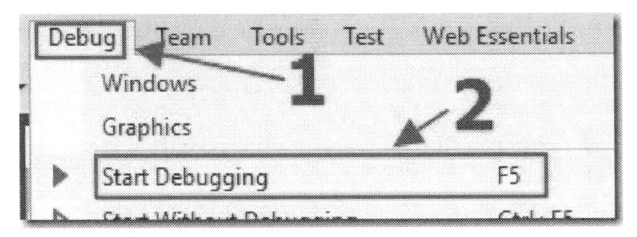

Hit **F5** to run the application.

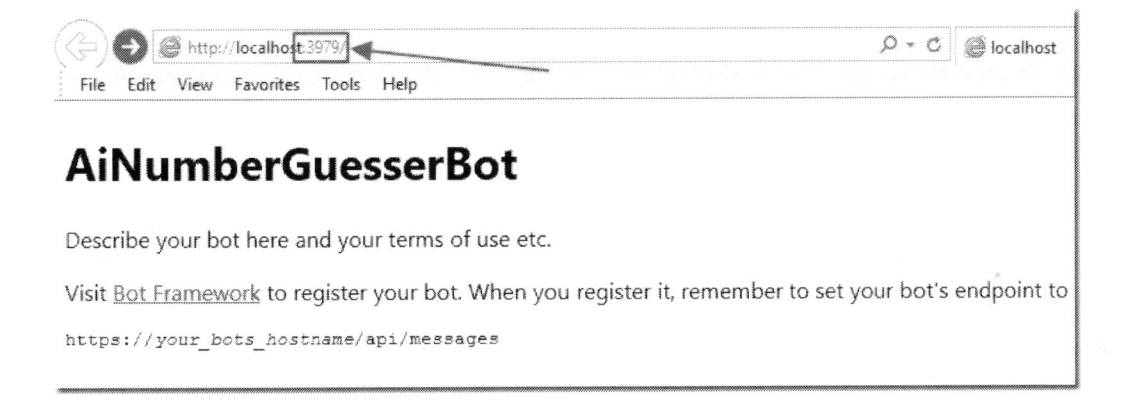

The web browser will open. Note the port number and the web address.

An Introduction to the Microsoft Bot Framework

Open and run the **Microsoft Bot Framework Emulator**.
When the emulator starts, connect to the **Bot** by setting the address to the one indicted in the web browser; however, add **/api/messages** to the end.

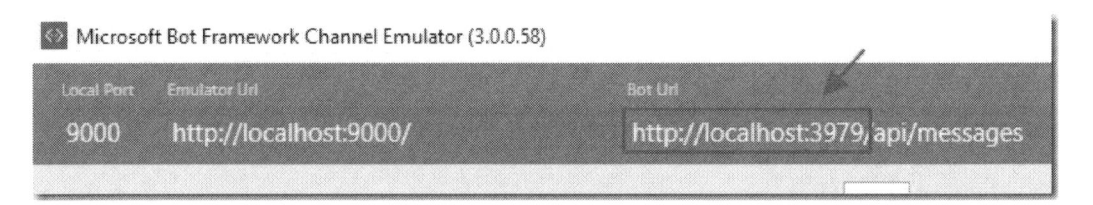

Ensure that the **Bot URL** is connecting to the correct address.

Type a message and click the **send** key (or press **Enter**).

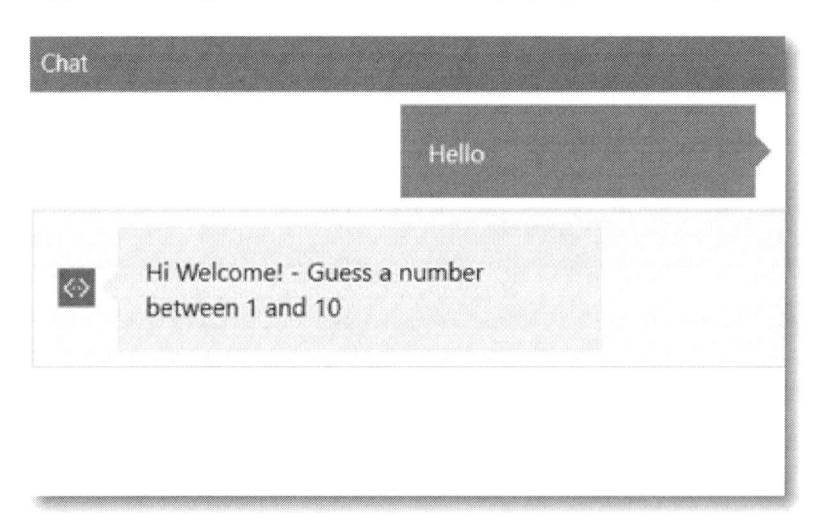

The **Bot** will respond.

This is all the **Bot** will do at this point; however, this example shows the minimal code to create and consume a **Dialog** class.

Dialog Prompts

A **PromptDialog** is essentially a **Dialog** factory for creating simple prompts. It allows you to ask the **User** for a response and indicate what code will run when the response is given. A **PromptDialog** spawns a *sub-dialog* that has its own private *state*. This sub-dialog is *suspended* by the **Microsoft Bot Framework service** while it waits for a response. When it gets a *response*, it *resumes* at the point in the code it was at when it was suspended.

This is the primary means of controlling program flow within a **Dialog** class.

A **PromptDialog** can be one of the following types:

- Prompt for an attachment
- Prompt for one of a set of choices
- Ask a yes/no question
- Prompt for a long
- Prompt for a double
- Prompt for a string

We will enhance our application to implement a **PromptDialog** that asks a *yes/no* question.

An Introduction to the Microsoft Bot Framework

First, add the following code to the **MessageReceivedAsync** method:

```
// This code will run when the user has entered a number
if (int.TryParse(message.Text, out intGuessedNumber))
{
    // A number was passed
    // See if it was the correct number
    if (intGuessedNumber != this.intNumberToGuess)
    {
        // The number was not correct
        this.intAttempts++;
        await context.PostAsync("Not correct. Guess again.");
        context.Wait(MessageReceivedAsync);
    }
    else
    {
        // Game completed
        StringBuilder sb = new StringBuilder();
        sb.Append("Congratulations! ");
        sb.Append("The number to guess was {0}. ");
        sb.Append("You needed {1} attempts. ");
        sb.Append("Would you like to play again?");
        string CongratulationsStringPrompt =
            string.Format(sb.ToString(),
            this.intNumberToGuess,
            this.intAttempts);
        // Put PromptDialog here
    }
}
```

This code will simply keep looping and counting the guessing attempts if the user does not guess the random number.

If the user does guess the number, the code in the *else* block will be called.

Right now, the code is not complete. We need to add a **PromptDialog** under the line **// Put PromptDialog here**.

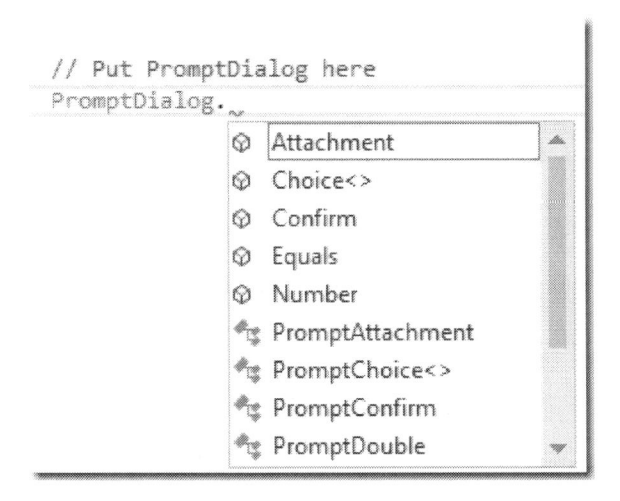

An Introduction to the Microsoft Bot Framework

```
// Put PromptDialog here
PromptDialog.
```
- Attachment
- Choice<>
- Confirm
- Equals
- Number
- PromptAttachment
- PromptChoice<>
- PromptConfirm
- PromptDouble

Type **PromptDialog** and press the *period* (.) key. The *autocomplete* options will show and we will see the option to implement the various types of **PromptDialogs**.

Choose the **Confirm** option.

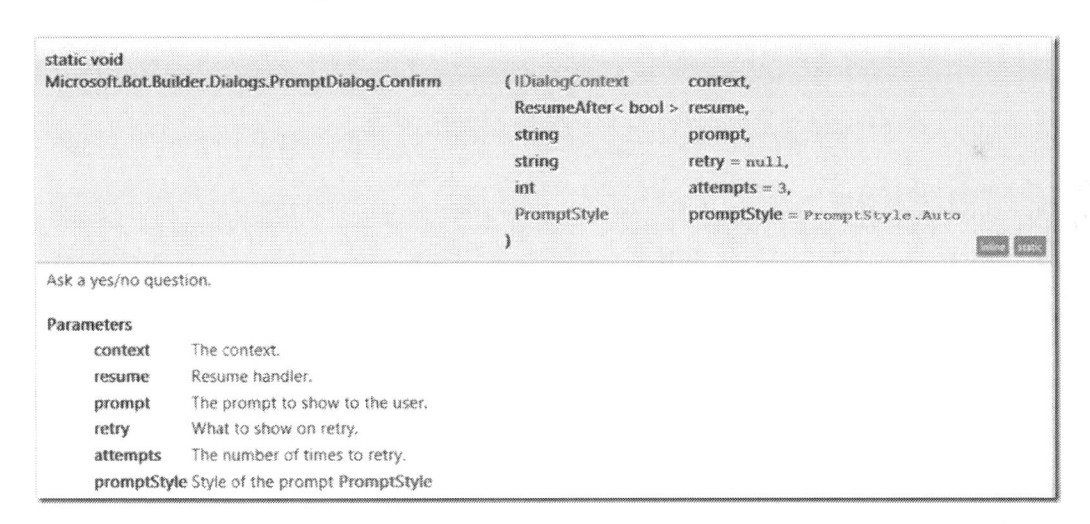

```
static void
Microsoft.Bot.Builder.Dialogs.PromptDialog.Confirm ( IDialogContext    context,
                                                     ResumeAfter< bool >  resume,
                                                     string            prompt,
                                                     string            retry = null,
                                                     int               attempts = 3,
                                                     PromptStyle       promptStyle = PromptStyle.Auto
                                                   )
```

Ask a yes/no question.

Parameters
- context   The context.
- resume   Resume handler.
- prompt   The prompt to show to the user.
- retry   What to show on retry.
- attempts   The number of times to retry.
- promptStyle Style of the prompt PromptStyle

We can look in the official documentation at https://docs.botframework.com/en-us/csharp/builder/sdkreference/ and see the method signature requires us to pass the current *context*, indicate the method to be called when we get a response (*resume handler*), provide a message to show the user (*prompt*), and provide a

An Introduction to the Microsoft Bot Framework

message to display if the response type is not correct (*retry*). The other parameters are optional.

The following shows the complete code for our implementation:

```
PromptDialog.Confirm(
    context,
    PlayAgainAsync,
    CongratulationsStringPrompt,
    "Didn't get that!");
```

We now need to implement the *resume handler* method to handle the response (**PlayAgainAsync**).

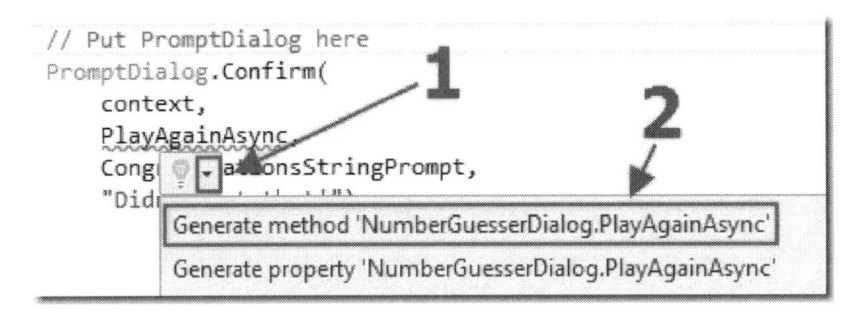

```
// Put PromptDialog here
PromptDialog.Confirm(
    context,
    PlayAgainAsync,
    CongratulationsStringPrompt,
    "Did
         Generate method 'NumberGuesserDialog.PlayAgainAsync'
         Generate property 'NumberGuesserDialog.PlayAgainAsync'
```

To implement it, hover the mouse over **PlayAgainAsync**, wait a few seconds, and the interface option window will appear.

Click the black arrow next to the light bulb and select **Generate method 'NumberGuesserDialog.PlayAgainAsync'**.

```
private Task PlayAgainAsync(IDialogContext context, IAwaitable<bool> result)
{
    throw new NotImplementedException();
}
```

The method will be created.

An Introduction to the Microsoft Bot Framework

```
private async Task PlayAgainAsync(IDialogContext context, IAwaitable<bool> result)
{
    throw new NotImplementedException();
}
```

Add **async** to the method signature.

Alter the method, so the complete code is as follows:

```
private async Task PlayAgainAsync(IDialogContext context, IAwaitable<bool> result)
{
    // Generate new random number
    Random random = new Random();
    this.intNumberToGuess = random.Next(1, 10);
    // Reset attempts
    this.intAttempts = 1;
    // Get the response from the user
    var confirm = await result;
    if (confirm) // They said yes
    {
        // Start a new Game
        await context.PostAsync("Hi Welcome! - Guess a number between 1 and 10");
        context.Wait(MessageReceivedAsync);
    }
    else // They said no
    {
        await context.PostAsync("Goodbye!");
        context.Wait(MessageReceivedAsync);
    }
}
```

Hit **F5** to run the program and connect to it, using the **Bot Framework Emulator**…

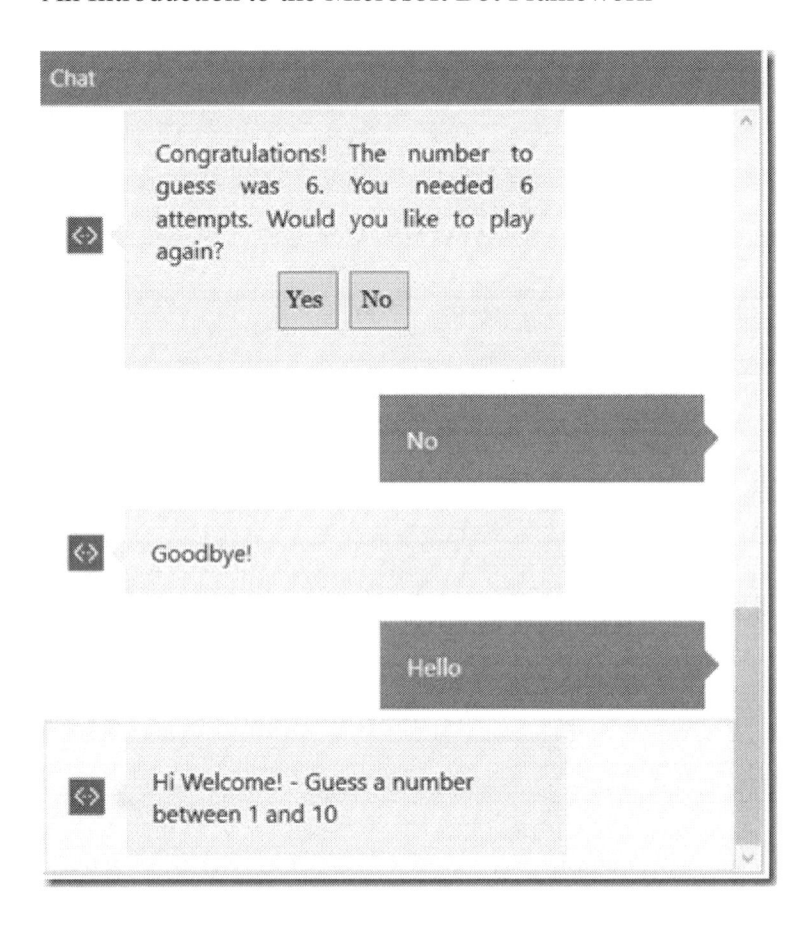

An Introduction to the Microsoft Bot Framework

[Chat screenshot showing:
- Bot: "Congratulations! The number to guess was 6. You needed 6 attempts. Would you like to play again?" with Yes/No buttons
- User: "No"
- Bot: "Goodbye!"
- User: "Hello"
- Bot: "Hi Welcome! - Guess a number between 1 and 10"]

When we guess the correct number, the **PromptDialog** will appear. When we provide an answer, the **PlayAgainAsync** method will immediately run to process our answer.

We can spawn another **PromptDialog** inside the **PlayAgainAsync** method if we choose, effectively creating an endless chain of **PromptDialogs** to create branches of code for a conversation.

An Introduction to the Microsoft Bot Framework

Chapter 5: Using Images, Cards, Carousels, and Buttons

The sample code for this chapter can be obtained at the link "Using Images, Cards, Carousels, and Buttons In The Microsoft Bot Framework" at http://AiHelpWebsite.com/Downloads

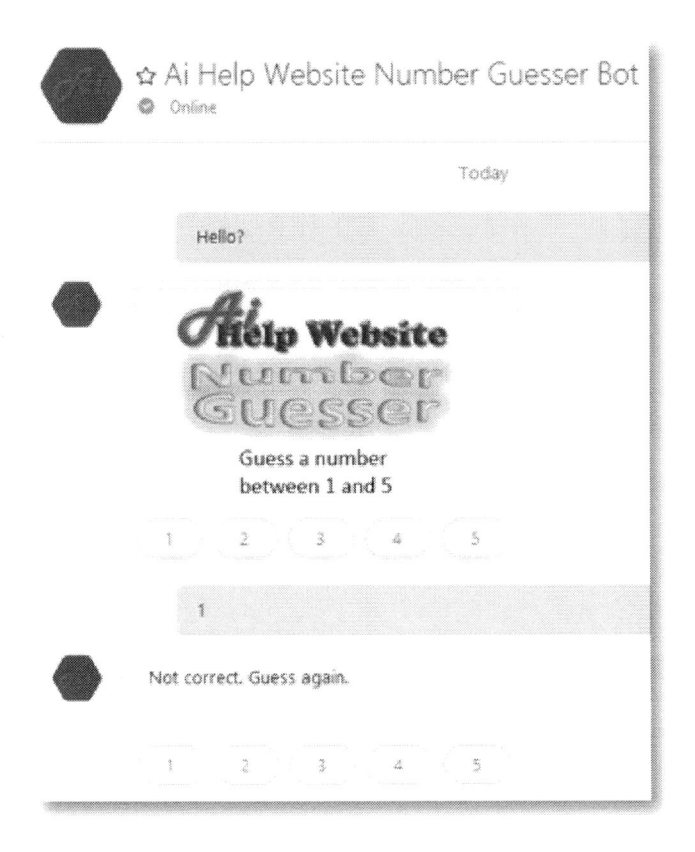

Note: *The image above shows the Bot in Skype. Deploying a Bot to Skype is covered in Chapter Ten.*

Implementing images in your **Microsoft Bot Framework** application adds a visual element to the interaction with your users.

An Introduction to the Microsoft Bot Framework

You can easily pass a *media attachment* (image/audio/video/file) to a message using code such as this:

```
activity.Attachments.Add(new Attachment()
{
    ContentUrl = "http://aihelpwebsite.com/portals/0/Images/AIHelpWebsiteLogo_Large.png",
    ContentType = "image/png",
    Name = "AIHelpWebsiteLogo_Large.png"
});
```

Depending on the channel used and the *media type*, an image will be displayed or a link will be displayed for the user to download the media element.

However, real power is provided when you use *rich card attachments*.

There are four **card** types:

Card Type	Description	Single or Carousel/List (Multiple Cards)
Hero Card	A big image with text	Single or Carousel/List
Thumbnail Card	A small image with text	Single or Carousel/List
Receipt Card	An invoice or receipt	Single
Sign-In Card	A user sign-in form	Single

An Introduction to the Microsoft Bot Framework

Hero Card

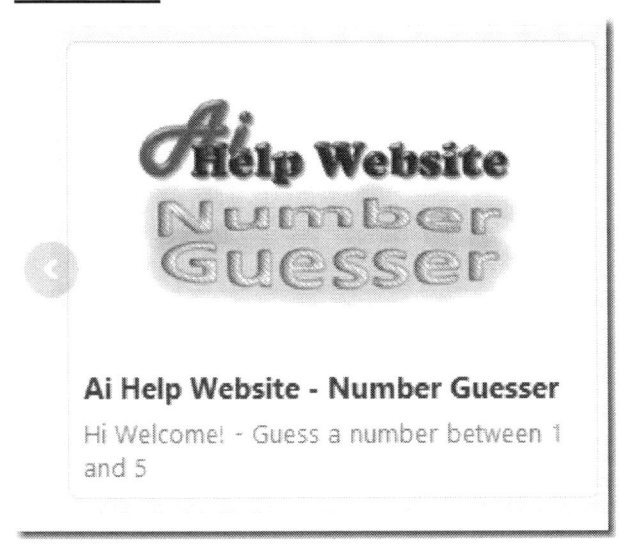

In this chapter, we will cover **Hero Card**.

A **Hero Card** and a **Thumbnail Card** differ only in the size of their *image* and *card*.

Each consists of the following **properties**:

Property	Description
Title	Title of the card
Text	Text to display on the card
Subtitle	A link for the title
Images	Actually, only a single image
Buttons	One or more buttons (In **Skype**, only 5 buttons will display on a card. If you have more buttons, it will create two cards.)
Tap	An action that is triggered when a user taps on the card (This does not work in some **Skype** clients, so for **Skype**, use a hyperlink for the *Subtitle* property.)

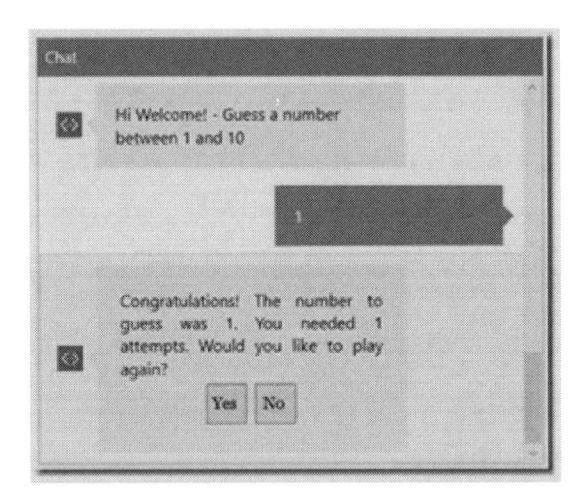

An Introduction to the Microsoft Bot Framework

To demonstrate implementing a **Hero Card**, we will start with the code from the previous chapter.

Note: *First, you will have to use **Manage NuGet Packages** in **Visual Studio** to update **Microsoft.Bot.Builder** to the latest stable version before you continue.*

Also, we will make some small changes, such as making the number to guess from **1** to **5** rather than **1** to **10**, so it shows up well in **Skype** because **Skype** will only display **5** buttons on a single card.

Open the project in **Visual Studio**.

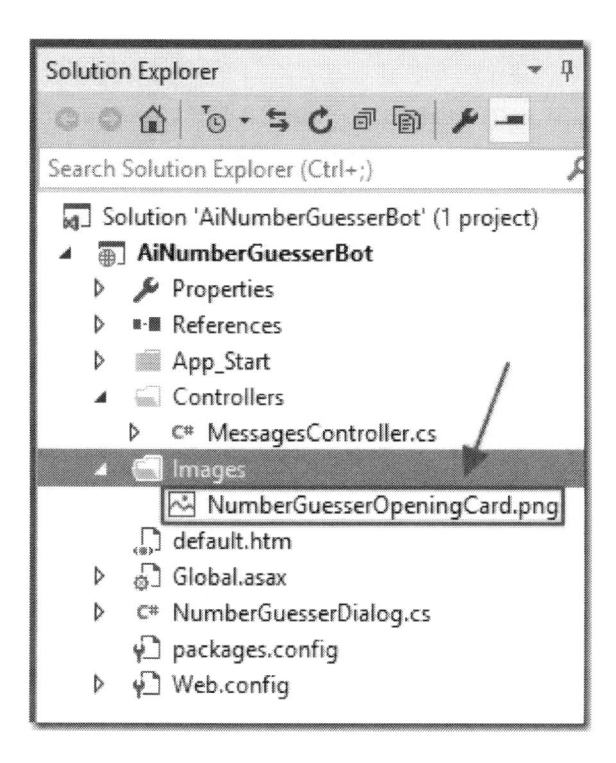

An Introduction to the Microsoft Bot Framework

Add a new folder and call it **Images.**

Add the **NumberGuesserOpeningCard.png** file (you can get the code on the *Downloads* page of the AiHelpWebsite.com) to the **Images** folder.

Open the **MessagesController.cs** file (in the **Controllers** directory), and add the following *using* statement to the top of the file:

```
using System.Collections.Generic;
```

An Introduction to the Microsoft Bot Framework

```
private Activity HandleSystemMessage(Activity message)
{
    if (message.Type == ActivityTypes.DeleteUserData)
    {
        // Implement user deletion here
        // If we handle user deletion, return a real message
    }
    else if (message.Type == ActivityTypes.ConversationUpdate)
    {
        // Handle conversation state changes, like members being adde
        // Use Activity.MembersAdded and Activity.MembersRemoved and
        // Not available in all channels
    }
    else if (message.Type == ActivityTypes.ContactRelationUpdate)
    {
        // Handle add/remove from contact lists
        // Activity.From + Activity.Action represent what happened
    }
    else if (message.Type == ActivityTypes.Typing)
```

Next, locate the **else if (message.Type == ActivityTypes.ContactRelationUpdate)** section in the **HandleSystemMessage** method.

This method fires when the **Bot** is added to the *Contact list* of a user.

Replace all the code in the section with the following code:

An Introduction to the Microsoft Bot Framework

```csharp
// Construct a base URL for Image
// To allow it to be found wherever the application is deployed
string strCurrentURL =
    this.Url.Request.RequestUri.AbsoluteUri.Replace(@"api/messages", "");
// Create a reply message
Activity replyToConversation = message.CreateReply();
replyToConversation.Recipient = message.From;
replyToConversation.Type = "message";
replyToConversation.Attachments = new List<Attachment>();
// AttachmentLayout options are list or carousel
replyToConversation.AttachmentLayout = "carousel";
#region Card One
// Full URL to the image
string strNumberGuesserOpeningCard =
    String.Format(@"{0}/{1}",
    strCurrentURL,
    "Images/NumberGuesserOpeningCard.png");
// Create a CardImage and add our image
List<CardImage> cardImages1 = new List<CardImage>();
cardImages1.Add(new CardImage(url: strNumberGuesserOpeningCard));
// Create a CardAction to make the HeroCard clickable
// Note this does not work in some Skype clients
CardAction btnAiHelpWebsite = new CardAction()
{
    Type = "openUrl",
    Title = "AiHelpWebsite.com",
    Value = "http://AiHelpWebsite.com"
};
// Finally create the Hero Card
// adding the image and the CardAction
HeroCard plCard1 = new HeroCard()
{
    Title = "Ai Help Website - Number Guesser",
    Subtitle = "Hi Welcome! - Guess a number between 1 and 5",
    Images = cardImages1,
    Tap = btnAiHelpWebsite
};
// Create an Attachment by calling the
// ToAttachment() method of the Hero Card
Attachment plAttachment1 = plCard1.ToAttachment();
// Add the Attachment to the reply message
replyToConversation.Attachments.Add(plAttachment1);
#endregion
// Create a ConnectorClient and use it to send the reply message
var connector =
    new ConnectorClient(new Uri(message.ServiceUrl));
var reply =
    connector.Conversations.SendToConversationAsync(replyToConversation);
```

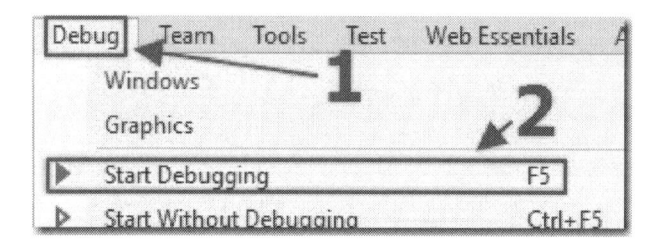

An Introduction to the Microsoft Bot Framework

Save the file and hit **F5** to run the application.

Open and run the **Bot** using the **Microsoft Bot Framework Emulator**.

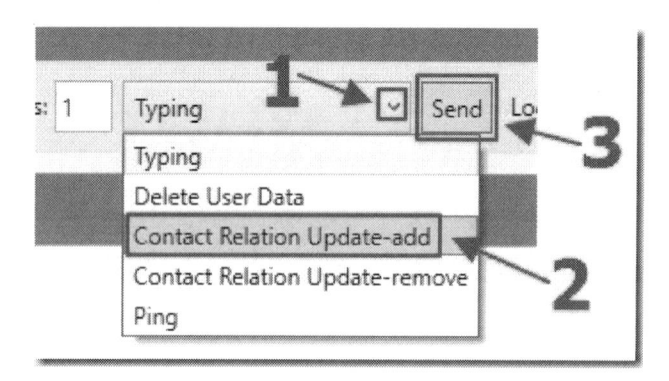

In the **Emulator**, invoke the **Contact Relation Update-add** event.

An Introduction to the Microsoft Bot Framework

The **Hero Card** will display.

Clicking on the card will take you to the **AiHelpWebsite.com** website.

An Introduction to the Microsoft Bot Framework

Carousel

A *carousel* displays multiple cards (either **Hero Cards** or **Thumbnail Cards**) *horizontally*.

A *List* (the default layout for multiple cards) displays the cards *vertically*.

The image above shows what a *carousel* of two **Hero Cards** looks like in the **Skype** client.

An Introduction to the Microsoft Bot Framework

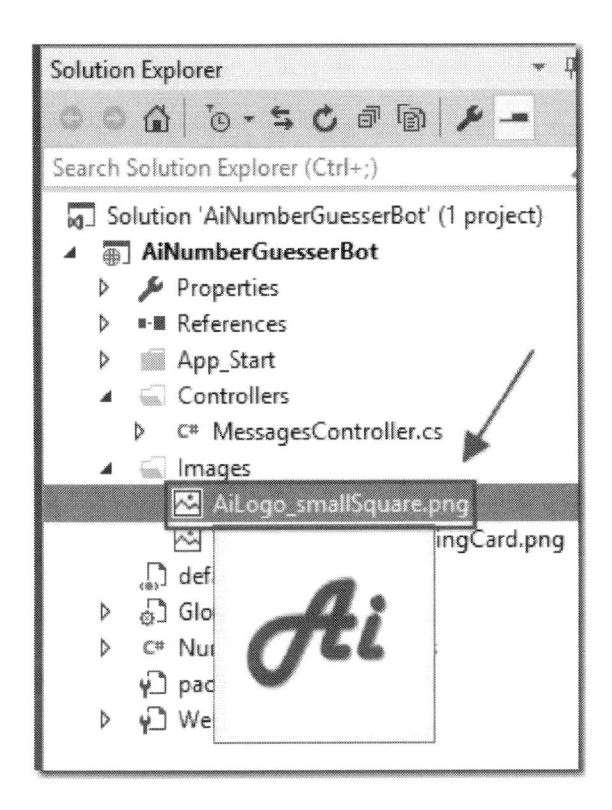

To implement this, first add the **AiLogo_smallSquare.png** file (you can get the code on the *Downloads* page of the AiHelpWebsite.com) to the **Images** folder.

Next, add the following code to the **HandleSystemMessage** method (above the **var connector = new ConnectorClient(new Uri(message.ServiceUrl));** line):

An Introduction to the Microsoft Bot Framework

```
#region Card Two
string strAiLogo_smallSquare =
    String.Format(@"{0}/{1}",
    strCurrentURL,
    "Images/AiLogo_smallSquare.png");
List<CardImage> cardImages2 = new List<CardImage>();
cardImages2.Add(new CardImage(url: strAiLogo_smallSquare));
// CardAction to make the HeroCard clickable
CardAction btnTutorial = new CardAction()
{
    Type = "openUrl",
    Title = "http://bit.ly/2bRyJMj",
    Value = "http://bit.ly/2bRyJMj"
};
HeroCard plCard2 = new HeroCard()
{
    Title = "Based on the Using Dialogs Tutorial",
    Subtitle = "http://bit.ly/2bRyJMj",
    Images = cardImages2,
    Tap = btnTutorial
};
Attachment plAttachment2 = plCard2.ToAttachment();
replyToConversation.Attachments.Add(plAttachment2);
#endregion
```

Save the file, run the application, and connect to it in the **Emulator**.

In the **Emulator**, invoke the **Contact Relation Update-add** event.

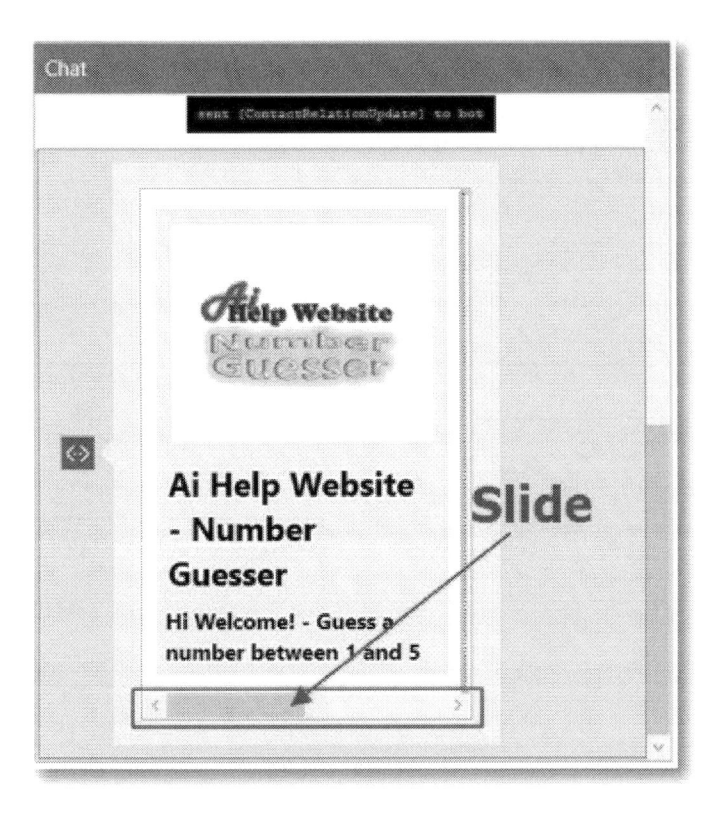

An Introduction to the Microsoft Bot Framework

The first card will show, but you will now see a *slider*.

Slide it to the *right*.

An Introduction to the Microsoft Bot Framework

You will then see the second **Hero Card**.

In **Skype**, the *Subtitle* property will display as a hyperlink and be clickable.

Rich Card Attachments In Dialogs

There are additional challenges when implementing **rich card attachments** in **Dialogs**.

Primarily, the biggest challenge is that, inside the **Dialog** class, you do not have access to the **base URL** of the application to determine where your images are.

We can address this by using the **Bot State Service**.

Open the **MessagesController.cs** file:

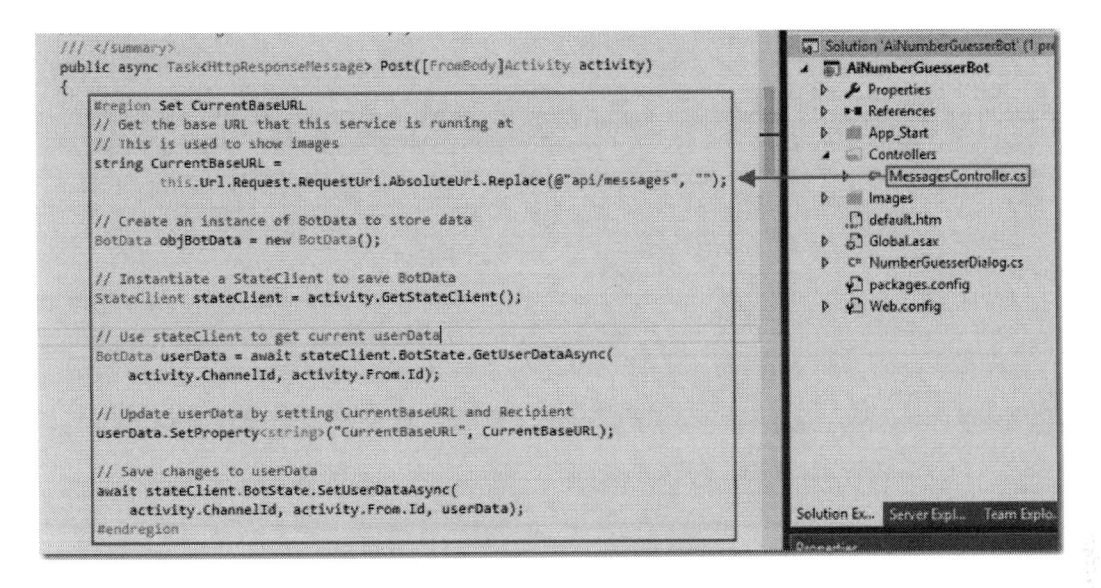

An Introduction to the Microsoft Bot Framework

Add the following code to the top of the **Post** method:

```
#region Set CurrentBaseURL
// Get the base URL that this service is running at
// This is used to show images
string CurrentBaseURL =
        this.Url.Request.RequestUri.AbsoluteUri.Replace(@"api/messages", "");
// Create an instance of BotData to store data
BotData objBotData = new BotData();
// Instantiate a StateClient to save BotData
StateClient stateClient = activity.GetStateClient();
// Use stateClient to get current userData
BotData userData = await stateClient.BotState.GetUserDataAsync(
    activity.ChannelId, activity.From.Id);
// Update userData by setting CurrentBaseURL and Recipient
userData.SetProperty<string>("CurrentBaseURL", CurrentBaseURL);
// Save changes to userData
await stateClient.BotState.SetUserDataAsync(
    activity.ChannelId, activity.From.Id, userData);
#endregion
```

This will store the *CurrentBaseURL* and the *Recipient* using the **Bot State Service**, so the values can later be retrieved in the **Dialog** class.

An Introduction to the Microsoft Bot Framework

```
namespace AiNumberGuesserBot
{
    [Serializable]
    public class NumberGuesserDialog : IDialog<object>
    {
        string strBaseURL;
        protected int intNumberToGuess;
        protected int intAttempts;

        public async Task StartAsync(IDialogContext context)

        public virtual async Task MessageReceivedAsync(
            IDialogContext context,
            IAwaitable<IMessageActivity> argument)
        {
            // Set BaseURL
            context.UserData.TryGetValue<string>(
                "CurrentBaseURL", out strBaseURL);

            int intGuessedNumber;
```

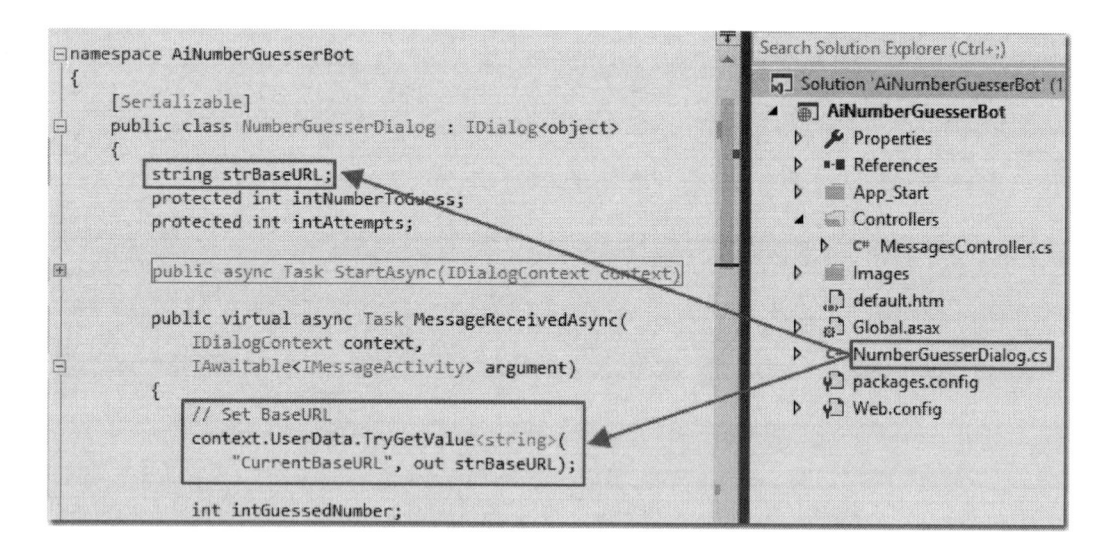

Solution Explorer:
- Solution 'AiNumberGuesserBot' (1
  - AiNumberGuesserBot
    - Properties
    - References
    - App_Start
    - Controllers
      - MessagesController.cs
    - Images
    - default.htm
    - Global.asax
    - NumberGuesserDialog.cs
    - packages.config
    - Web.config

Open the **NumberGuesserDialog.cs** file.

Add the following code above the namespace:

```
using System.Collections.Generic;
```

Add this to the top of the class:

```
string strBaseURL;
```

This will provide a global variable that will be automatically serialized and persisted between calls to store the **Base URL**.

Add the following code to the top of the **MessageReceivedAsync** method:

```
// Set BaseURL
context.UserData.TryGetValue<string>(
    "CurrentBaseURL", out strBaseURL);
```

An Introduction to the Microsoft Bot Framework

This will retrieve the value of **CurrentBaseURL** that was stored in **Bot State Service** in the **MessagesController** class and store it in the **strBaseURL** global variable.

Add the following *Utility* method to the class. This method will create 5 **CardAction** buttons that will be attached to the **Hero Card** (that we will create in a later step):

```
#region private static List<CardAction> CreateButtons()
private static List<CardAction> CreateButtons()
{
    // Create 5 CardAction buttons
    // and return to the calling method
    List<CardAction> cardButtons = new List<CardAction>();
    for (int i = 1; i < 6; i++)
    {
        string CurrentNumber = Convert.ToString(i);
        CardAction CardButton = new CardAction()
        {
            Type = "imBack",
            Title = CurrentNumber,
            Value = CurrentNumber
        };
        cardButtons.Add(CardButton);
    }
    return cardButtons;
}
#endregion
```

The buttons are set to the *Type* "imBack", which makes the button (**CardAction**) simply post the *value* (in this case, the button number) back to the **Bot**.

An Introduction to the Microsoft Bot Framework

Create The Hero Card In The Dialog Class

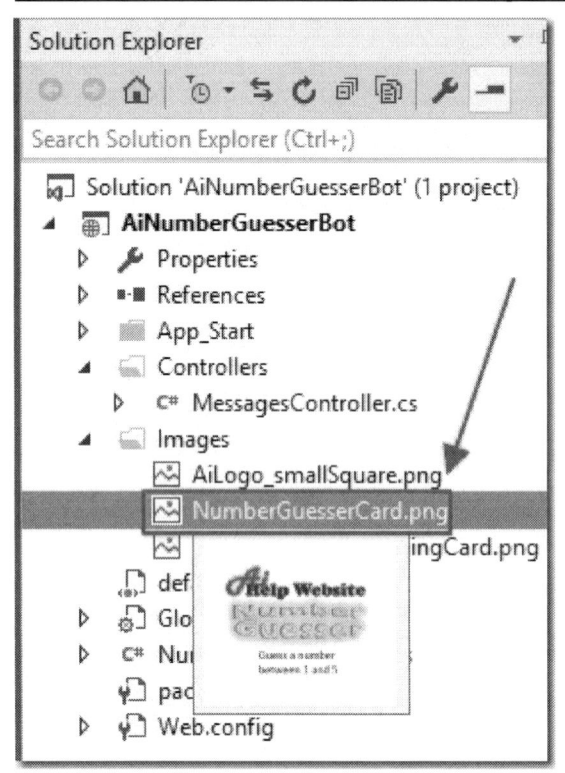

We will now display a **Hero Card** with **5** buttons in the **Dialog** class.

First, add the **NumberGuesserCard.png** file (you can get the code on the *Downloads* page of the AiHelpWebsite.com) to the **Images** folder.

An Introduction to the Microsoft Bot Framework

Next, find the following code in the **MessageReceivedAsync** method:

```
// See if a number was passed
if (!int.TryParse(message.Text, out intGuessedNumber))
{
    // A number was not passed
    await context.PostAsync("Hi Welcome! - Guess a number between 1 and 10");
    context.Wait(MessageReceivedAsync);
}
```

An Introduction to the Microsoft Bot Framework

Replace it with the following code:

```csharp
// See if a number was passed
if (!int.TryParse(message.Text, out intGuessedNumber))
{
    // A number was not passed
    // Create a reply Activity
    Activity replyToConversation = (Activity)context.MakeMessage();
    replyToConversation.Recipient = replyToConversation.Recipient;
    replyToConversation.Type = "message";
    string strNumberGuesserCard =
        String.Format(@"{0}/{1}",
        strBaseURL,
        "Images/NumberGuesserCard.png");
    List<CardImage> cardImages = new List<CardImage>();
    cardImages.Add(new CardImage(url: strNumberGuesserCard));
    // Create the Buttons
    // Call the CreateButtons utility method
    List<CardAction> cardButtons = CreateButtons();
    // Create the Hero Card
    // Set the image and the buttons
    HeroCard plCard = new HeroCard()
    {
        Images = cardImages,
        Buttons = cardButtons,
    };
    // Create an Attachment by calling the
    // ToAttachment() method of the Hero Card
    Attachment plAttachment = plCard.ToAttachment();
    // Attach the Attachment to the reply
    replyToConversation.Attachments.Add(plAttachment);
    // set the AttachmentLayout as 'list'
    replyToConversation.AttachmentLayout = "list";
    // Send the reply
    await context.PostAsync(replyToConversation);
    context.Wait(MessageReceivedAsync);
}
```

Save the file, hit **F5** to run the project, and connect to it in the **Emulator**.

An Introduction to the Microsoft Bot Framework

The **Bot** will now display an *image* and *buttons*.

We can either click one of the buttons or enter a number to play the game.

An Introduction to the Microsoft Bot Framework

The following image shows what it looks like in **Skype**:

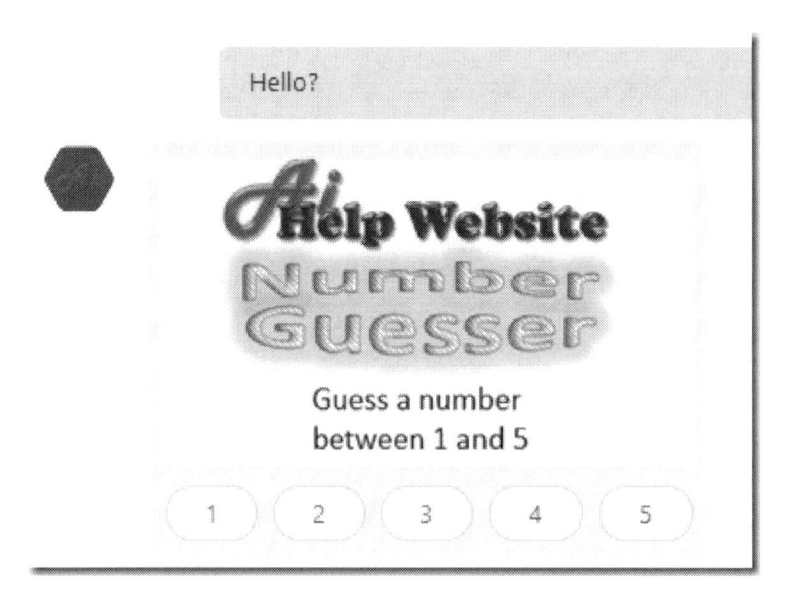

Creating A Re-Usable Hero Card

If there are a few more places we need to display the **Hero Card** with the buttons, we will want to create a re-usable **Hero Card**.

This **Hero Card** will not have an image, only buttons.

An Introduction to the Microsoft Bot Framework

First, add the following *utility* method to the **Dialog** class:

```
#region private static Activity ShowButtons(IDialogContext context, string strText)
private static Activity ShowButtons(IDialogContext context, string strText)
{
    // Create a reply Activity
    Activity replyToConversation = (Activity)context.MakeMessage();
    replyToConversation.Text = strText;
    replyToConversation.Recipient = replyToConversation.Recipient;
    replyToConversation.Type = "message";
    // Call the CreateButtons utility method
    // that will create 5 buttons to put on the Here Card
    List<CardAction> cardButtons = CreateButtons();
    // Create a Hero Card and add the buttons
    HeroCard plCard = new HeroCard()
    {
        Buttons = cardButtons
    };
    // Create an Attachment
    // set the AttachmentLayout as 'list'
    Attachment plAttachment = plCard.ToAttachment();
    replyToConversation.Attachments.Add(plAttachment);
    replyToConversation.AttachmentLayout = "list";
    // Return the reply to the calling method
    return replyToConversation;
}
#endregion
```

Note that it calls the **CreateButtons** *utility* method that we created earlier.

An Introduction to the Microsoft Bot Framework

Now, locate the following code:

```csharp
// A number was passed
// See if it was the correct number
if (intGuessedNumber != this.intNumberToGuess)
{
    // The number was not correct
    this.intAttempts++;
    await context.PostAsync("Not correct. Guess again.");
    context.Wait(MessageReceivedAsync);
}
```

Replace it with:

```csharp
// A number was passed
// See if it was the correct number
if (intGuessedNumber != this.intNumberToGuess)
{
    // The number was not correct
    this.intAttempts++;
    // Create a response
    // This time call the ** ShowButtons ** method
    Activity replyToConversation =
        ShowButtons(context, "Not correct. Guess again.");
    await context.PostAsync(replyToConversation);
    context.Wait(MessageReceivedAsync);
}
```

The code will now call the **ShowButtons** method that will return the **Hero Card**.

Finally, find the following code:

```csharp
// Start a new Game
await context.PostAsync("Hi Welcome! - Guess a number between 1 and 10");
context.Wait(MessageReceivedAsync);
```

An Introduction to the Microsoft Bot Framework

Replace it with:

```
// Start a new Game
// Create a response
// This time call the ** ShowButtons ** method
Activity replyToConversation =
    ShowButtons(context, "Hi Welcome! - Guess a number between 1 and 5");
await context.PostAsync(replyToConversation);
context.Wait(MessageReceivedAsync);
```

An Introduction to the Microsoft Bot Framework

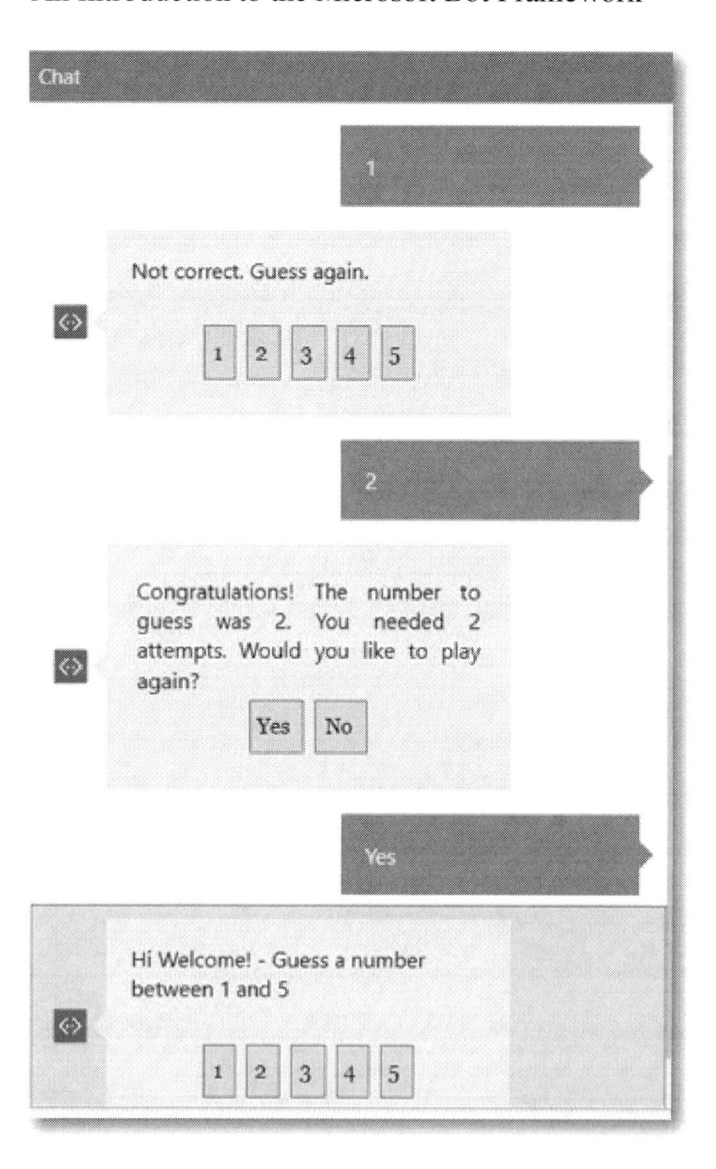

The Bot will now display the **Hero Card**, with only the buttons, in each situation where we called the *utility* method.

Chapter 6: Implementing A SQL Server Database With Your Bot

The sample code for this chapter can be obtained at the link "Implementing A SQL Server Database With The Microsoft Bot Framework" at http://AiHelpWebsite.com/Downloads

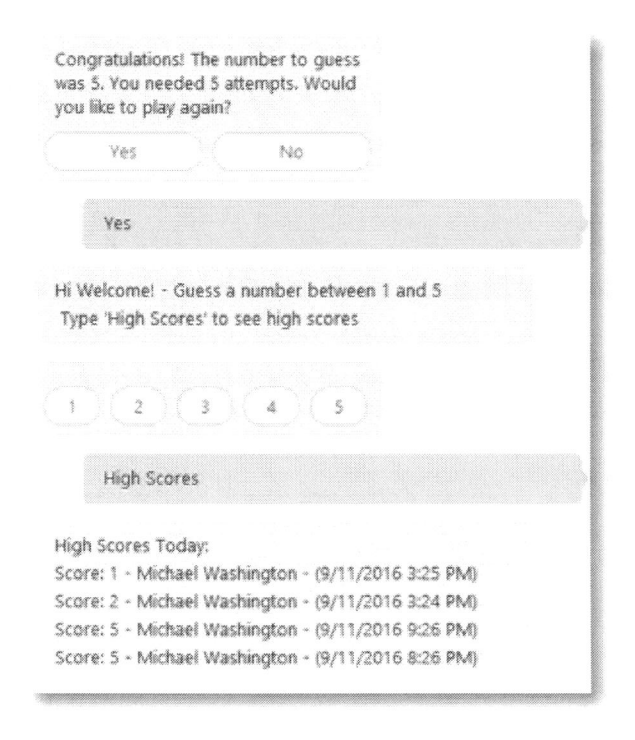

Microsoft Bot Framework *Chatbot* applications that require information to be stored, queried, and shared with multiple users will require a central storage repository.

Using **Microsoft SQL Server** and **Microsoft Azure** will allow you to easily implement this feature.

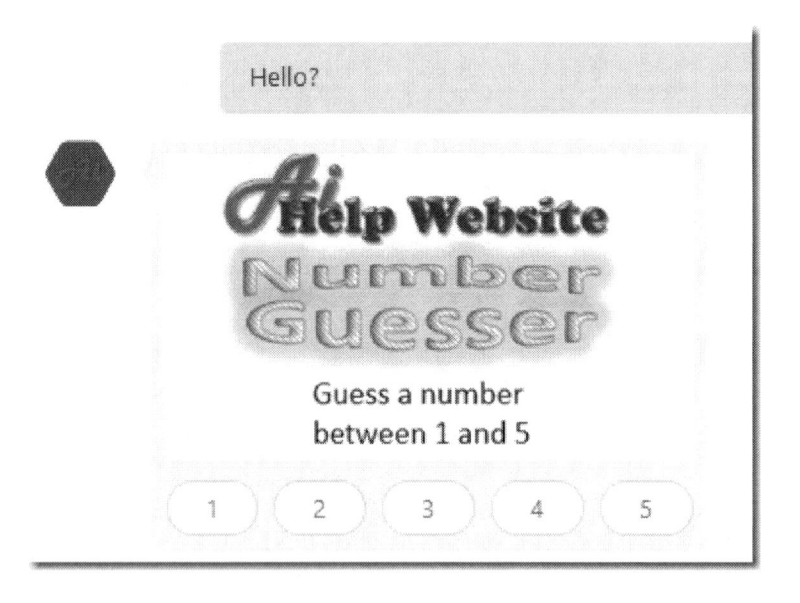

An Introduction to the Microsoft Bot Framework

To demonstrate implementing a database with a **Microsoft Bot Framework** application, we will start with the code from the previous chapter.

Create The SQL Server Database

We will start by creating a **database** and logging the messages sent *to* and *from* the **Bot**.

An Introduction to the Microsoft Bot Framework

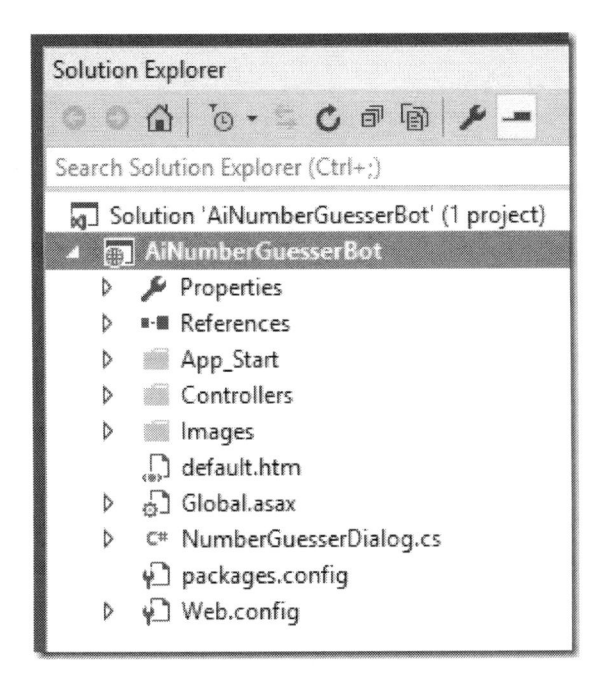

```
Solution Explorer
Search Solution Explorer (Ctrl+;)
⌐ Solution 'AiNumberGuesserBot' (1 project)
  ▲ AiNumberGuesserBot
    ▷ Properties
    ▷ References
    ▷ App_Start
    ▷ Controllers
    ▷ Images
      default.htm
    ▷ Global.asax
    ▷ C# NumberGuesserDialog.cs
      packages.config
    ▷ Web.config
```

Open the project in **Visual Studio**.

An Introduction to the Microsoft Bot Framework

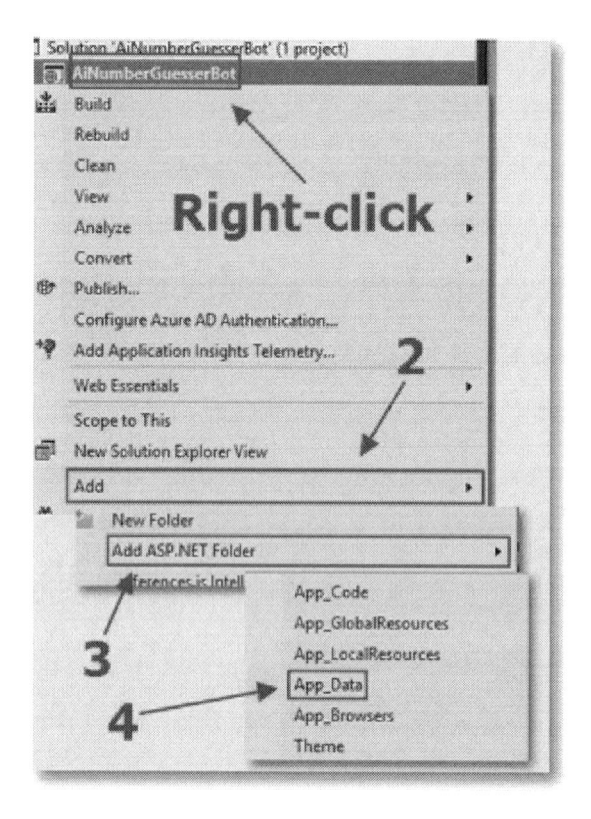

In the **Solution Explorer** in **Visual Studio**, *right-click* on the **Project** (not the **Solution**), and select **Add**, then **Add ASP.NET Folder**, then **App_Data**.

Note: **App_Data** *is a special folder that will contain the database we will create. We use this folder because we will have an option to not deploy this folder (and the database that it will contain) when we publish the application to* **Azure.** *This will be covered later.*

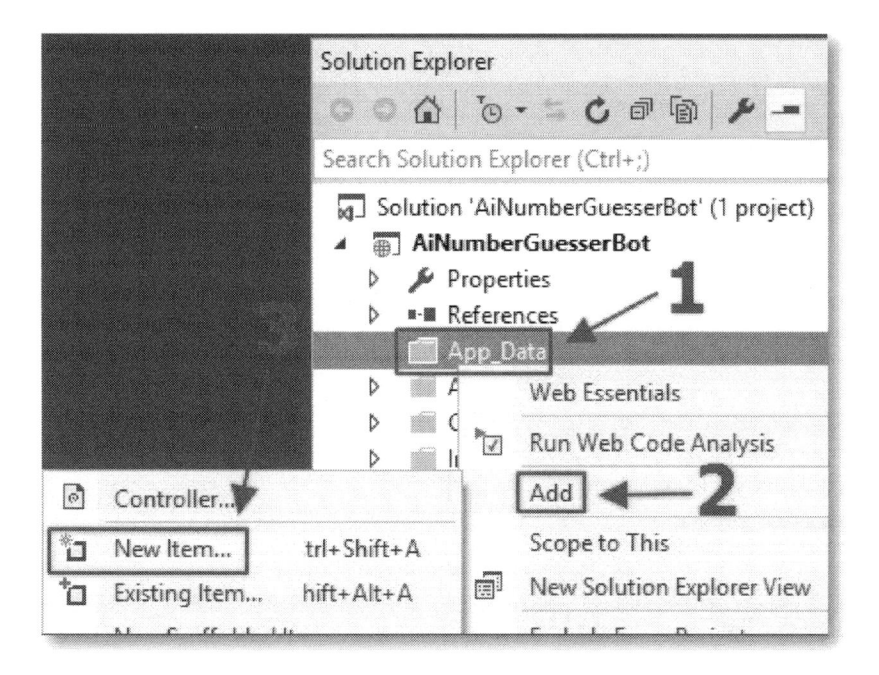

An Introduction to the Microsoft Bot Framework

Right-click on the **App_Data** folder. Select **Add** and then **New Item**.

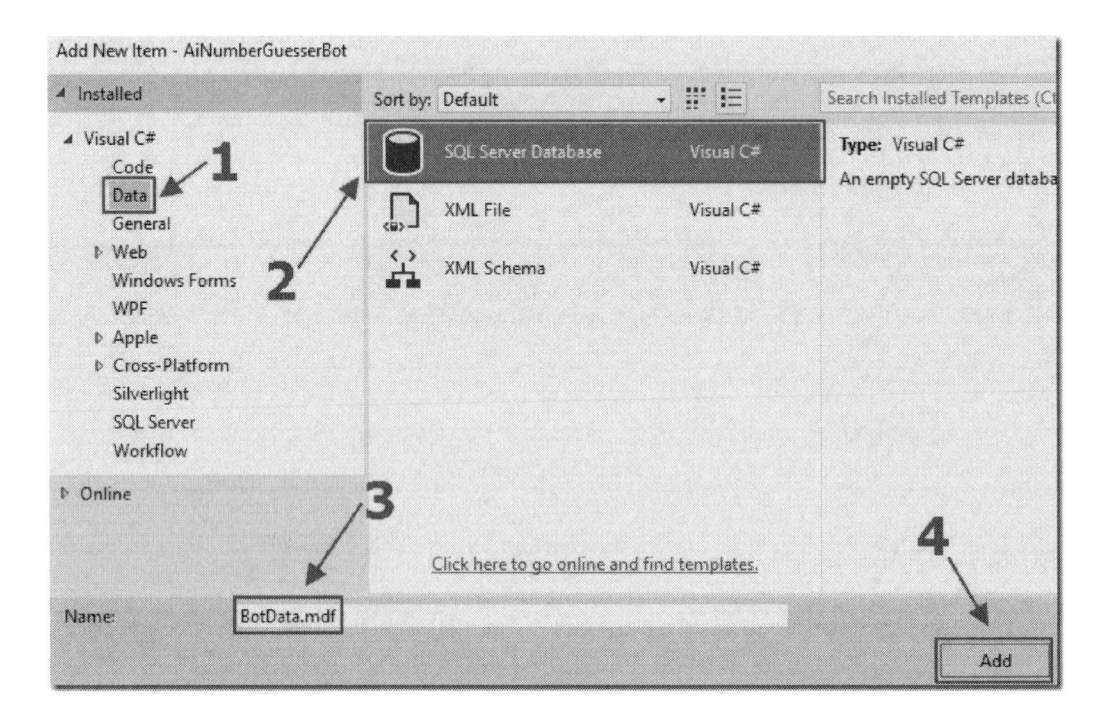

An Introduction to the Microsoft Bot Framework

Add a **SQL Server Database**.

Name it **BotData.mdf**.

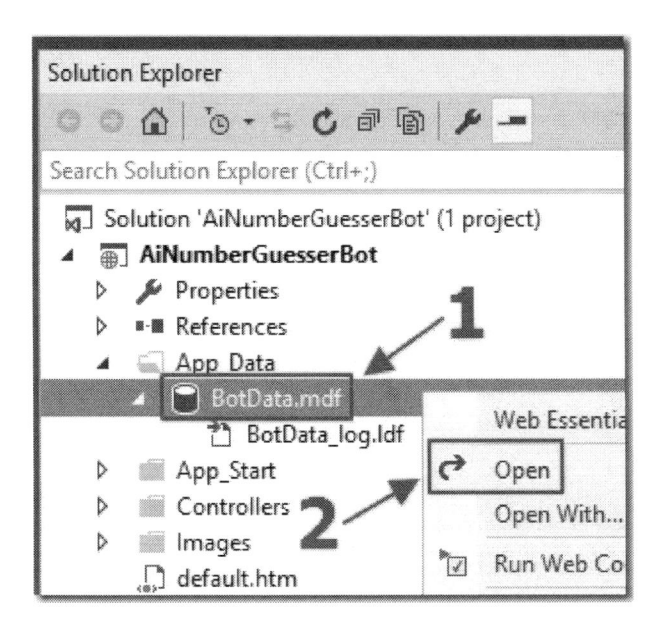

An Introduction to the Microsoft Bot Framework

We will now create a table in the database to hold our data.

Right-click on the database and select **Open**.

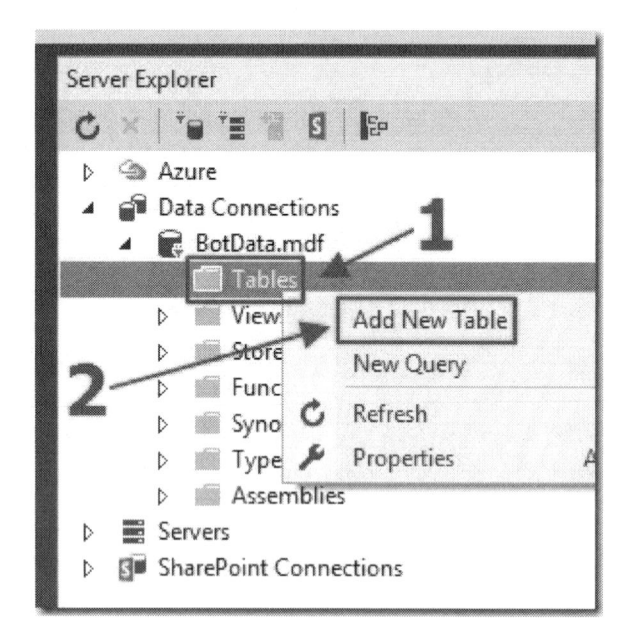

An Introduction to the Microsoft Bot Framework

Expand the database elements in the tree.

Right-click on **Tables** and select **Add New Table**.

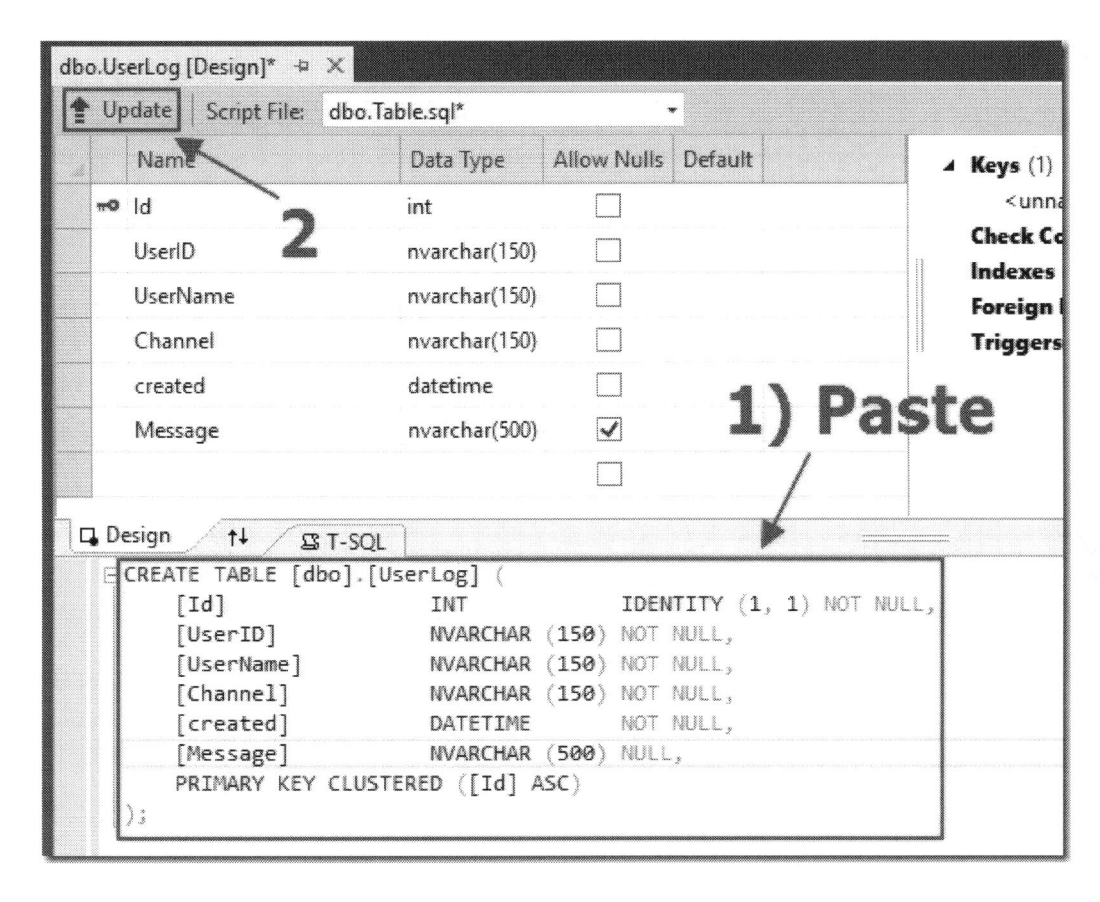

An Introduction to the Microsoft Bot Framework

Paste the following *script* in and click the **Update** button:

```
CREATE TABLE [dbo].[UserLog] (
    [Id]            INT             IDENTITY (1, 1) NOT NULL,
    [UserID]        NVARCHAR (150) NOT NULL,
    [UserName]      NVARCHAR (150) NOT NULL,
    [Channel]       NVARCHAR (150) NOT NULL,
    [created]       DATETIME        NOT NULL,
    [Message]       NVARCHAR (500) NULL,
    PRIMARY KEY CLUSTERED ([Id] ASC)
);
```

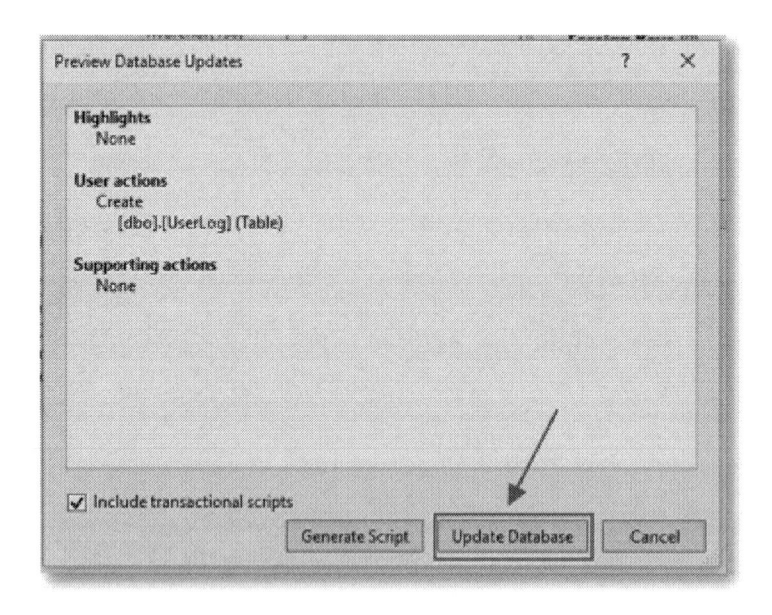

An Introduction to the Microsoft Bot Framework

Click **Update Database**.

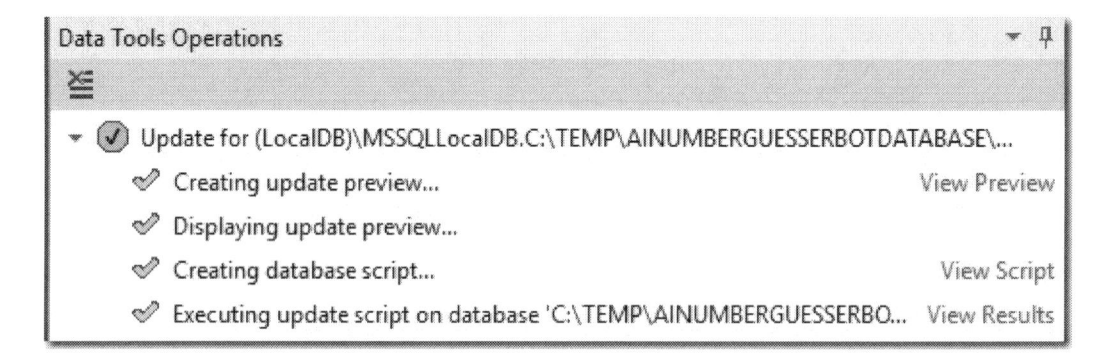

The table will be created.

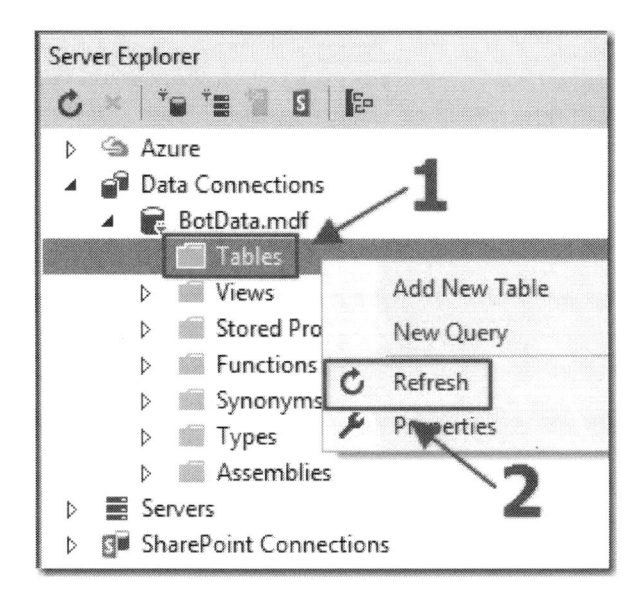

An Introduction to the Microsoft Bot Framework

Right-click on the **Tables** node and select **Refresh**.

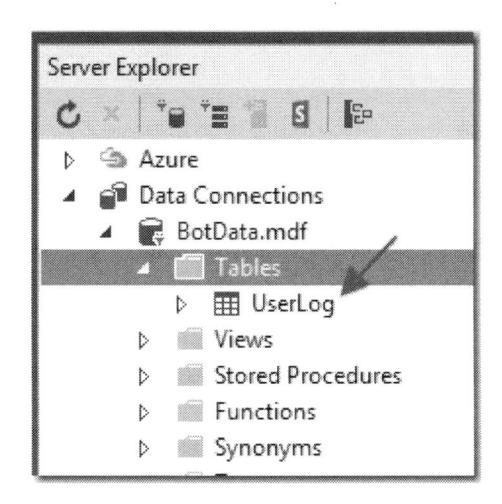

The table will show.

An Introduction to the Microsoft Bot Framework

Create An ADO.NET Entity Data Model

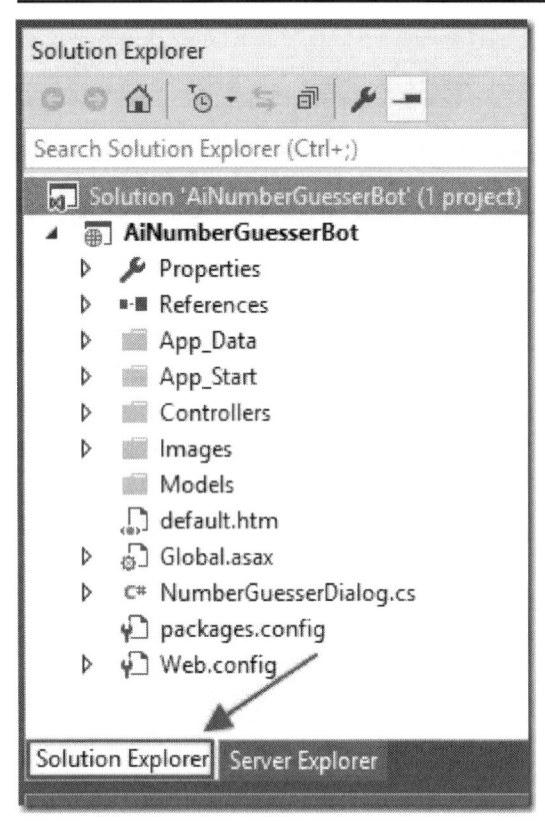

We will now create an **Entity Data Model** to allow *programmatic* access to the database.

Switch to **Solution Explorer** view.

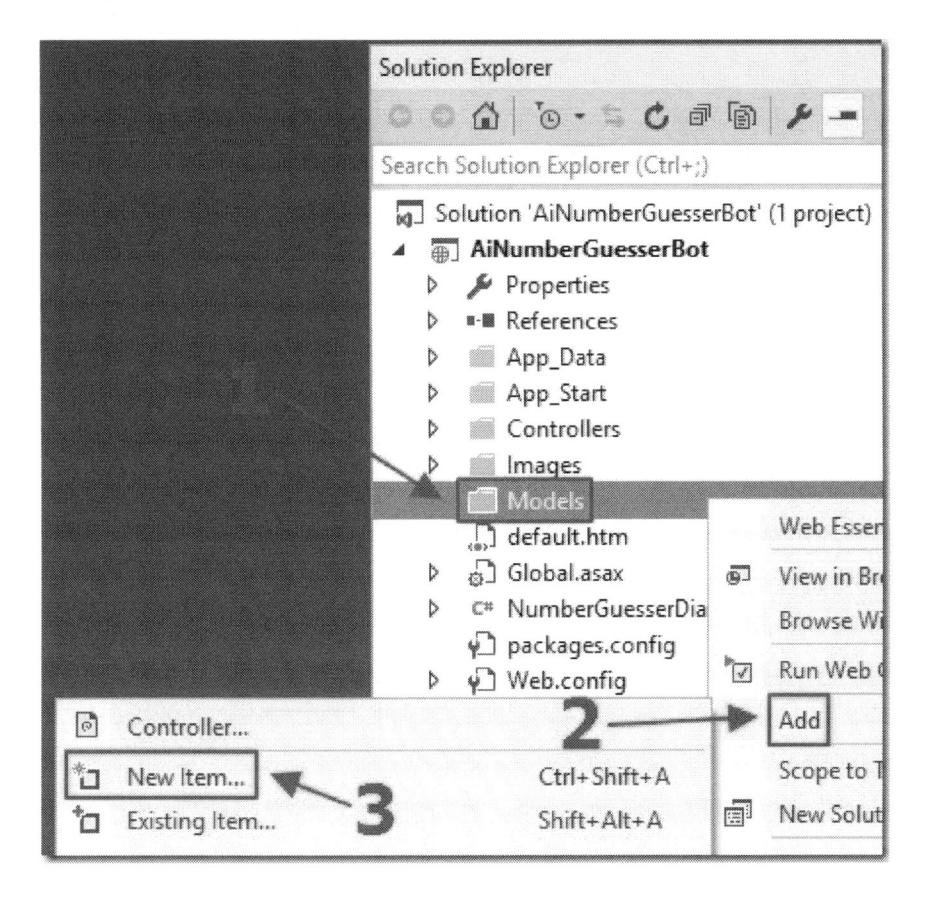

An Introduction to the Microsoft Bot Framework

Create a folder called **Models**.

Right-click on the **Models** folder. Select **Add** and then **New Item**.

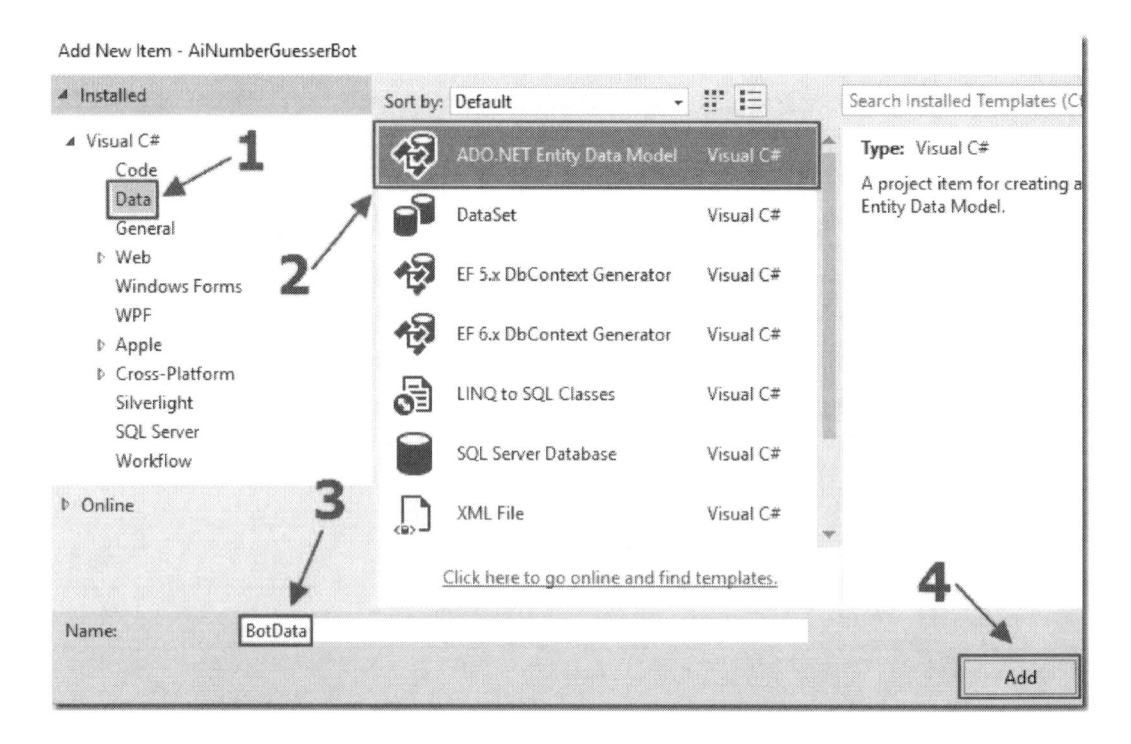

An Introduction to the Microsoft Bot Framework

Add an **ADO.NET Entity Data Model** and call it **BotData**.

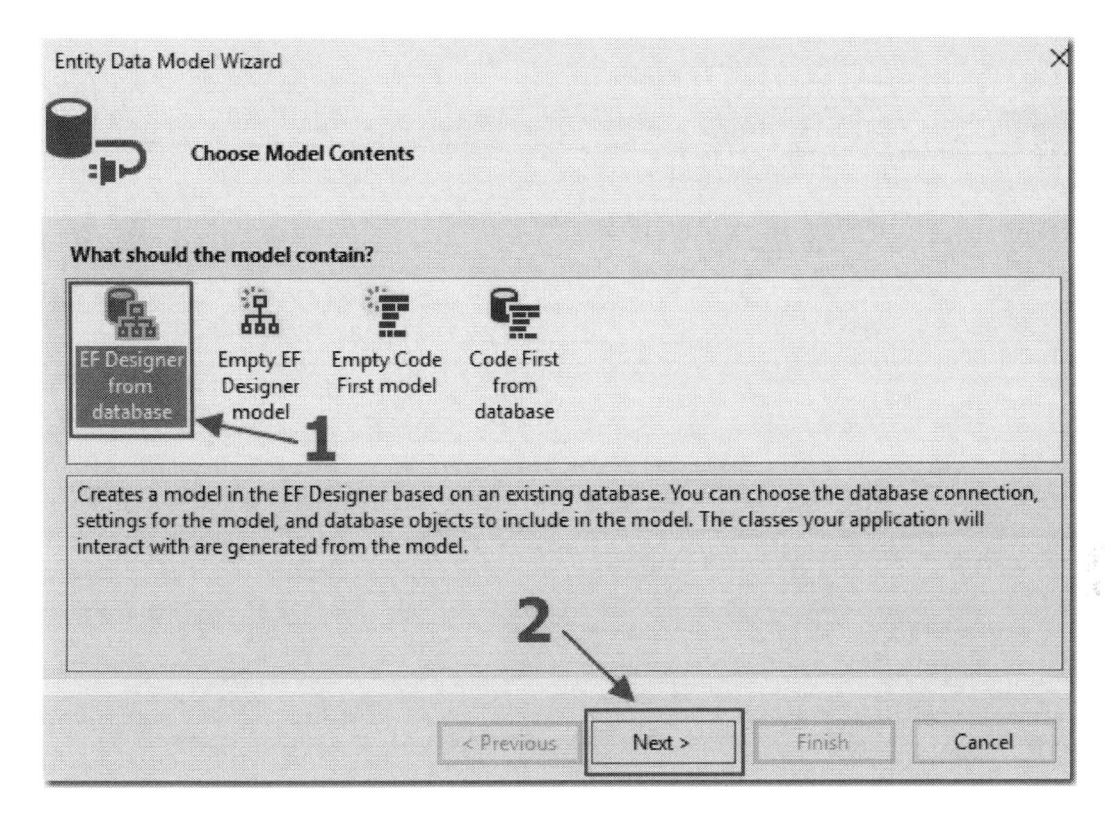

An Introduction to the Microsoft Bot Framework

When the **Entity Data Model Wizard** opens, select **EF Designer from database**.

Click **Next**.

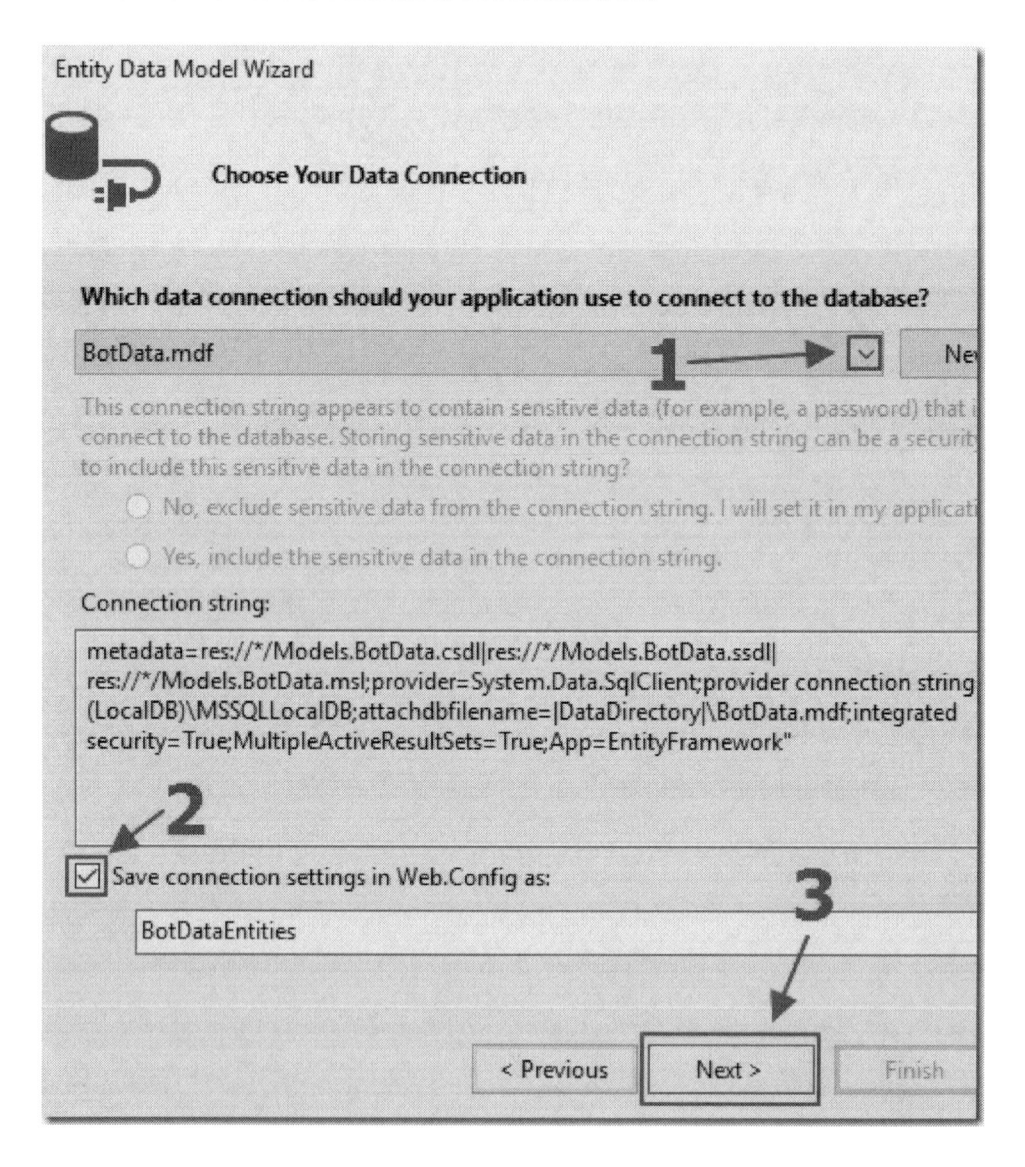

An Introduction to the Microsoft Bot Framework

Select **BotData.mdf** in the database dropdown (if it is not already selected).

Check the box next to **Save connection settings in Web.Config**.

Click **Next**.

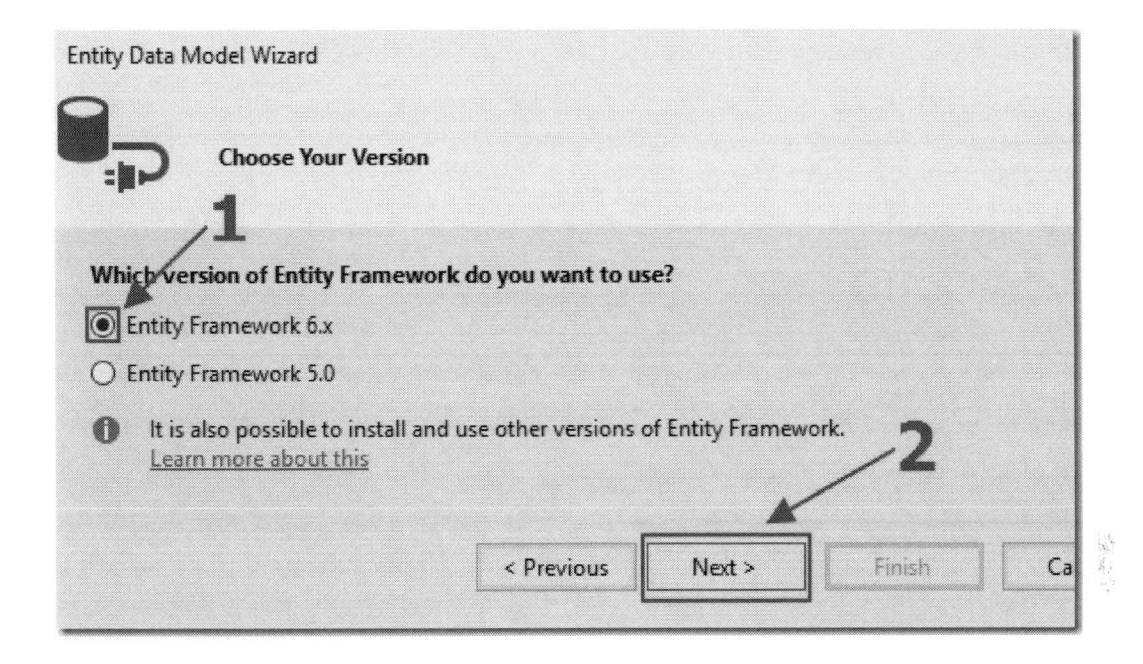

An Introduction to the Microsoft Bot Framework

Select **Entity Framework 6.x**.

Click **Next**.

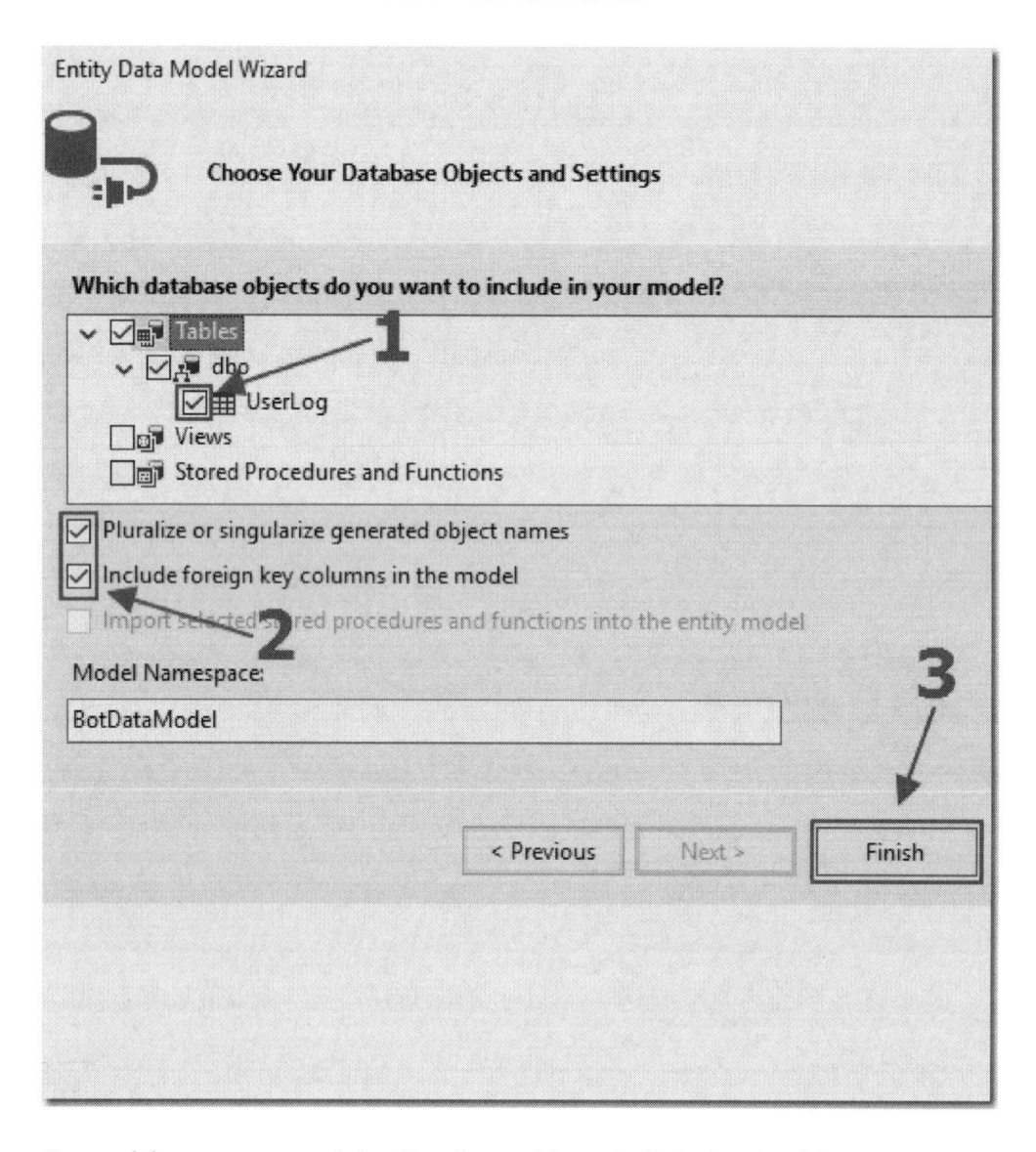

An Introduction to the Microsoft Bot Framework

![Entity Data Model Wizard screenshot showing Choose Your Database Objects and Settings with UserLog table checked (1), Pluralize and Include foreign key options checked (2), and Finish button highlighted (3)]

Expand the tree to reveal the **UserLog** table and click the checkbox next to it. Accept the other default values.

Click **Finish**.

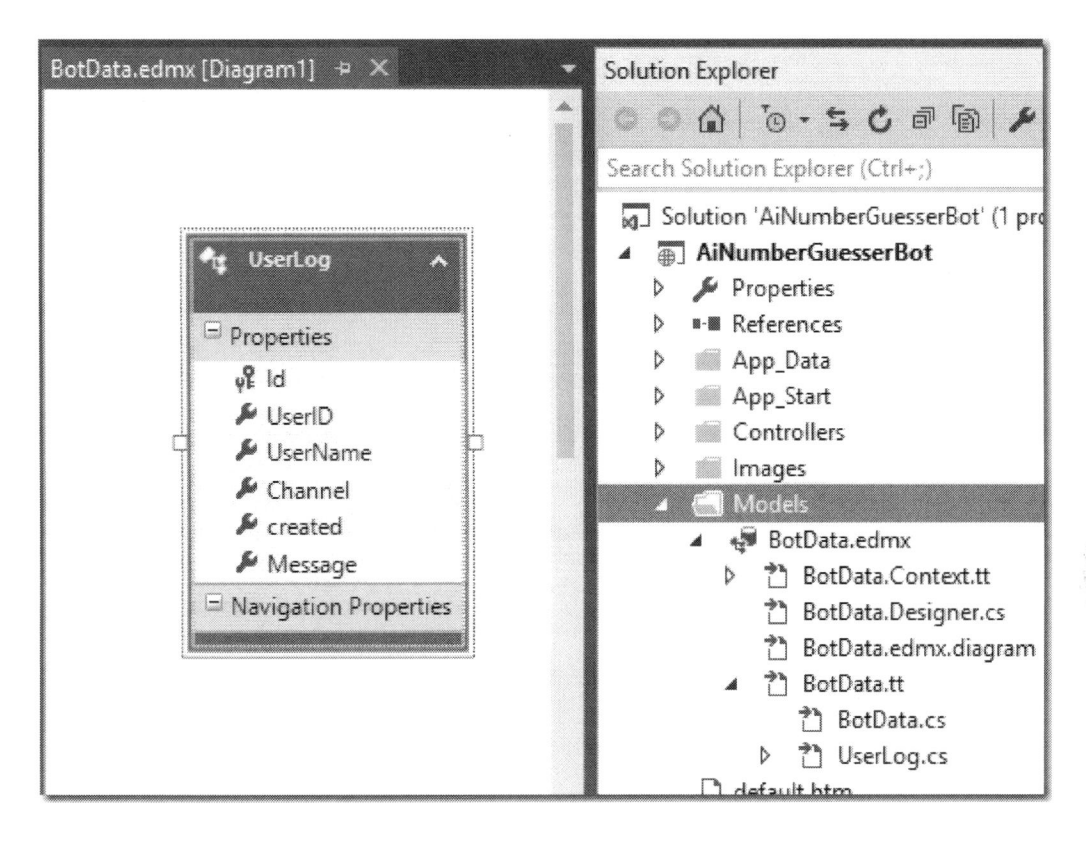

An Introduction to the Microsoft Bot Framework

The **BotData.edmx** an **Entity Data Model** will be created.

You can close the **BotData.edmx** for now.

Log To The Database

We will now create code that will log (most of) the messages *to* and *from* the **Bot** to the database.

An Introduction to the Microsoft Bot Framework

First, create a file called **Utility.cs** and use the following code:

```csharp
namespace AiNumberGuesserBot
{
    public static class Utility
    {
        public static string Truncate(this string value, int maxLength)
        {
            if (string.IsNullOrEmpty(value)) return value;
            return value.Length <= maxLength ? value : value.Substring(0, maxLength);
        }
    }
}
```

This creates a *utility* method to allow us to trim any text we store in the database. This ensures that no message is too long to be stored in the database. This would cause an error.

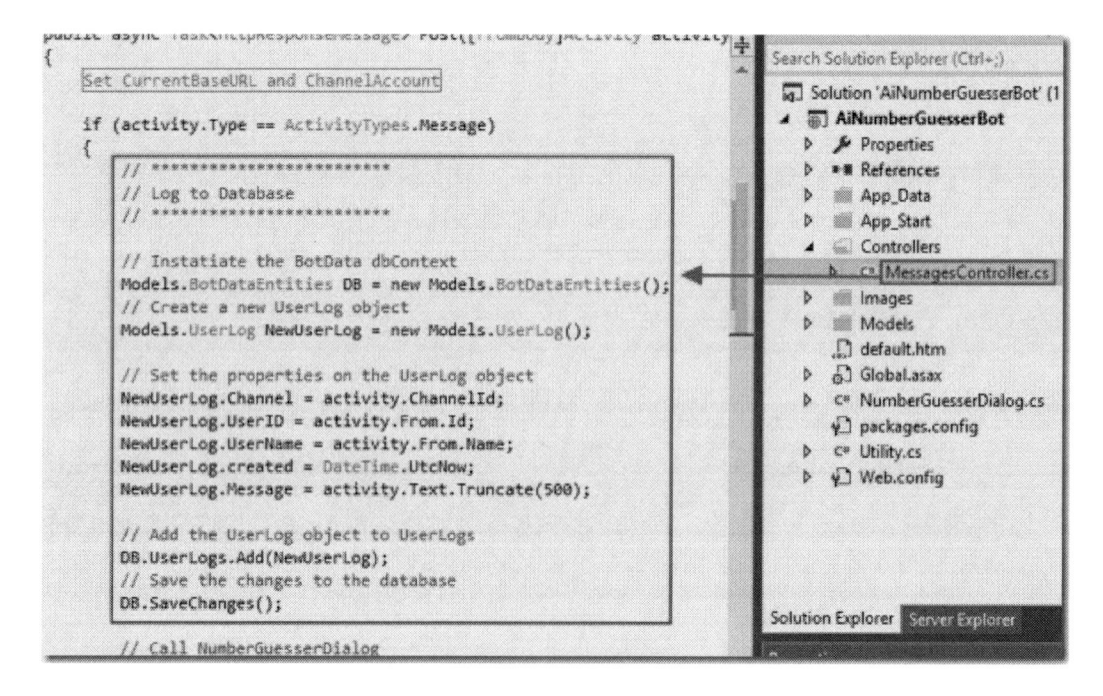

```
public async Task<HttpResponseMessage> Post([FromBody]Activity activity)
{
    Set CurrentBaseURL and ChannelAccount

    if (activity.Type == ActivityTypes.Message)
    {
        // ***************************
        // Log to Database
        // ***************************

        // Instatiate the BotData dbContext
        Models.BotDataEntities DB = new Models.BotDataEntities();
        // Create a new UserLog object
        Models.UserLog NewUserLog = new Models.UserLog();

        // Set the properties on the UserLog object
        NewUserLog.Channel = activity.ChannelId;
        NewUserLog.UserID = activity.From.Id;
        NewUserLog.UserName = activity.From.Name;
        NewUserLog.created = DateTime.UtcNow;
        NewUserLog.Message = activity.Text.Truncate(500);

        // Add the UserLog object to UserLogs
        DB.UserLogs.Add(NewUserLog);
        // Save the changes to the database
        DB.SaveChanges();

        // Call NumberGuesserDialog
```

Solution Explorer:
- Solution 'AiNumberGuesserBot' (1
  - AiNumberGuesserBot
    - Properties
    - References
    - App_Data
    - App_Start
    - Controllers
      - MessagesController.cs
    - Images
    - Models
    - default.htm
    - Global.asax
    - NumberGuesserDialog.cs
    - packages.config
    - Utility.cs
    - Web.config

An Introduction to the Microsoft Bot Framework

Next, find the following code in **MessagesController.cs**:

```
// Call NumberGuesserDialog
await Conversation.SendAsync(activity, () => new NumberGuesserDialog());
```

Replace it with:

```
// ***************************
// Log to Database
// ***************************
// Instantiate the BotData dbContext
Models.BotDataEntities DB = new Models.BotDataEntities();
// Create a new UserLog object
Models.UserLog NewUserLog = new Models.UserLog();
// Set the properties on the UserLog object
NewUserLog.Channel = activity.ChannelId;
NewUserLog.UserID = activity.From.Id;
NewUserLog.UserName = activity.From.Name;
NewUserLog.created = DateTime.UtcNow;
NewUserLog.Message = activity.Text.Truncate(500);
// Add the UserLog object to UserLogs
DB.UserLogs.Add(NewUserLog);
// Save the changes to the database
DB.SaveChanges();
// Call NumberGuesserDialog
await Conversation.SendAsync(activity, () => new NumberGuesserDialog());
```

This code logs the messages being sent *from* the user *to* the **Bot**.

An Introduction to the Microsoft Bot Framework

Log Messages In The Dialog Class

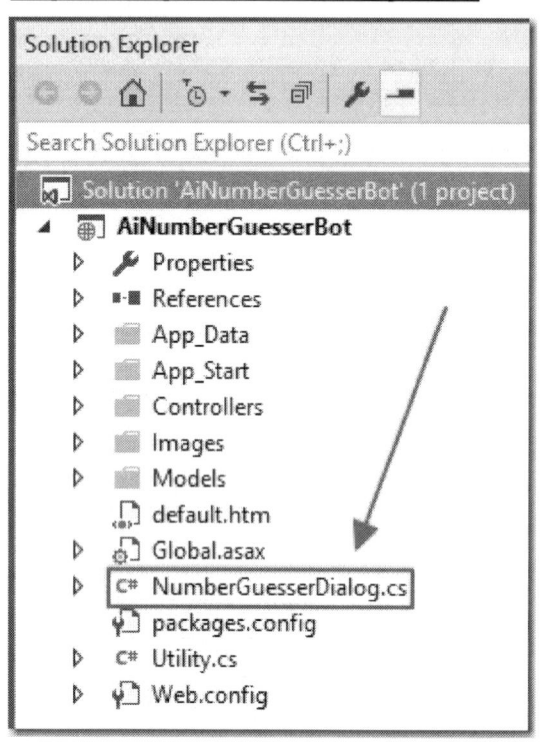

The **Dialog** class creates a response to the user.

Find *all* code in the **NumberGuessserDialog.cs** file (there will be multiple places) that send a text response to the user, which contain these lines:

```
await context.PostAsync(replyToConversation);
context.Wait(MessageReceivedAsync);
```

An Introduction to the Microsoft Bot Framework

Add the following code above the existing lines of code (again, there will be *multiple* places you will do this):

```
// ***************************
// Log to Database
// ***************************
// Instantiate the BotData dbContext
Models.BotDataEntities DB = new Models.BotDataEntities();
// Create a new UserLog object
Models.UserLog NewUserLog = new Models.UserLog();
// Set the properties on the UserLog object
NewUserLog.Channel = replyToConversation.ChannelId;
NewUserLog.UserID = replyToConversation.From.Id;
NewUserLog.UserName = replyToConversation.From.Name;
NewUserLog.created = DateTime.UtcNow;
// This logs the message being sent to the user
NewUserLog.Message = replyToConversation.Text.Truncate(500);
// Add the UserLog object to UserLogs
DB.UserLogs.Add(NewUserLog);
// Save the changes to the database
DB.SaveChanges();
```

When we have a **PromptDialog**, we don't have a *reply* **Activity**. In this case, we need to make one, so we have the values we need to log to the database.

Find the following code in the **Dialog** class:

```
PromptDialog.Confirm(
    context,
    PlayAgainAsync,
    CongratulationsStringPrompt,
    "Didn't get that!");
```

An Introduction to the Microsoft Bot Framework

Add the following code above the existing lines of code:

```
// **************************
// Log to Database
// **************************
// Create a reply Activity
Activity replyToConversation = (Activity)context.MakeMessage();
// Instantiate the BotData dbContext
Models.BotDataEntities DB = new Models.BotDataEntities();
// Create a new UserLog object
Models.UserLog NewUserLog = new Models.UserLog();
// Set the properties on the UserLog object
NewUserLog.Channel = replyToConversation.ChannelId;
NewUserLog.UserID = replyToConversation.From.Id;
NewUserLog.UserName = replyToConversation.From.Name;
NewUserLog.created = DateTime.UtcNow;
// This logs the message being sent to the user
NewUserLog.Message = CongratulationsStringPrompt.Truncate(500);
// Add the UserLog object to UserLogs
DB.UserLogs.Add(NewUserLog);
// Save the changes to the database
DB.SaveChanges();
```

Note: The **CongratulationsStringPrompt** *is set by the existing code to indicate that the user has won the game.*

Test The Database Logging Code

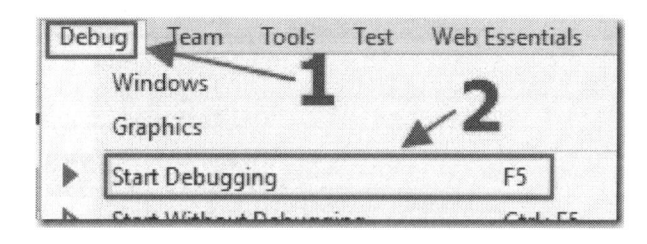

Hit **F5** to run the application.

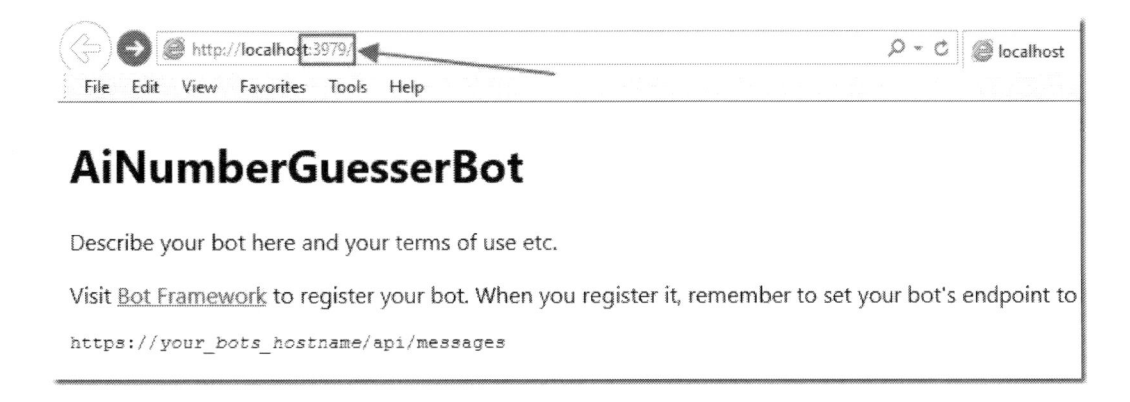

An Introduction to the Microsoft Bot Framework

AiNumberGuesserBot

Describe your bot here and your terms of use etc.

Visit Bot Framework to register your bot. When you register it, remember to set your bot's endpoint to

https://your_bots_hostname/api/messages

The web browser will open.

Note the port number and the web address.

Open and run the **Microsoft Bot Framework Emulator**.

When the emulator starts, connect to the **Bot** by setting the address to the one indicted in the web browser; however, add **/api/messages** to the end.

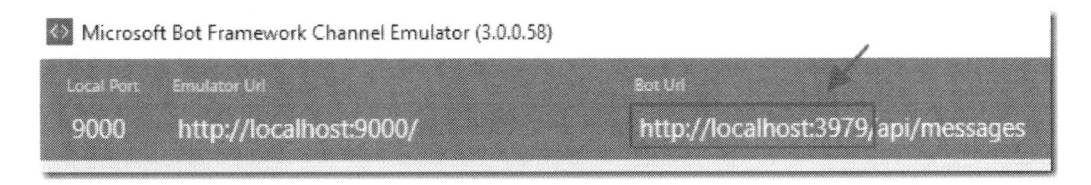

Ensure that the **Bot URL** is connecting to the correct address.

An Introduction to the Microsoft Bot Framework

Enter *Hello* and click the *send* button to start a conversation with the **Bot**.

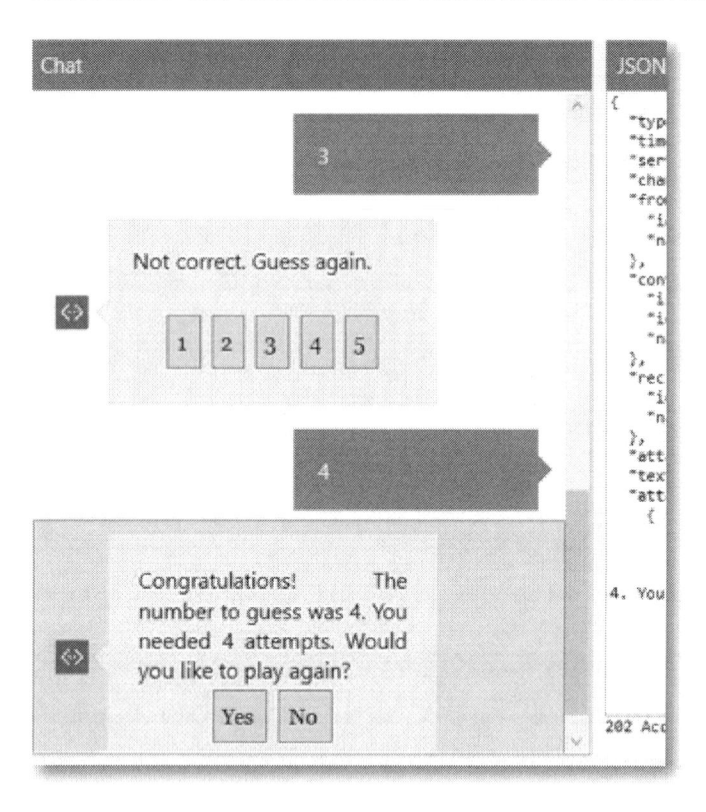

Play the game with the **Bot**.

Close the web browser to stop the application and return to **Visual Studio**.

An Introduction to the Microsoft Bot Framework

View The Data

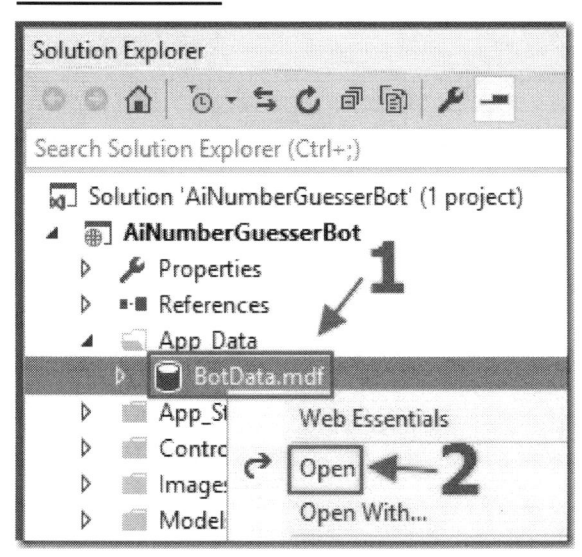

We will now view the data that was logged to the database.

In the **Solution Explorer** in **Visual Studio**, *right-click* on **BotData.mdf** and select **Open**.

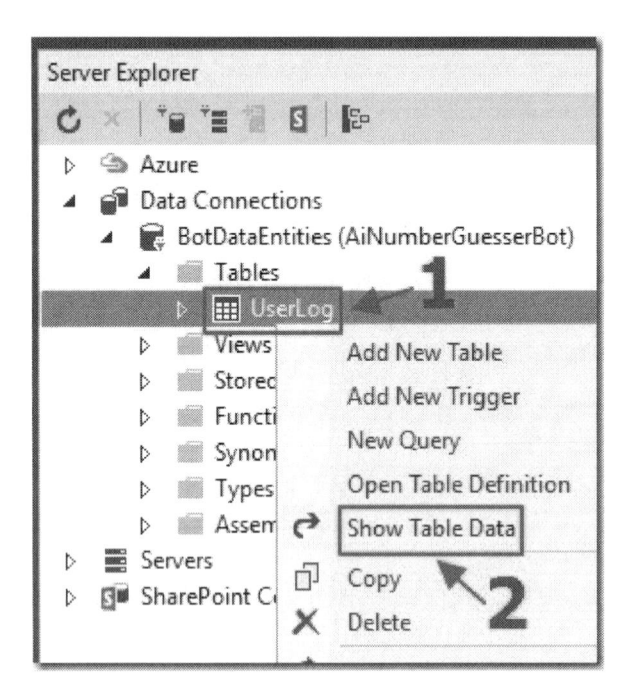

An Introduction to the Microsoft Bot Framework

This will open the **Server Explorer**.

Right-click on the **UserLog** table and select **Show Table Data**.

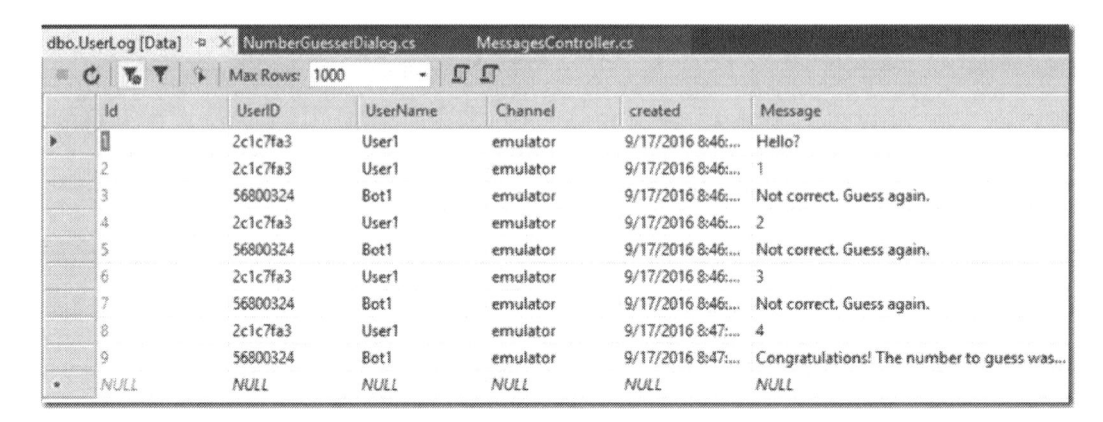

The logged data will be displayed.

An Introduction to the Microsoft Bot Framework

Logging High Scores

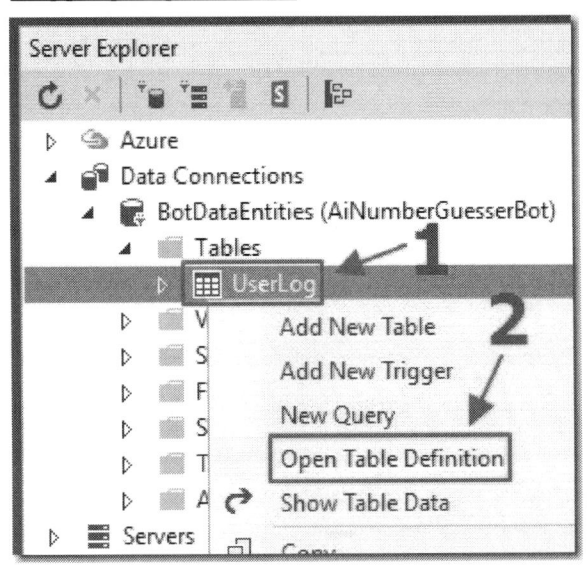

We will now add code to log and display **High Scores**.

We have to alter the database first to store the number of turns required to win and the name of the winner.

In the **Server Explorer**, *right-click* on the **UserLog** table and select **Open Table Definition**.

Note: *If you don't have this option, install the latest SQL Server Data Tools (SSDT) from* https://msdn.microsoft.com/library/mt204009.aspx

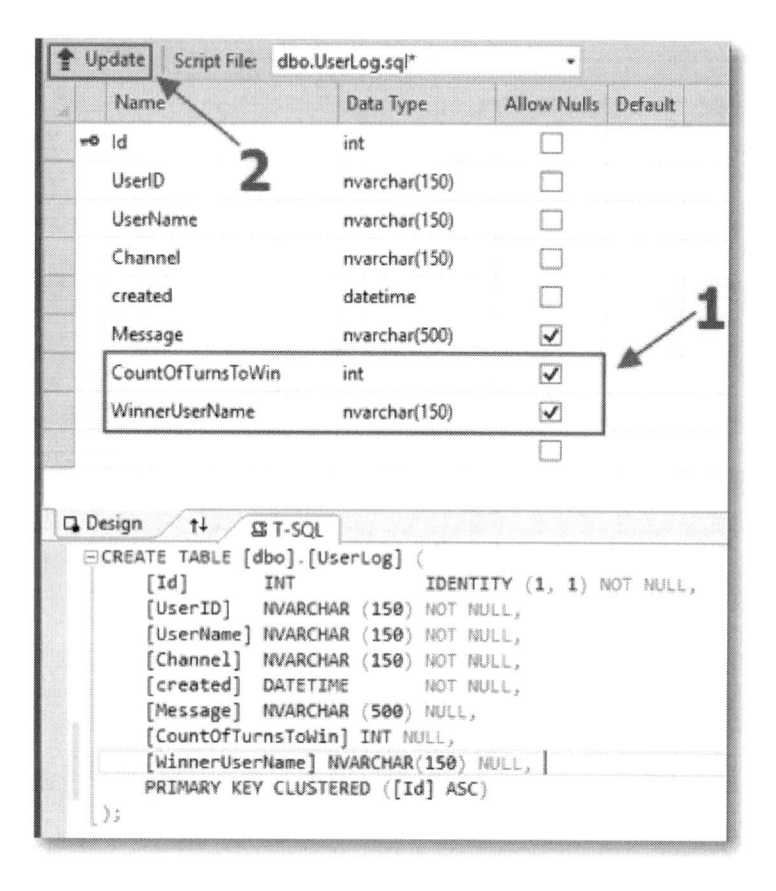

An Introduction to the Microsoft Bot Framework

[Screenshot of SQL table designer for dbo.UserLog.sql showing columns: Id (int), UserID (nvarchar(150)), UserName (nvarchar(150)), Channel (nvarchar(150)), created (datetime), Message (nvarchar(500)), CountOfTurnsToWin (int), WinnerUserName (nvarchar(150)), with the last two fields highlighted (marker 1) and the Update button marked (marker 2). T-SQL panel shows:]

```sql
CREATE TABLE [dbo].[UserLog] (
    [Id]              INT            IDENTITY (1, 1) NOT NULL,
    [UserID]          NVARCHAR (150) NOT NULL,
    [UserName]        NVARCHAR (150) NOT NULL,
    [Channel]         NVARCHAR (150) NOT NULL,
    [created]         DATETIME       NOT NULL,
    [Message]         NVARCHAR (500) NULL,
    [CountOfTurnsToWin] INT NULL,
    [WinnerUserName]  NVARCHAR(150) NULL,
    PRIMARY KEY CLUSTERED ([Id] ASC)
);
```

Add the following fields:

- **CountOfTurnsToWin** [int]
- **WinnerUserName** [nvarchar(150)]

Click the **Update** button.

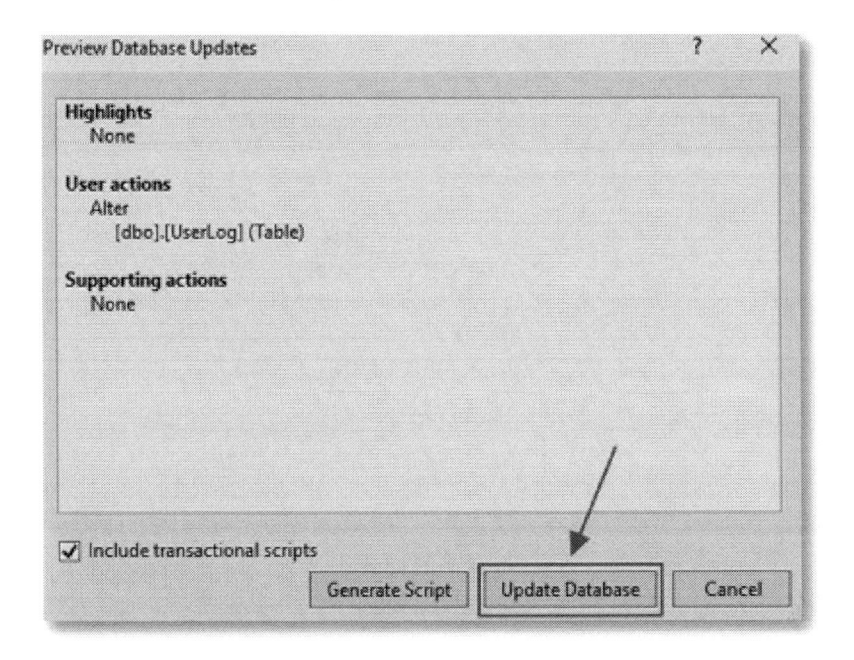

An Introduction to the Microsoft Bot Framework

When the **Preview Database Updates** box shows, click **Update Database**.

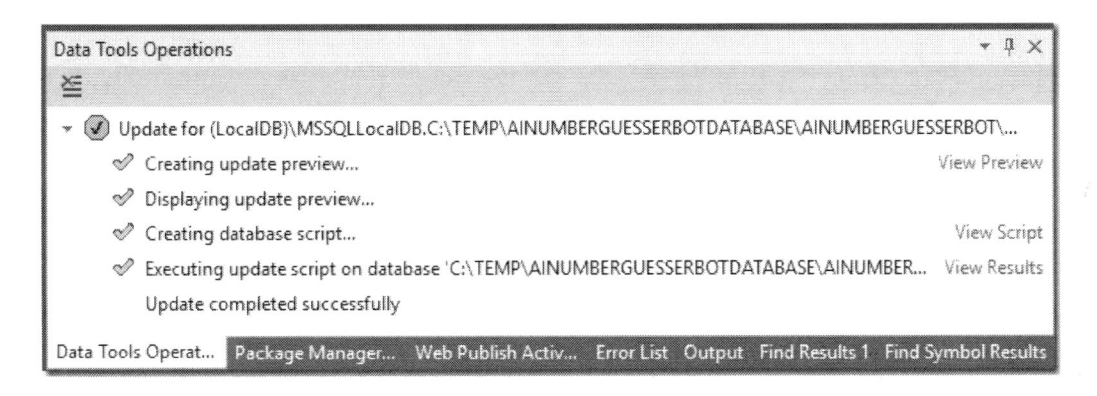

The **Data Tools Operations** window will indicate when the update is complete.

An Introduction to the Microsoft Bot Framework

Update ADO.NET Entity Data Model

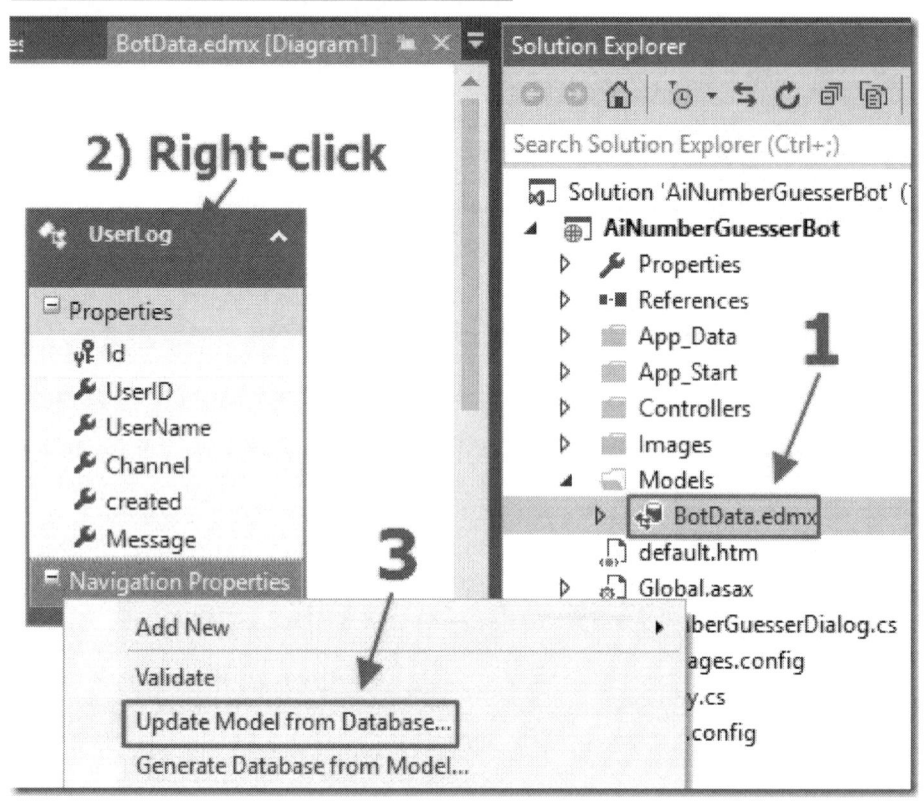

We have to update the **ADO.NET Entity Data Model** to have programmatic access to the newly added fields.

In the **Solution Explorer**, click on **BotData.edmx** to open it in the designer.

In the designer, *right-click* on the **UserLog** table and select **Update Model from Database**.

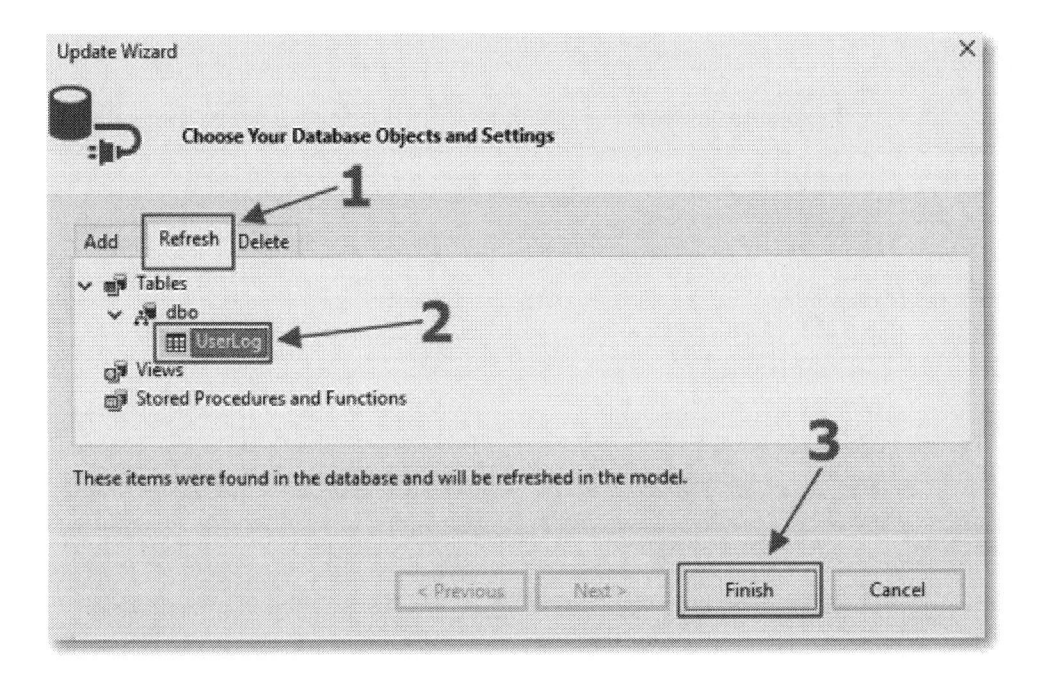

An Introduction to the Microsoft Bot Framework

When the **Update Wizard** shows, select the **Refresh** tab and then select the **UserLog** table. Click **Finish**.

An Introduction to the Microsoft Bot Framework

Alter Code To Log High Scores

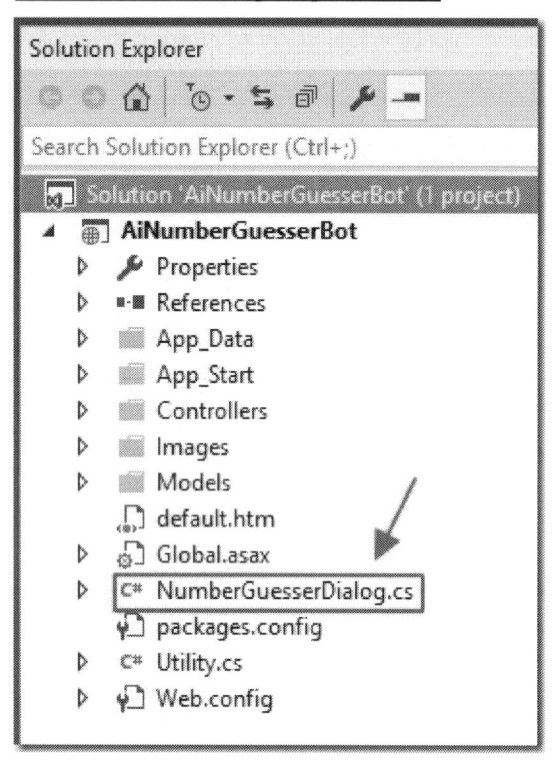

We will now alter the code in the **Dialog** class to log the winning user and the number of turns they required to win.

In the **NumberGuesserDialog.cs** file, locate the following code:

An Introduction to the Microsoft Bot Framework

```
// ***************************
// Log to Database
// ***************************
// Create a reply Activity
Activity replyToConversation = (Activity)context.MakeMessage();
// Instantiate the BotData dbContext
Models.BotDataEntities DB = new Models.BotDataEntities();
// Create a new UserLog object
Models.UserLog NewUserLog = new Models.UserLog();
// Set the properties on the UserLog object
NewUserLog.Channel = replyToConversation.ChannelId;
NewUserLog.UserID = replyToConversation.From.Id;
NewUserLog.UserName = replyToConversation.From.Name;
NewUserLog.created = DateTime.UtcNow;
// This logs the message being sent to the user
NewUserLog.Message = CongratulationsStringPrompt.Truncate(500);
```

Add the following lines of code *below* the code above:

```
// Log the number of turns it took to win
NewUserLog.CountOfTurnsToWin = this.intAttempts;
// Log the name of the user who won
NewUserLog.WinnerUserName = replyToConversation.Recipient.Name;
```

An Introduction to the Microsoft Bot Framework

<u>Display The High Scores</u>

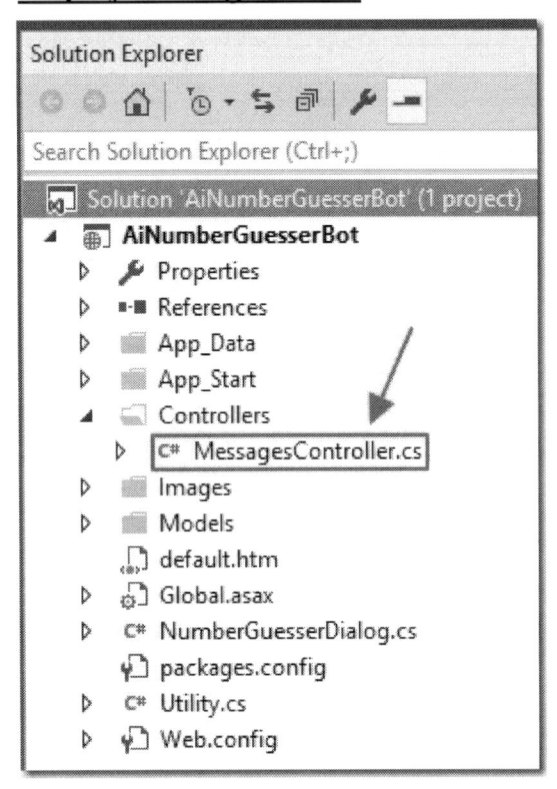

```
Solution Explorer
Solution 'AiNumberGuesserBot' (1 project)
    AiNumberGuesserBot
        Properties
        References
        App_Data
        App_Start
        Controllers
            C# MessagesController.cs
        Images
        Models
        default.htm
        Global.asax
        C# NumberGuesserDialog.cs
        packages.config
        C# Utility.cs
        Web.config
```

We will now add code to display the **High Scores** whenever the user types *High Scores*.

An Introduction to the Microsoft Bot Framework

Open the **MessagesController.cs** file and add the following method to the class:

```csharp
private void ShowHighScores(Activity activity)
{
    // This method will take an Activity and return a response
    // that will contain the current High Scores
    // Connect to the database
    Models.BotDataEntities DB = new Models.BotDataEntities();
    // Get Yesterday
    var ParamYesterday = DateTime.Now.AddDays(-1);
    // Get the top 5 high scores since yesterday
    var HighScores = (from UserLog in DB.UserLogs
                      where UserLog.CountOfTurnsToWin != null
                      where UserLog.created > ParamYesterday
                      select UserLog)
                      .OrderBy(x => x.CountOfTurnsToWin)
                      .Take(5)
                      .ToList();
    // Create a response
    System.Text.StringBuilder sb = new System.Text.StringBuilder();
    sb.Append("High Scores Today:\n\n");
    // Loop through each high score
    foreach (var Score in HighScores)
    {
        // Add the High Score to the response
        sb.Append(String.Format("Score: {0} - {1} - ({2} {3})\n\n"
            , Score.CountOfTurnsToWin
            , Score.WinnerUserName
            , Score.created.ToLocalTime().ToShortDateString()
            , Score.created.ToLocalTime().ToShortTimeString()));
    }
    // Create a reply message
    Activity replyToConversation = activity.CreateReply();
    replyToConversation.Recipient = activity.From;
    replyToConversation.Type = "message";
    // Set the text containg the High Scores as the response
    replyToConversation.Text = sb.ToString();
    // Create a ConnectorClient and use it to send the reply message
    var connector =
        new ConnectorClient(new Uri(activity.ServiceUrl));
    // Send the reply
    connector.Conversations.SendToConversationAsync(replyToConversation);
}
```

An Introduction to the Microsoft Bot Framework

We will now add the code that will call the **ShowHighScores** method we just added.

In the **MessagesController.cs** file, locate the following code:

```
// Call NumberGuesserDialog
await Conversation.SendAsync(activity, () => new NumberGuesserDialog());
```

Replace it with the following code:

```
// Detect if the user enters the words "high score"
if (activity.Text.ToLower().Contains("high score"))
{
    // Call the ShowHighScores method
    // passing to it, the current Activity
    ShowHighScores(activity);
}
else
{
    // Call NumberGuesserDialog
    await Conversation.SendAsync(activity, () => new NumberGuesserDialog());
}
```

Finally, to let the user know they can type *High Scores* to see the high scores, find the following code in the **Dialog** class:

```
Activity replyToConversation =
    ShowButtons(context, "Hi Welcome! - Guess a number between 1 and 5");
```

Change it to:

```
Activity replyToConversation =
    ShowButtons(context,
    "Hi Welcome! - Guess a number between 1 and 5 \n\n Type 'High Scores' to see high scores");
```

An Introduction to the Microsoft Bot Framework

Test The Code

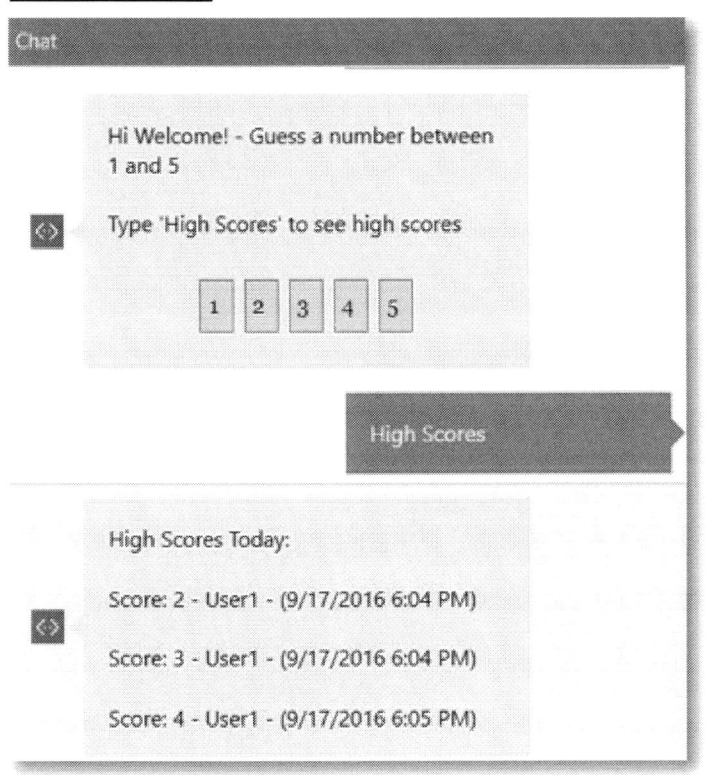

[Chat screenshot showing: "Hi Welcome! - Guess a number between 1 and 5. Type 'High Scores' to see high scores" with buttons 1, 2, 3, 4, 5. User types "High Scores" and bot responds with "High Scores Today: Score: 2 - User1 - (9/17/2016 6:04 PM), Score: 3 - User1 - (9/17/2016 6:04 PM), Score: 4 - User1 - (9/17/2016 6:05 PM)"]

Now when we type *High Scores*, we can see the high scores for the past day.

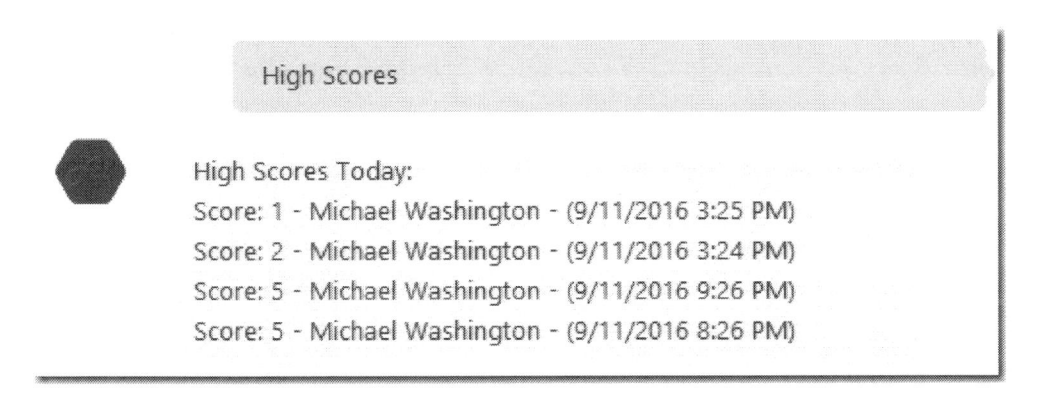

[Chat screenshot showing: "High Scores" and response "High Scores Today: Score: 1 - Michael Washington - (9/11/2016 3:25 PM), Score: 2 - Michael Washington - (9/11/2016 3:24 PM), Score: 5 - Michael Washington - (9/11/2016 9:26 PM), Score: 5 - Michael Washington - (9/11/2016 8:26 PM)"]

An Introduction to the Microsoft Bot Framework

The image above shows what the high scores look like when the **Bot** is published and viewed through the **Skype** client.

Publishing A Microsoft Bot Framework Application That Uses a Database

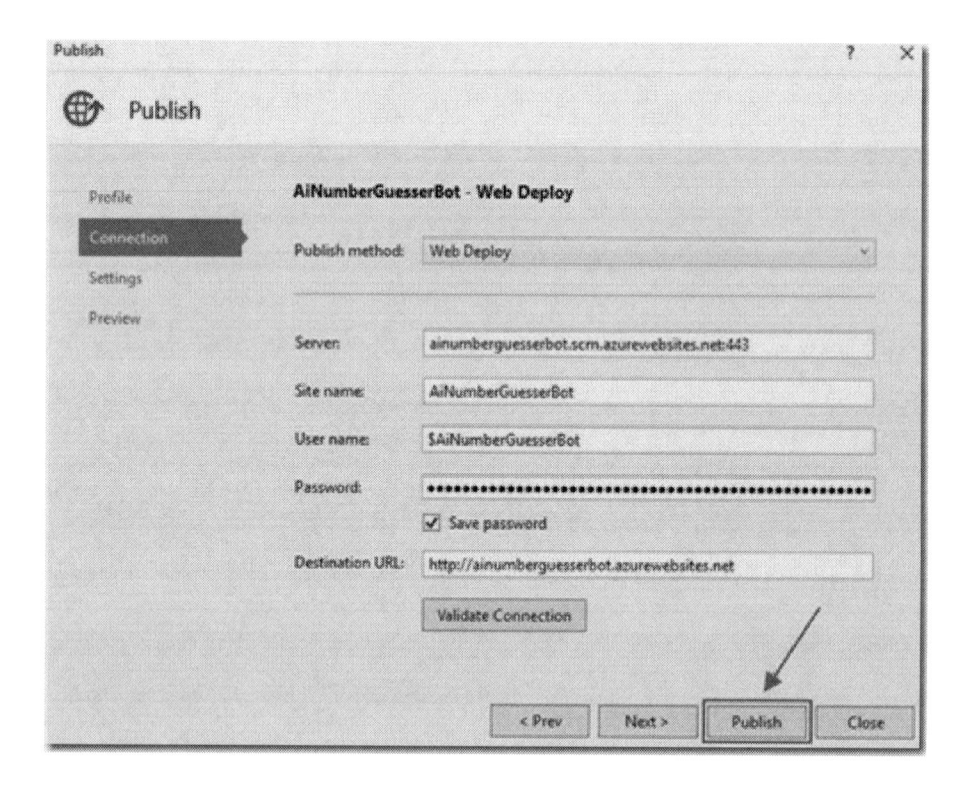

To publish the **Bot**, we can follow the directions in *Chapter 2: Create a Hello World! Bot*.

However, unlike this chapter, that chapter does not cover publishing a **Bot** that uses a database.

An Introduction to the Microsoft Bot Framework

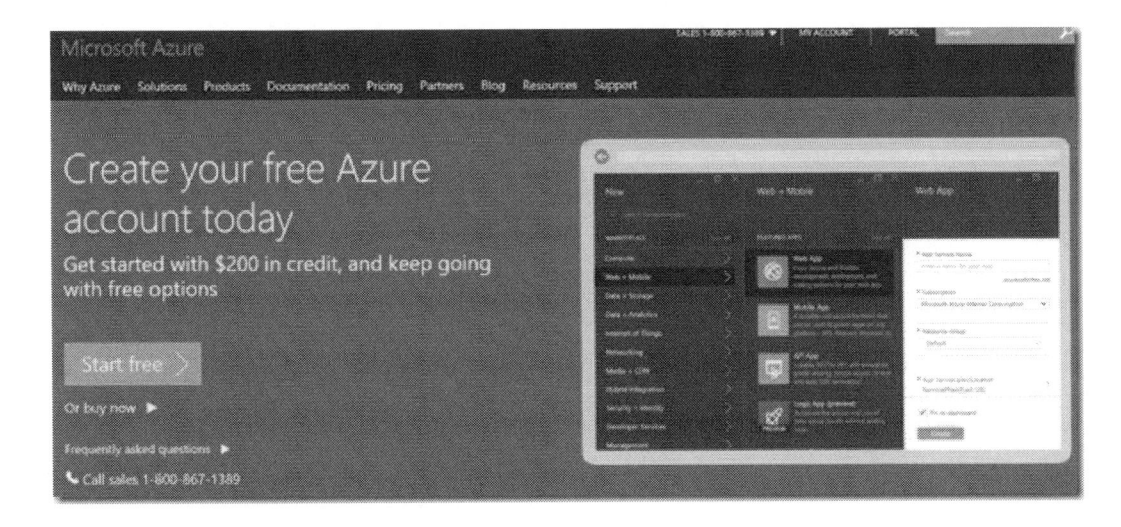

If you do not have a **Microsoft Azure** account, go to htttps://azure.microsoft.com and create an account and a subscription.

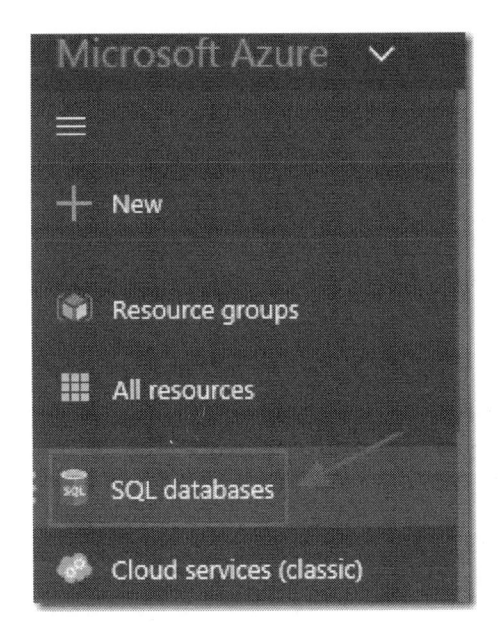

Log into the **Azure** web portal and select **SQL databases**.

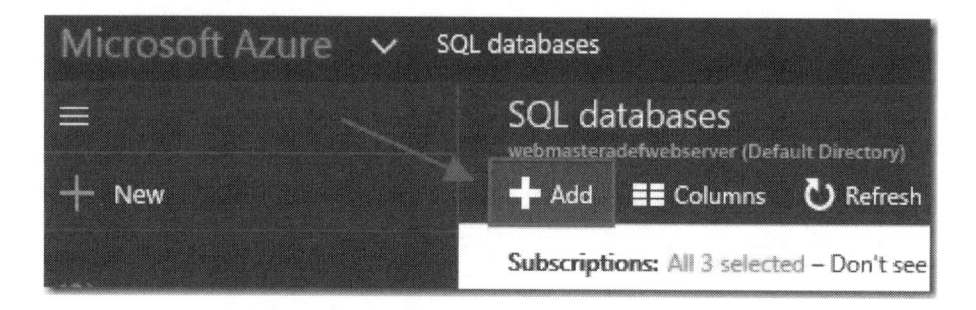

An Introduction to the Microsoft Bot Framework

Add a new database.

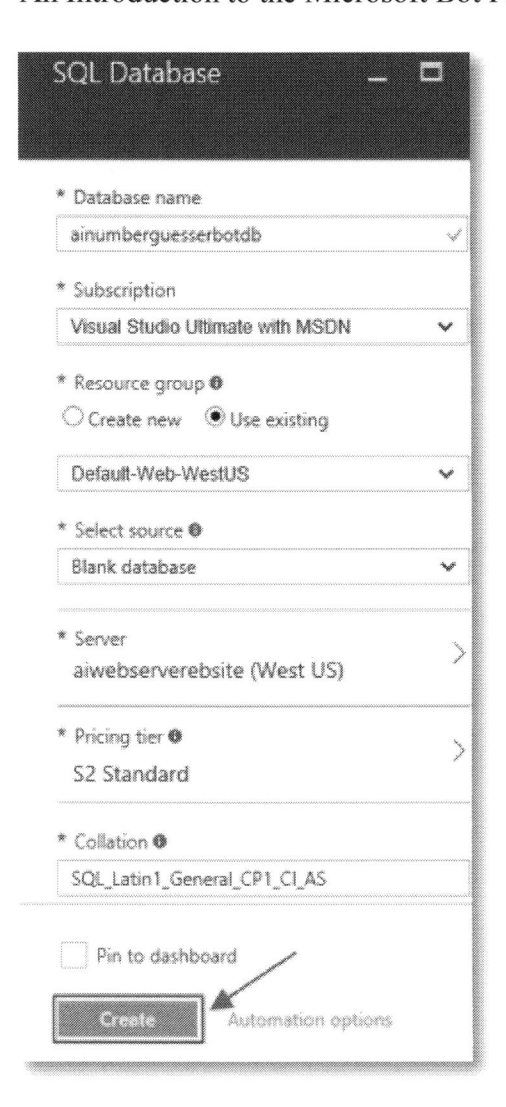

An Introduction to the Microsoft Bot Framework

Fill in the form to create a new database.

Note: *If you do not already have a server to put the database on, you will be prompted to create one. At that time, you will create a user name and password. This is the user name and password you will use in the connection string to connect to the database when you use the deployment wizard in* **Visual Studio** *(covered later).*

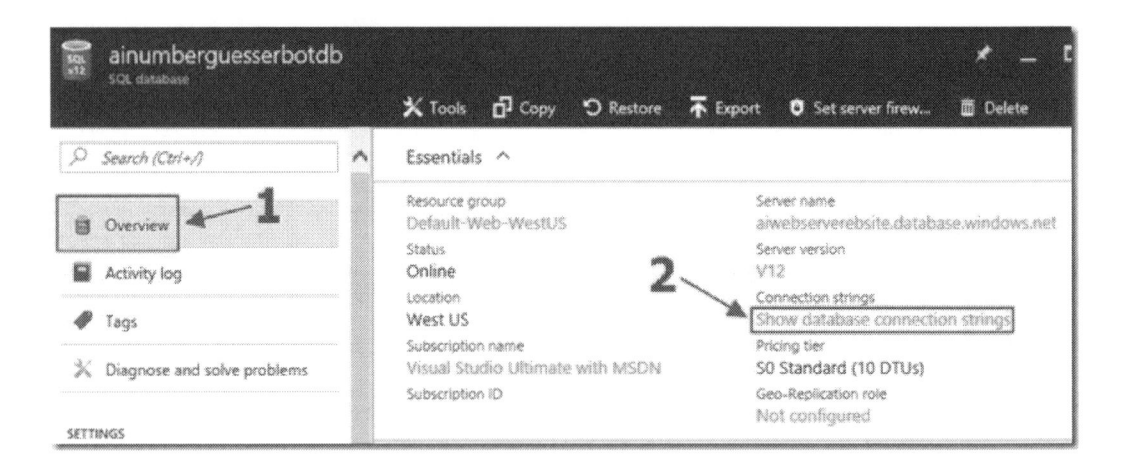

An Introduction to the Microsoft Bot Framework

After you create the database, you can view the **ADO.NET(SQL authentication)** connection string for the database in the **Overview** section.

Note: *The connection string will not have the username and password. You will use the username and password of the* **Azure** *server that contains the database.*

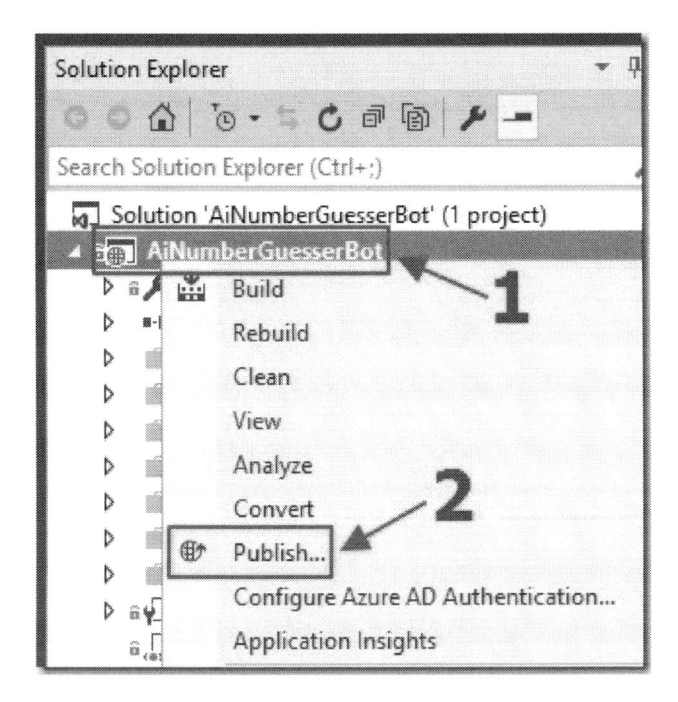

An Introduction to the Microsoft Bot Framework

In the **Solution Explorer** in **Visual Studio**, *right-click* on the project node and select **Publish**.

An Introduction to the Microsoft Bot Framework

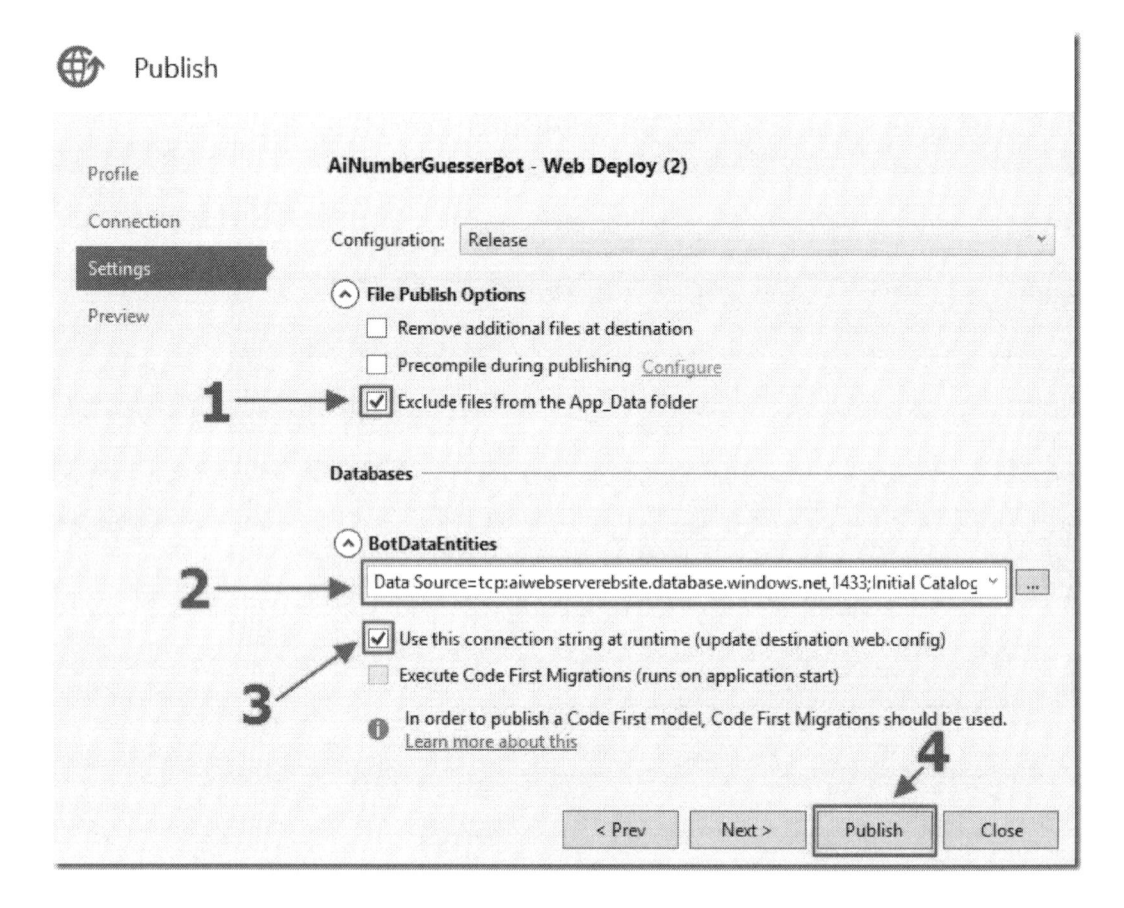

In the **Publish** wizard, fill out the fields to publish your **Bot** to **Azure**.

On the **Settings** tab:

1. Select **Exclude files from the App_Data folder**.
   This will prevent the **BotData.mdf** database file from being published to **Azure**. You are doing this because the **.mdf** file cannot be used on **Azure**.
2. Enter the connection string to the database (running on **Azure**) in **BotDataEntities.**
   You can get the **ADO.NET(SQL authentication)** connection string for the database in the **Overview** section for the database in the **Azure** portal. Use the "**…**" button to help you connect to the database and construct the connection string.

An Introduction to the Microsoft Bot Framework

3. Check **Use this connection string at runtime**.
   This will update the **web.config** of the published application, so the published application will connect to the database on **Azure**.
4. Click the **Publish** button.

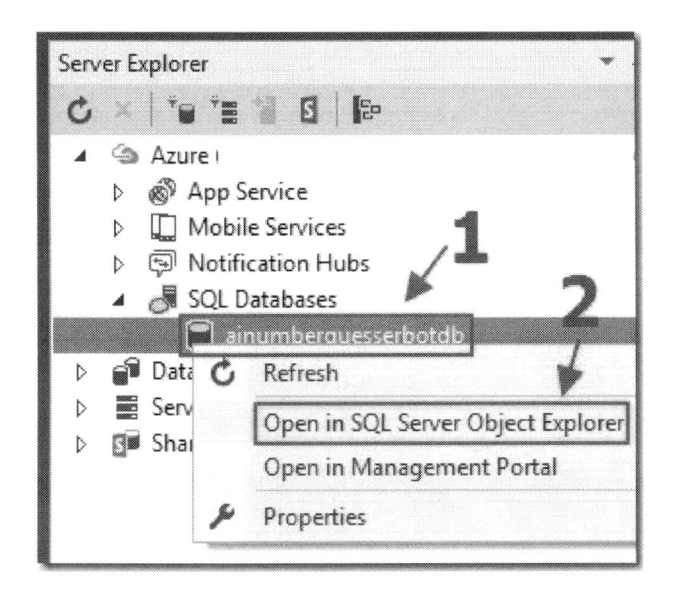

In the **Server Explorer** in **Visual Studio**, *right-click* on the database and select **Open in SQL Server Object Explorer**.

Note: *If you don't have this option, install the latest SQL Server Data Tools (SSDT) from* https://msdn.microsoft.com/library/mt204009.aspx

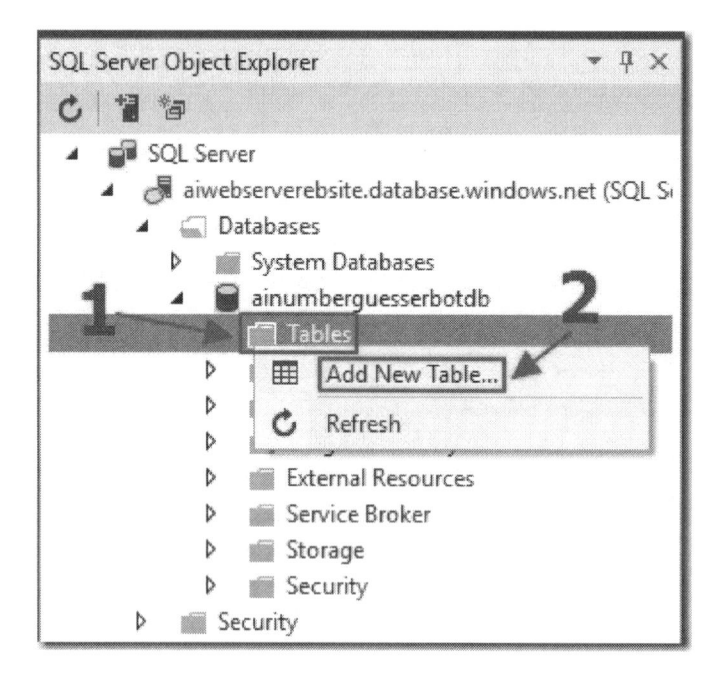

An Introduction to the Microsoft Bot Framework

This will open the **SQL Server Object Explorer**.

Right-click on the **Tables** node under the database and select **Add New Table**.

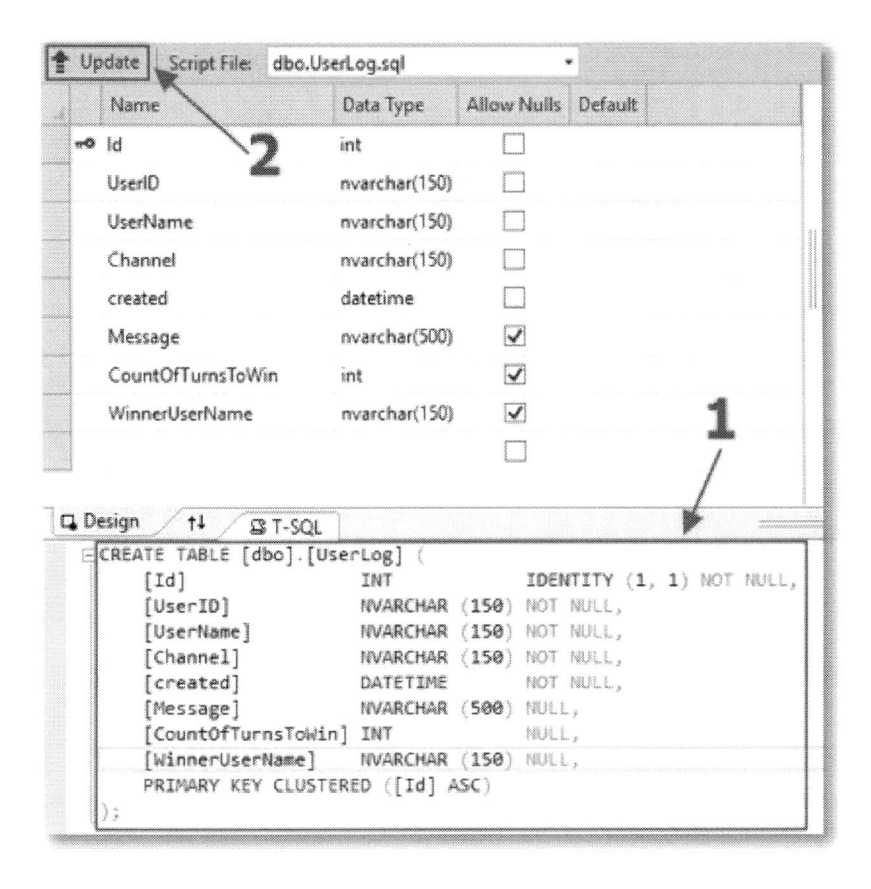

An Introduction to the Microsoft Bot Framework

Use the following script to create the required table and click the **Update** button:

```
CREATE TABLE [dbo].[UserLog] (
    [Id]                INT             IDENTITY (1, 1) NOT NULL,
    [UserID]            NVARCHAR (150)  NOT NULL,
    [UserName]          NVARCHAR (150)  NOT NULL,
    [Channel]           NVARCHAR (150)  NOT NULL,
    [created]           DATETIME        NOT NULL,
    [Message]           NVARCHAR (500)  NULL,
    [CountOfTurnsToWin] INT             NULL,
    [WinnerUserName]    NVARCHAR (150)  NULL,
    PRIMARY KEY CLUSTERED ([Id] ASC)
);
```

An Introduction to the Microsoft Bot Framework

When the **Preview Database Updates** box shows, click **Update Database**.

Note: *You can also use the **Cloud Explorer for Visual Studio 2015** extension to manage your **Azure** databases inside **Visual Studio**.*

An Introduction to the Microsoft Bot Framework

Chapter 7: Implementing Language Understanding Intelligent Service (LUIS)

The sample code for this chapter can be obtained at the link "Implementing Language Understanding Intelligent Service (LUIS) In Microsoft Bot Framework" at http://AiHelpWebsite.com/Downloads

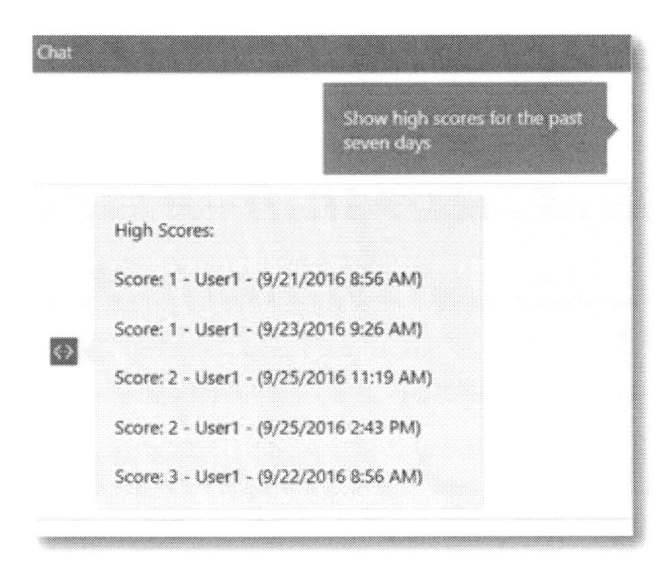

Using **Language Understanding Intelligent Service (LUIS)** in your **Microsoft Bot Framework** application allows you to create chat bots that are easier for your end-users to interact with.

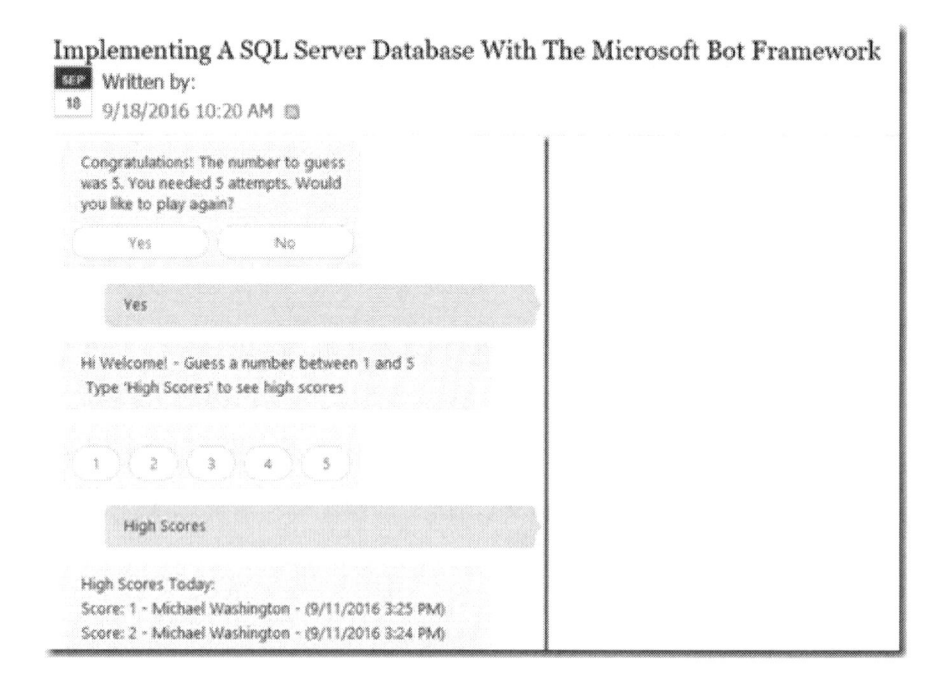

An Introduction to the Microsoft Bot Framework

Implementing A SQL Server Database With The Microsoft Bot Framework

Written by:
9/18/2016 10:20 AM

> Congratulations! The number to guess was 5. You needed 5 attempts. Would you like to play again?
>
> Yes / No

Yes

> Hi Welcome! - Guess a number between 1 and 5
> Type 'High Scores' to see high scores
>
> 1 2 3 4 5

High Scores

> High Scores Today:
> Score: 1 - Michael Washington - (9/11/2016 3:25 PM)
> Score: 2 - Michael Washington - (9/11/2016 3:24 PM)

For this example, we will start with the code created in the previous chapter.

This chapter covers how to create a number guessing game and storing and displaying the high scores. In the previous chapter, the user is required to type in the exact words *High Scores*, and they could only see the high scores for the past day.

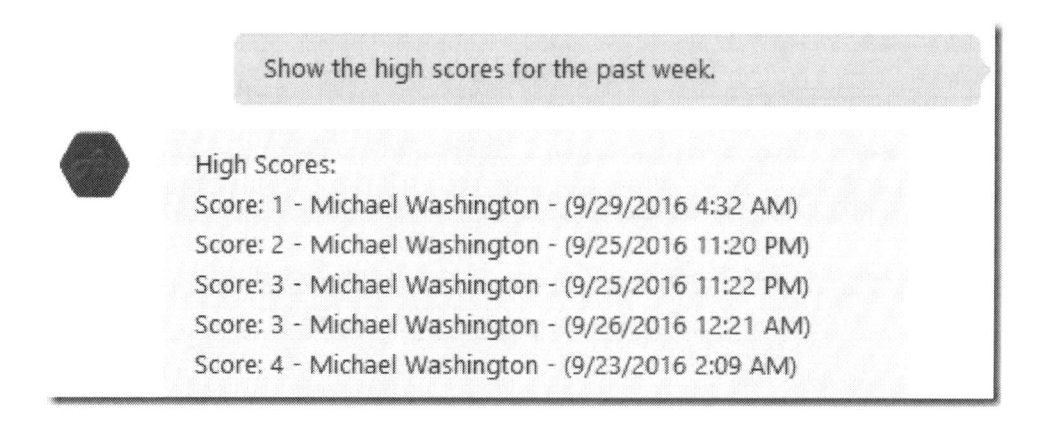

Show the high scores for the past week.

> High Scores:
> Score: 1 - Michael Washington - (9/29/2016 4:32 AM)
> Score: 2 - Michael Washington - (9/25/2016 11:20 PM)
> Score: 3 - Michael Washington - (9/25/2016 11:22 PM)
> Score: 3 - Michael Washington - (9/26/2016 12:21 AM)
> Score: 4 - Michael Washington - (9/23/2016 2:09 AM)

An Introduction to the Microsoft Bot Framework

In this chapter, we will alter the code to allow the user to see the high scores for the past week, the past month, or the past days they specify (up to 30 days).

Most importantly, we will allow the user to type their request using normal language and then detect the *intent* of the user and the important related *entities* (such as the number of days).

We will do this by creating an application using the **Language Understanding Intelligent Service (LUIS)** and then interfacing that application with our existing **Bot**.

Create The LUIS Application

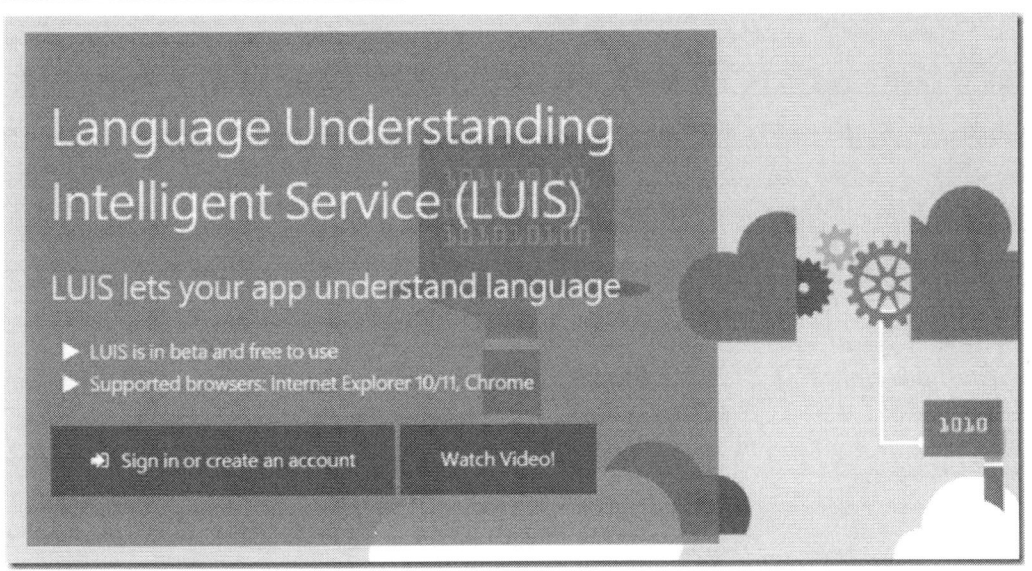

The first step is to go to https://www.luis.ai/ and create an account on the **Language Understanding Intelligent Service (LUIS)** site and log in.

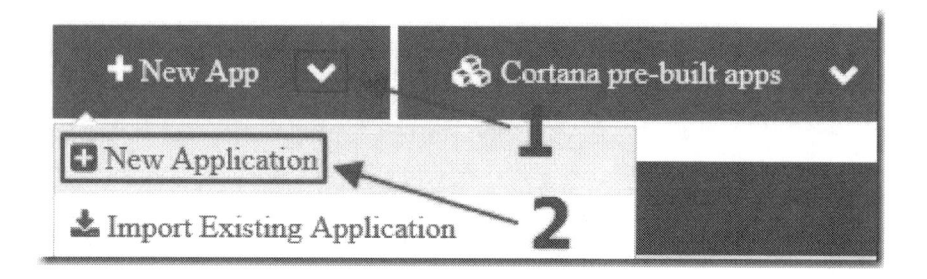

An Introduction to the Microsoft Bot Framework

Create a **New Application**.

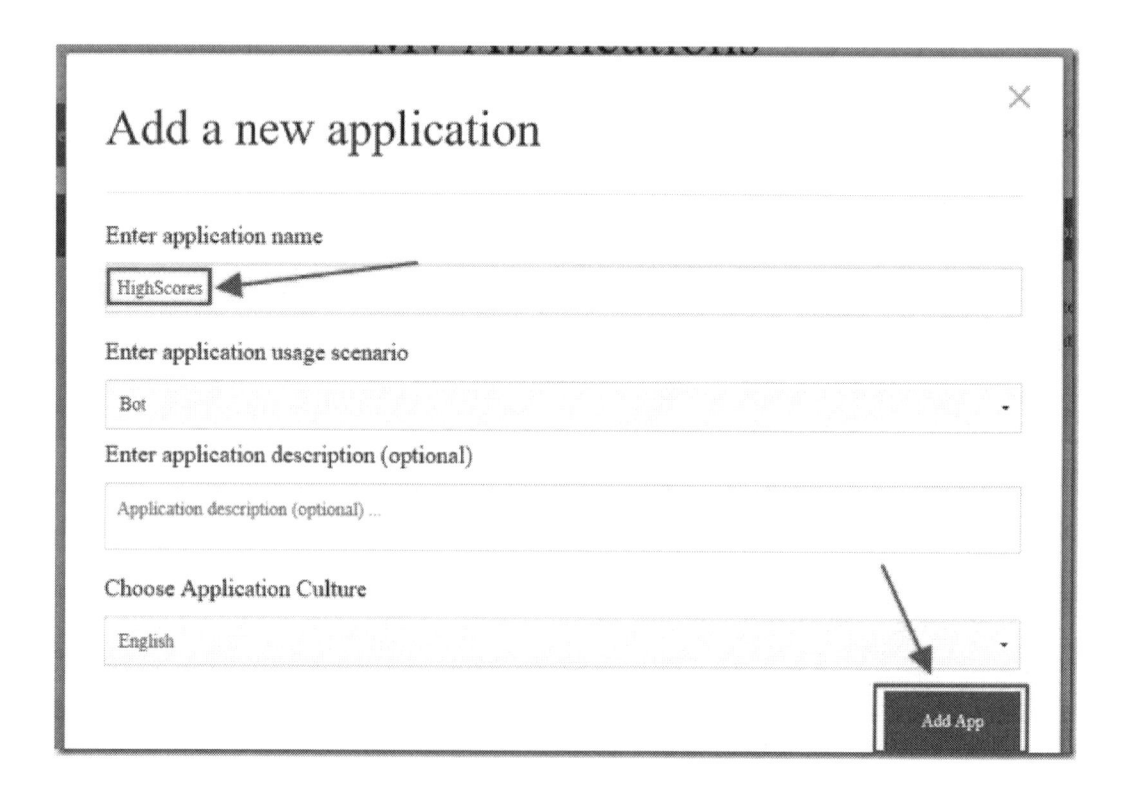

We will call it **HighScores**, and after filling out the other fields, we click **Add App**.

An Introduction to the Microsoft Bot Framework

Now we need to create **Entities**. These are elements we will need to identify and gather, so our **Bot** can perform operations based on their value. In our example, we want to create two **Entities**:

- **PeriodOfTime** – Detect if the user entered a word describing the amount of days (but not the actual days), for example, *week* or *month*
- **Days** – Detect if the user entered the actual days such as *3* or *three*

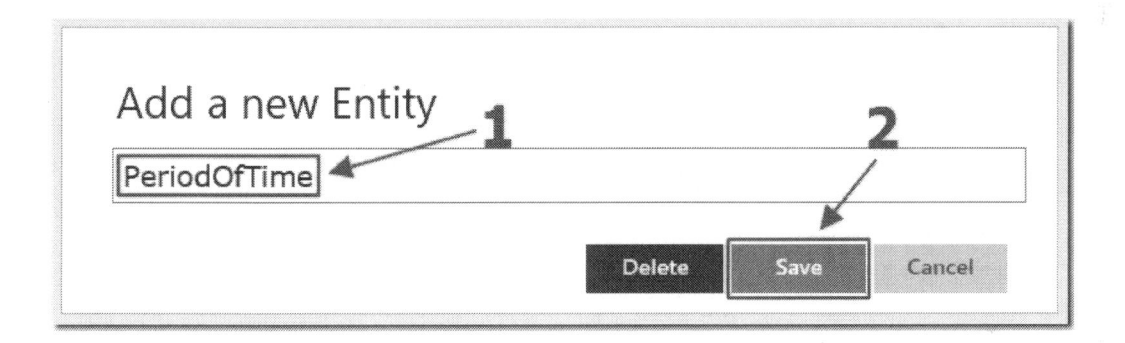

Click the *plus* button next to the **Entities** label (on the left-hand side of the editor) to open a box that will allow you to add each **Entity** (one at a time).

149

An Introduction to the Microsoft Bot Framework

When you're done, the **Entities** will be displayed.

Next, we will add an **Intent**.

*Note: The "None" **Intent**, to be triggered when an **utterance** by the user does not match a programmed intent, will be automatically created)*

Click the *plus* button next to the **Intents** label.

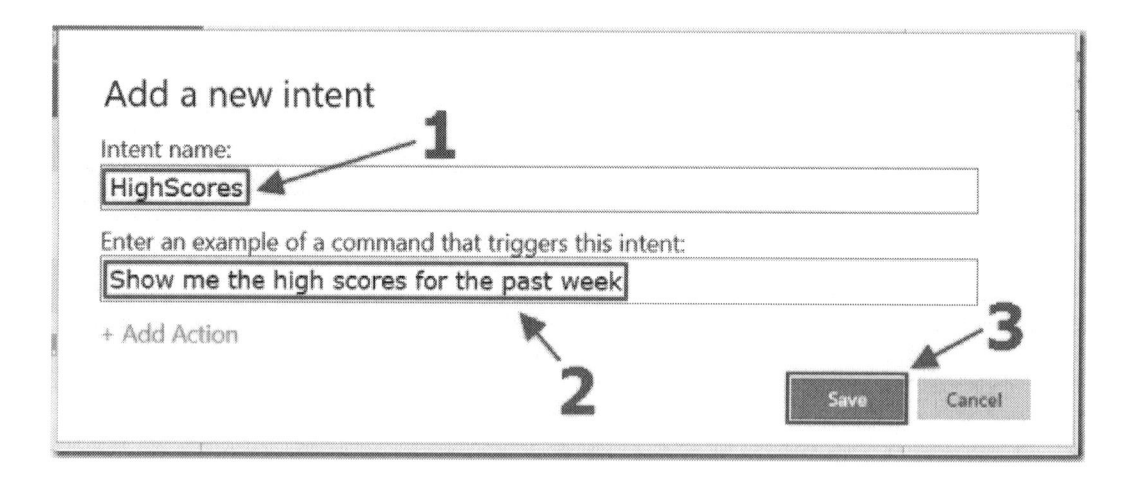

Enter *HighScores* for the **Intent** name.

Enter *Show me the high scores for the past week* for **Enter an example of a command that triggers this intent**. (This is also known as a sample *utterance*.)

Click **Save**.

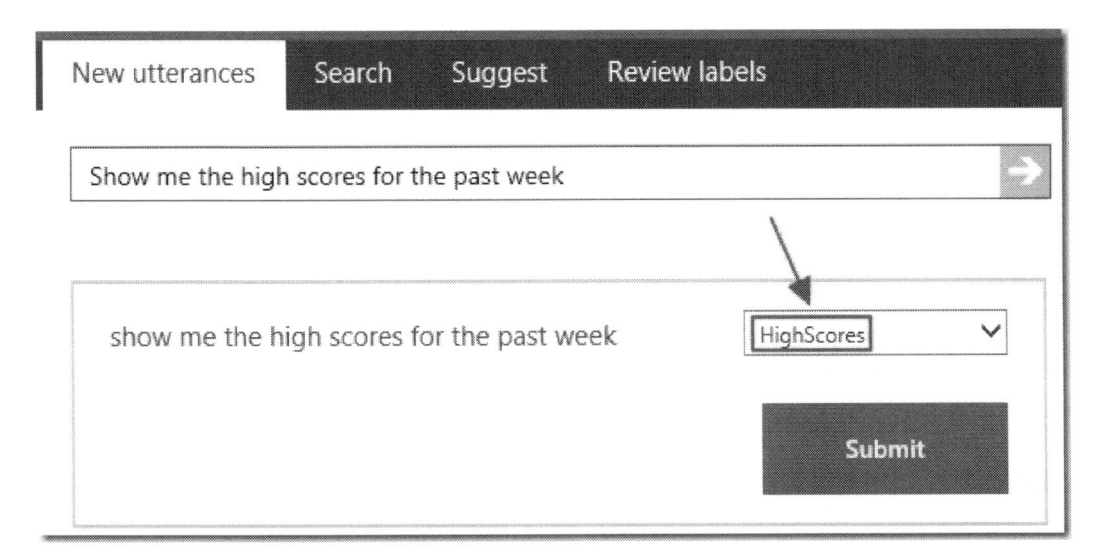

An Introduction to the Microsoft Bot Framework

The utterance will now display in the **New utterances** tab.

We want this *utterance* to trigger the *HighScores* **Intent**, so select it from the dropdown.

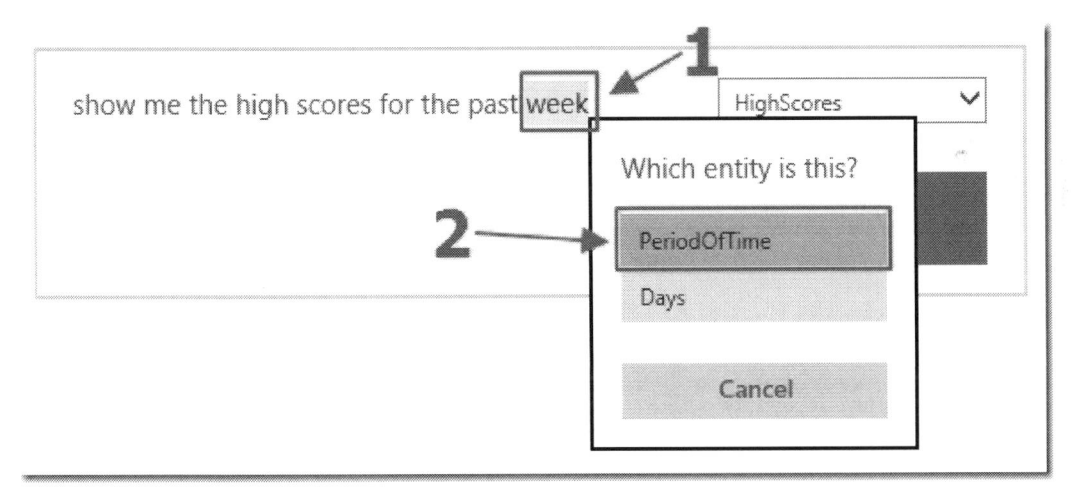

We also want to detect the associated *Entity*.

Click on the word **week**, it will then be highlighted, and a popup box will appear.

Select **PeriodOfTime**.

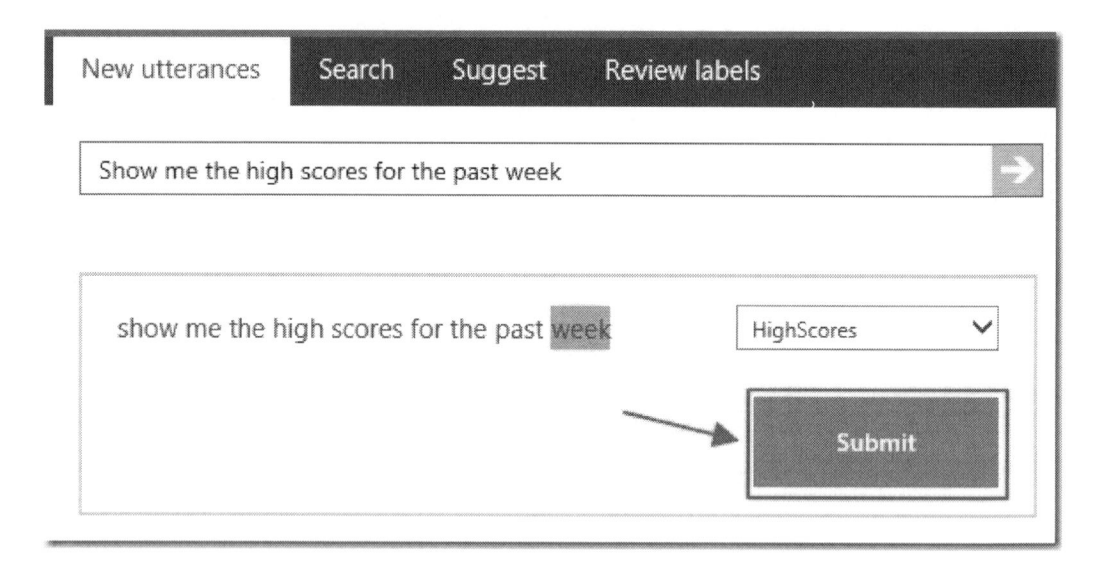

An Introduction to the Microsoft Bot Framework

Finally, click **Submit**.

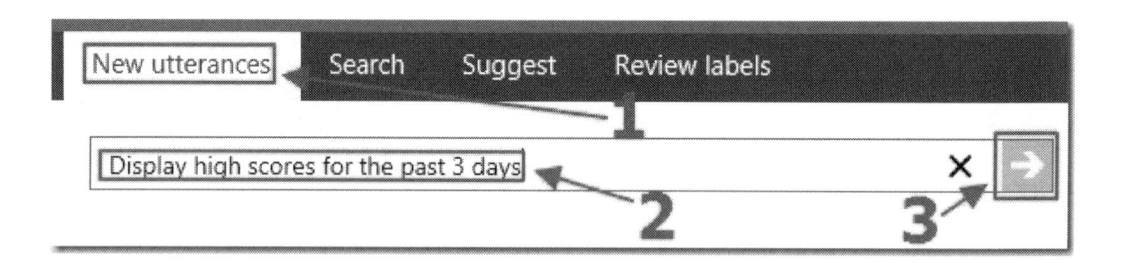

Continue to enter and label additional utterances.

Note: *Remember to label any* ***Entities*** *that indicate a number as* ***Days****.*

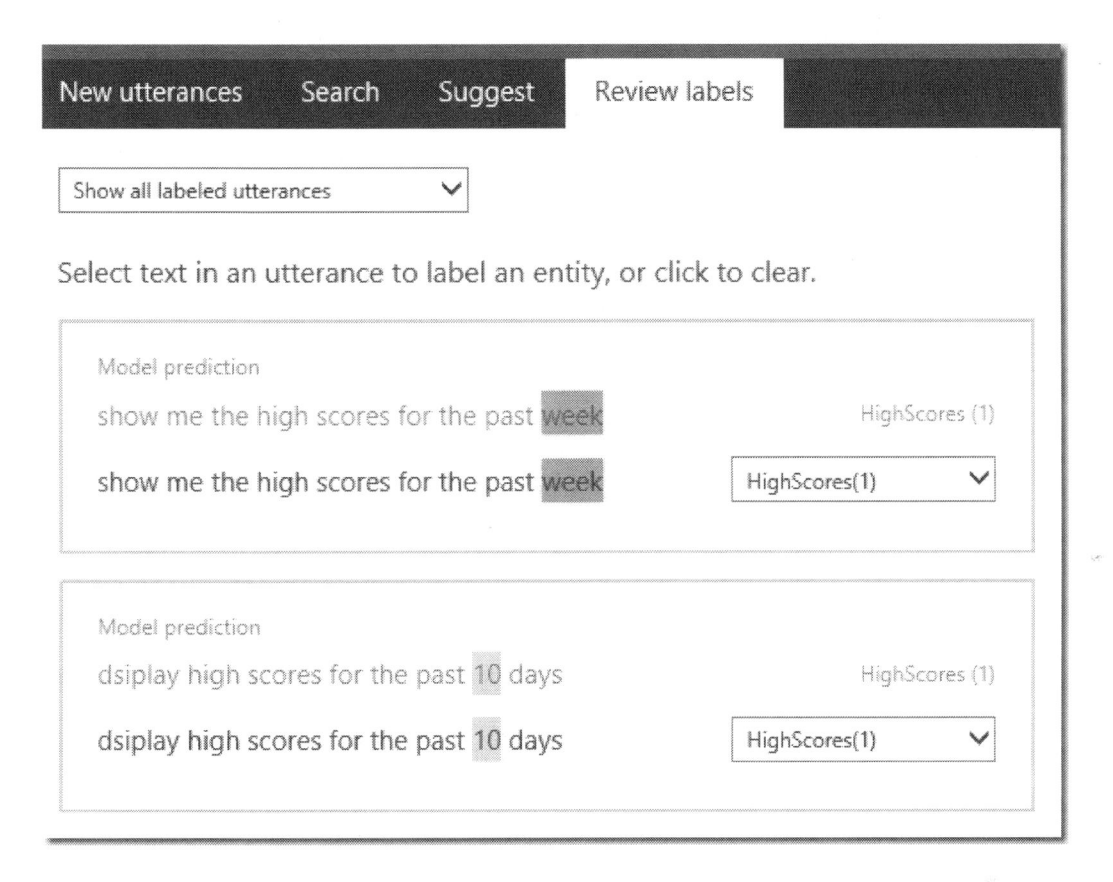

An Introduction to the Microsoft Bot Framework

Continue to train the service.

You will notice that eventually it will start detecting the **Entities** on its own.

However, many times you will still have to correct it.

Enter and correct at least ten different utterances.

Click the **Train** button in the bottom *left-hand* corner of the interface to train the model.

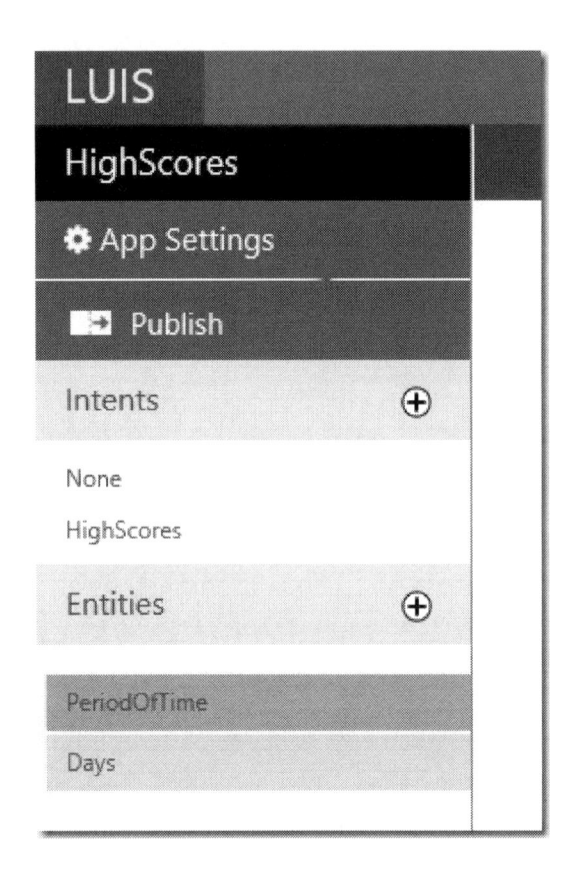

An Introduction to the Microsoft Bot Framework

Next, click the **Publish** button.

Finally, click the **Publish web service** button.

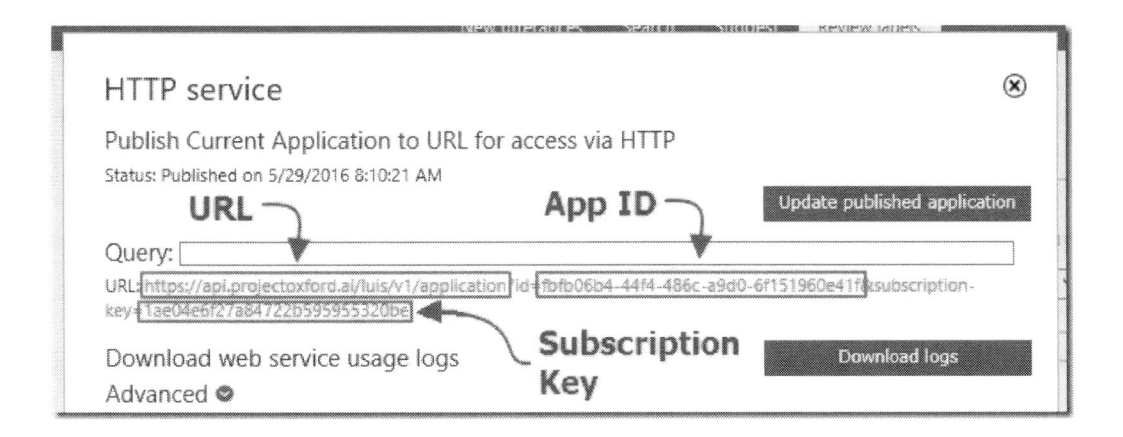

An Introduction to the Microsoft Bot Framework

The published end-point will be displayed.

Make note of the **App ID** and **Subscription Key**. You will need these later to be used in the **Bot** application.

Note: *Starting 12/31/2016,* ***App ID*** *will no longer be used. You will only use a* ***Subscription Key*** *to connect to your* ***LUIS*** *application.*

Note: *For a production application, you will obtain your subscription key from Azure.*

Now, we need to update the **Bot** to call the **LUIS** service...

155

An Introduction to the Microsoft Bot Framework

Update The Bot Application

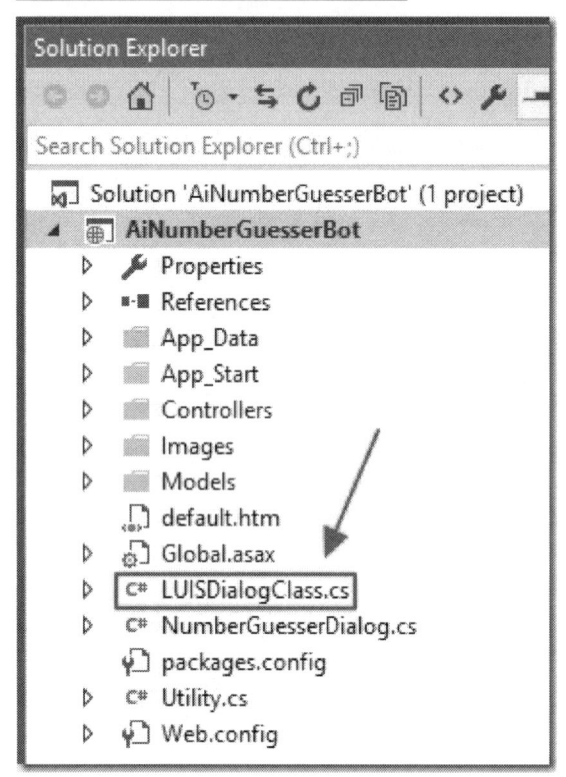

Open the project from the previous chapter in **Visual Studio**.

An Introduction to the Microsoft Bot Framework

Add a new file called **LUISDialogClass.cs**, using the following code:

```csharp
using Microsoft.Bot.Builder.Dialogs;
using Microsoft.Bot.Builder.Luis;
using Microsoft.Bot.Builder.Luis.Models;
using Microsoft.Bot.Connector;
using System;
using System.Collections.Generic;
using System.Linq;
using System.Threading.Tasks;
using System.Web;
namespace AiNumberGuesserBot
{
    [LuisModel("{Your App ID}", "{Your Subscription Key}")]
    [Serializable]
    public class LUISDialogClass : LuisDialog<object>
    {
        #region public async Task None(IDialogContext context, LuisResult result)
        [LuisIntent("")]
        [LuisIntent("None")]
        public async Task None(IDialogContext context, LuisResult result)
        {
            // Not a match -- Start a new Game
            context.Call(new NumberGuesserDialog(), null);
        }
        #endregion
```

An Introduction to the Microsoft Bot Framework

```csharp
#region public async Task HighScores(IDialogContext context, LuisResult result)
[LuisIntent("HighScores")]
public async Task HighScores(IDialogContext context, LuisResult result)
{
    // See if the intent has a > .99 match
    bool boolIntentMatch = false;
    foreach (var objIntent in result.Intents)
    {
        // If the HighScores Intent is detected
        // and it's score is greater than or = to .99
        // set boolIntentMatch = true
        if (
            (objIntent.Intent == "HighScores")
            && (objIntent.Score >= .99f)
            )
        {
            boolIntentMatch = true;
        }
    }
    if (boolIntentMatch)
    {
        // ** To Do: Code to handle a Match **
    }
    else
    {
        // Not a match -- Start a new Game
        var objNumberGuesserDialog = new NumberGuesserDialog();
        context.Call(objNumberGuesserDialog, null);
    }
}
#endregion
```

This code will pass text entered into the **Bot** to the **LUIS** application and trigger the **None** or **HighScores** methods based on what the **LUIS** application determines the *Intent* is, which the entered text matches.

We decorate each method with a **LuisIntent** decoration, setting the name of an *Intent* (for example, *[LuisIntent("HighScores")]*) to indicate which method should be triggered.

Note: *The code is not complete at this point. We will complete the code in later steps.*

An Introduction to the Microsoft Bot Framework

```
11  namespace AiNumberGuesserBot
12  {
13      [LuisModel("{Your App ID}", "{Your Subscription Key}")]
14      [Serializable]
15      public class LUISDialogClass : LuisDialog<object>
16      {
```

Ensure that you enter the **App ID** and **Subscription Key** from your **LUIS** application in the **LuisModel** decoration at the top of the class.

This is how the code knows what **LUIS** application to connect to.

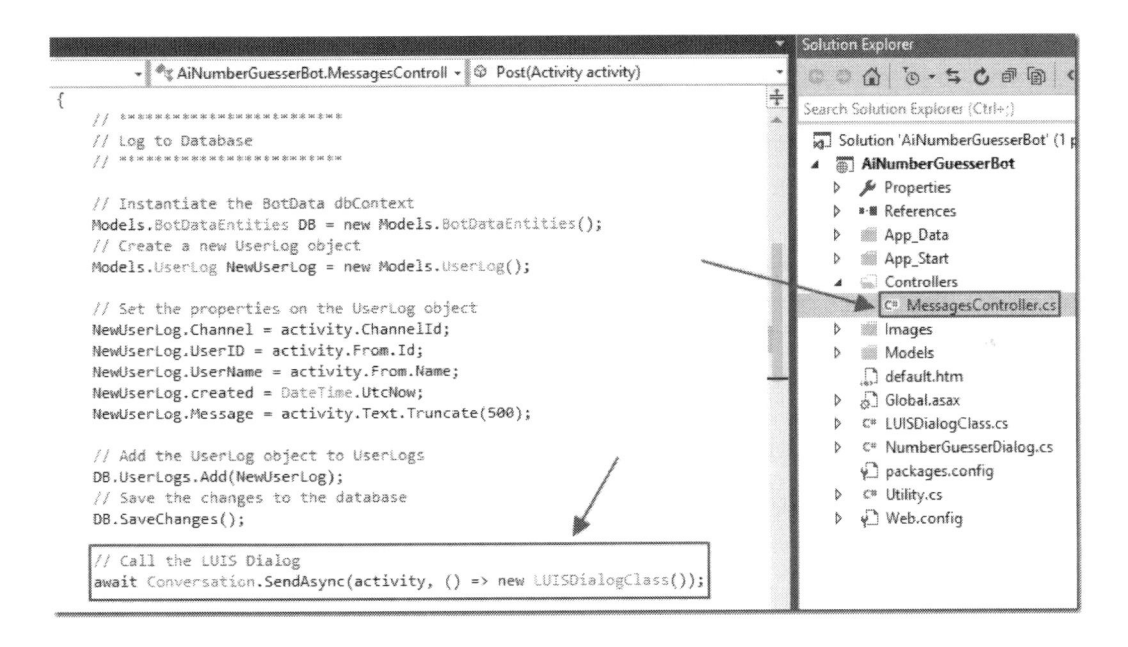

```
// ***********************
// Log to Database
// ***********************

// Instantiate the BotData dbContext
Models.BotDataEntities DB = new Models.BotDataEntities();
// Create a new UserLog object
Models.UserLog NewUserLog = new Models.UserLog();

// Set the properties on the UserLog object
NewUserLog.Channel = activity.ChannelId;
NewUserLog.UserID = activity.From.Id;
NewUserLog.UserName = activity.From.Name;
NewUserLog.created = DateTime.UtcNow;
NewUserLog.Message = activity.Text.Truncate(500);

// Add the UserLog object to UserLogs
DB.UserLogs.Add(NewUserLog);
// Save the changes to the database
DB.SaveChanges();

// Call the LUIS Dialog
await Conversation.SendAsync(activity, () => new LUISDialogClass());
```

We now need to call the **LUISDialogClass**, instead of the previously configured **NumberGuesserDialog** class, when a user communicates with the **Bot**.

The new **LUIS** code (**LUISDialogClass**) will call the **NumberGuesserDialog** class when needed, for example, when the user has not triggered the *HighScores* intent.

An Introduction to the Microsoft Bot Framework

Open the **MessagesController.cs** file in the **Controllers** folder.

Replace the following code:

```
// Detect if the user enters the words "high score"
if (activity.Text.ToLower().Contains("high score"))
{
    // Call the ShowHighScores method
    // passing to it, the current Activity
    ShowHighScores(activity);
}
else
{
    // Call NumberGuesserDialog
    await Conversation.SendAsync(activity, () => new NumberGuesserDialog());
}
```

With:

```
// Call the LUIS Dialog
await Conversation.SendAsync(activity, () => new LUISDialogClass());
```

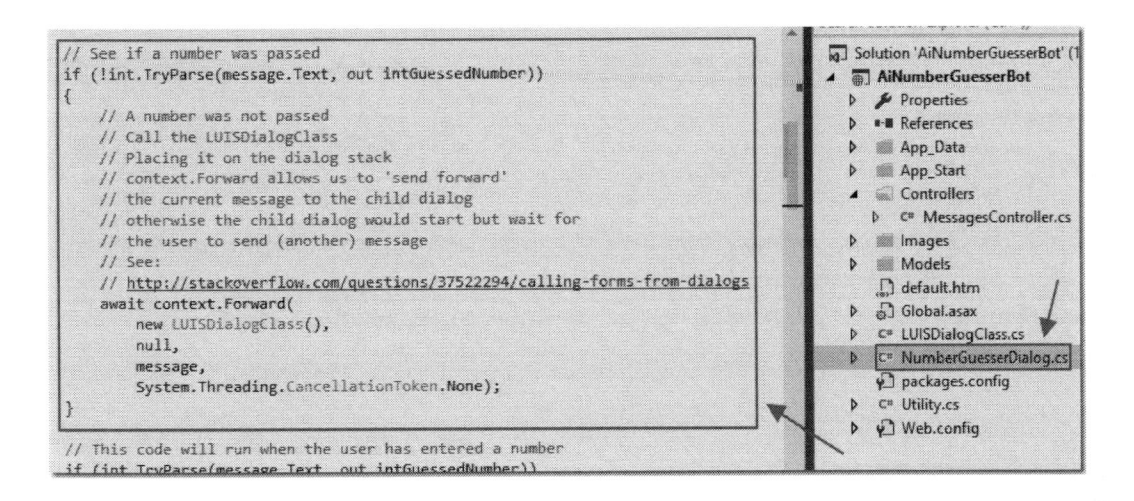

An Introduction to the Microsoft Bot Framework

```
// See if a number was passed
if (!int.TryParse(message.Text, out intGuessedNumber))
{
    // A number was not passed
    // Call the LUISDialogClass
    // Placing it on the dialog stack
    // context.Forward allows us to 'send forward'
    // the current message to the child dialog
    // otherwise the child dialog would start but wait for
    // the user to send (another) message
    // See:
    // http://stackoverflow.com/questions/37522294/calling-forms-from-dialogs
    await context.Forward(
        new LUISDialogClass(),
        null,
        message,
        System.Threading.CancellationToken.None);
}
// This code will run when the user has entered a number
if (int.TryParse(message.Text, out intGuessedNumber))
```

There are places where the **NumberGuesserDialog** will need to call **LUISDialogClass**, for example, when the user has entered a response that is not a number being guessed as part of the game.

The **NumberGuesserDialog** class will need to return control back to the **LUISDialogClass**.

Replace the code in the **NumberGuesserDialog** class (encapsulated in the brackets) that begins like the text below:

```
// See if a number was passed
if (!int.TryParse(message.Text, out intGuessedNumber))
{
    ...
}
```

An Introduction to the Microsoft Bot Framework

With the following code:

```csharp
// See if a number was passed
if (!int.TryParse(message.Text, out intGuessedNumber))
{
    // A number was not passed
    // Call the LUISDialogClass
    // Placing it on the dialog stack
    // context.Forward allows us to 'send forward'
    // the current message to the child dialog
    // otherwise the child dialog would start but wait for
    // the user to send (another) message
    // See:
    // http://stackoverflow.com/questions/37522294/calling-forms-from-dialogs
    await context.Forward(
        new LUISDialogClass(),
        null,
        message,
        System.Threading.CancellationToken.None);
}
```

An Introduction to the Microsoft Bot Framework

```
Activity replyToConversation = (Activity)context.MakeMessage();
replyToConversation.Recipient = replyToConversation.Recipient;
replyToConversation.Type = "message";

string strAiHelpWebsite_Small =
    String.Format(@"{0}/{1}",
    strBaseURL,
    "Images/NumberGuesserCard.png");

List<CardImage> cardImages = new List<CardImage>();
cardImages.Add(new CardImage(url: strAiHelpWebsite_Small));

// Create the Buttons
List<CardAction> cardButtons = CreateButtons();

HeroCard plCard = new HeroCard()
{
    Images = cardImages,
    Buttons = cardButtons,
};

Attachment plAttachment = plCard.ToAttachment();
replyToConversation.Attachments.Add(plAttachment);
replyToConversation.AttachmentLayout = "list";

await context.PostAsync(replyToConversation);

// Start the Game
context.Wait(MessageReceivedAsync);
```

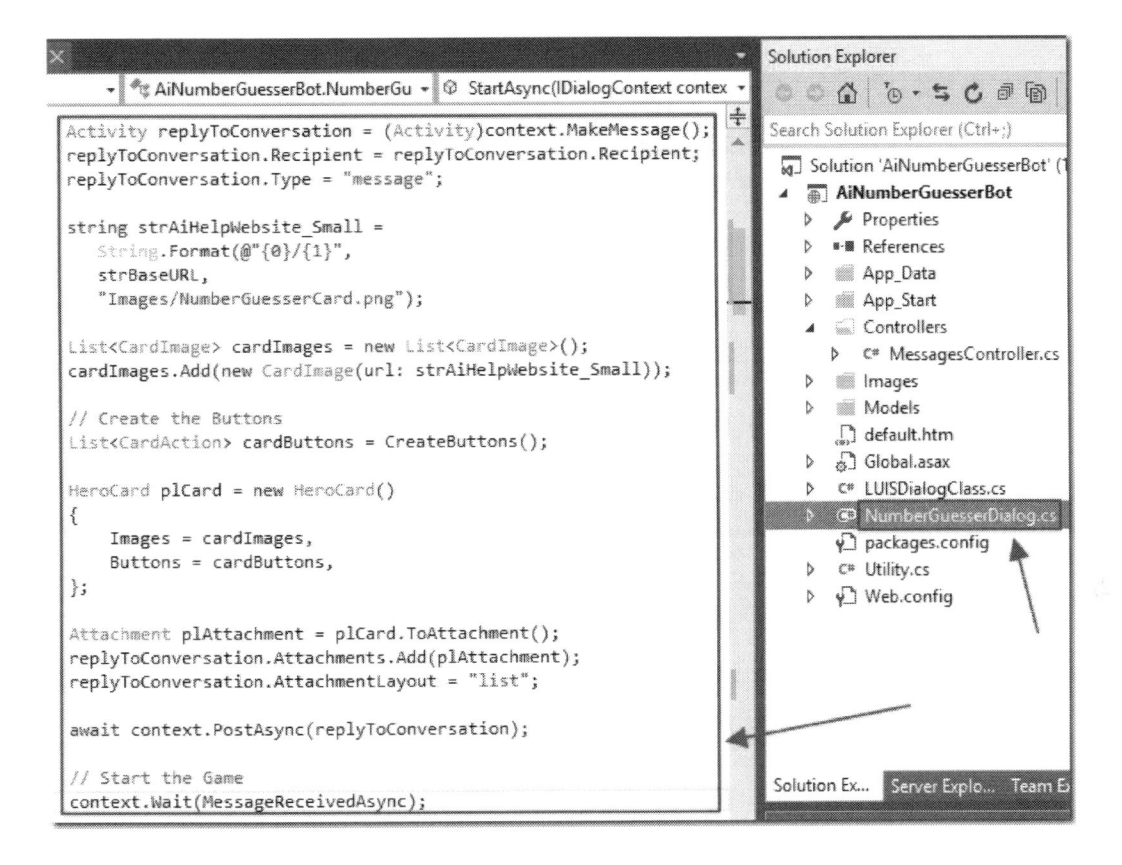

The **NumberGuesserDialog** class is no longer the root class, so we will need to alter it slightly again, so it starts up the game properly when it is triggered by the **LUISDialogClass**.

Locate the following code in the *StartAsync* method:

```
// Start the Game
context.Wait(MessageReceivedAsync);
```

An Introduction to the Microsoft Bot Framework

Replace it with:

```
Activity replyToConversation = (Activity)context.MakeMessage();
replyToConversation.Recipient = replyToConversation.Recipient;
replyToConversation.Type = "message";
string strAiHelpWebsite_Small =
    String.Format(@"{0}/{1}",
    strBaseURL,
    "Images/NumberGuesserCard.png");
List<CardImage> cardImages = new List<CardImage>();
cardImages.Add(new CardImage(url: strAiHelpWebsite_Small));
// Create the Buttons
List<CardAction> cardButtons = CreateButtons();
HeroCard plCard = new HeroCard()
{
    Images = cardImages,
    Buttons = cardButtons,
};
Attachment plAttachment = plCard.ToAttachment();
replyToConversation.Attachments.Add(plAttachment);
replyToConversation.AttachmentLayout = "list";
await context.PostAsync(replyToConversation);
// Start the Game
context.Wait(MessageReceivedAsync);
```

This code shows the welcome screen to start the number guessing game.

An Introduction to the Microsoft Bot Framework

Implement High Scores

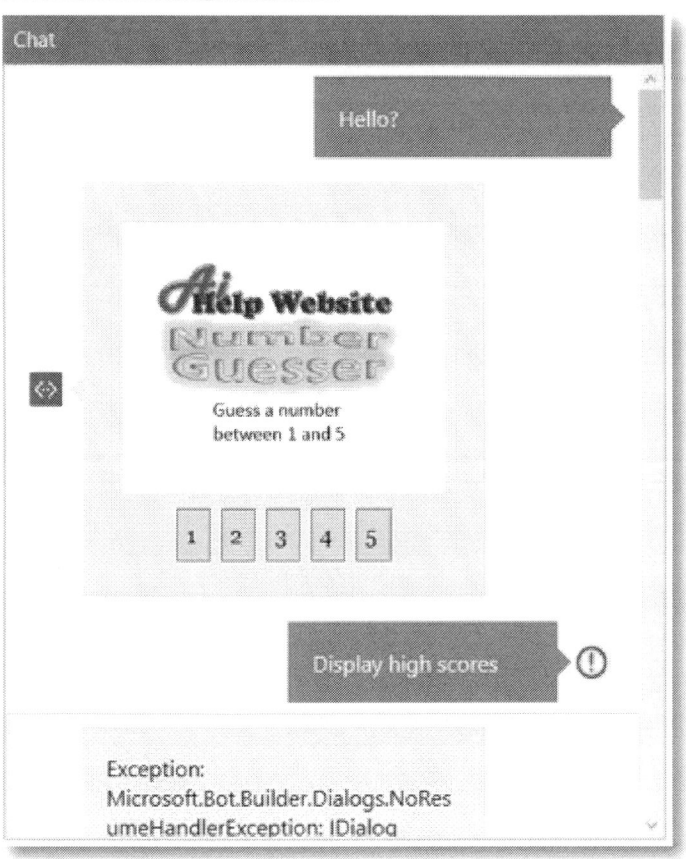

At this point, if we run the application and connect to it in the **Microsoft Bot Framework Emulator**, we can play the game.

However, if we type anything that triggers the *HighScores* **LUIS** Intent, we will receive an error because the code to handle this has not been implemented yet.

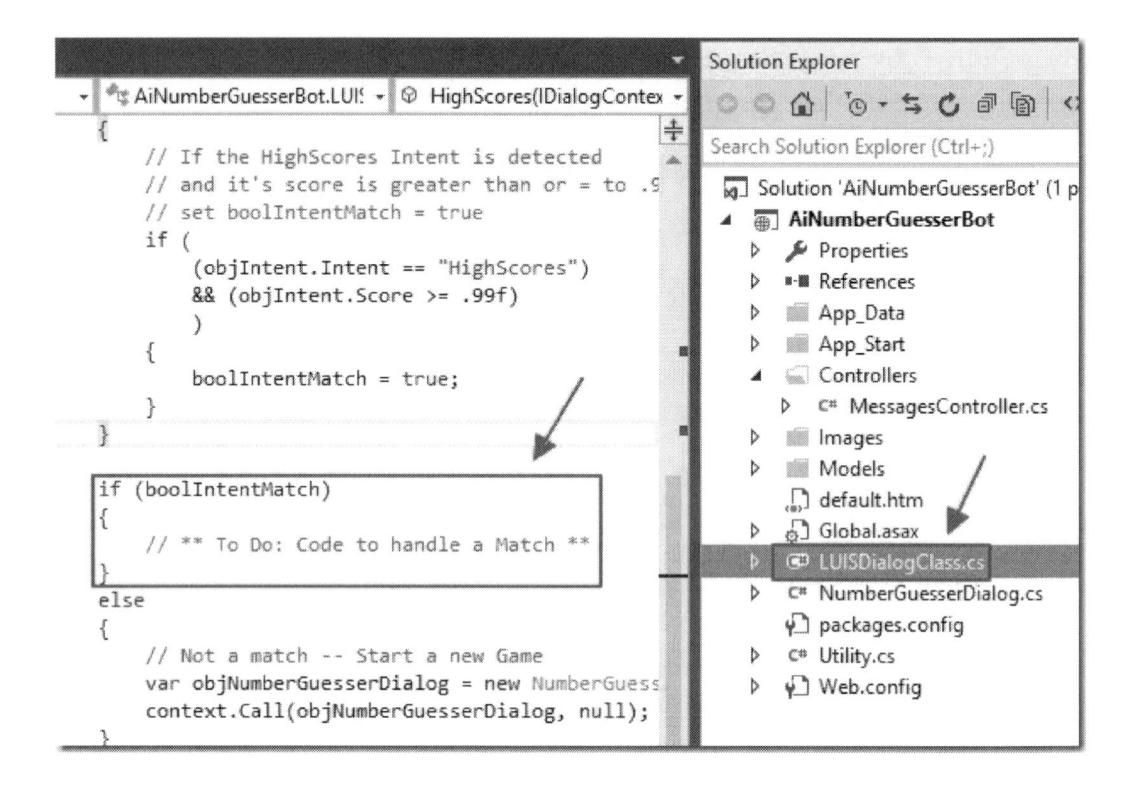

An Introduction to the Microsoft Bot Framework

Open the **LUISDialogClass.cs** file and locate the following code:

```
if (boolIntentMatch)
{
    // ** To Do: Code to handle a Match **
}
```

An Introduction to the Microsoft Bot Framework

Replace it with:

```csharp
if (boolIntentMatch)
{
    // Determine the days in the past
    // to search for High Scores
    int intDays = -1;
    #region PeriodOfTime
    EntityRecommendation PeriodOfTime;
    if (result.TryFindEntity("PeriodOfTime", out PeriodOfTime))
    {
        switch (PeriodOfTime.Entity)
        {
            case "month":
                intDays = -30;
                break;
            case "day":
                intDays = -1;
                break;
            case "week":
                intDays = -7;
                break;
            default:
                intDays = -1;
                break;
        }
    }
    #endregion
    #region Days
    EntityRecommendation Days;
    if (result.TryFindEntity("Days", out Days))
    {
        // Set Days
        int intTempDays;
        if (int.TryParse(Days.Entity, out intTempDays))
        {
            // A Number was passed
            intDays = (Convert.ToInt32(intTempDays) * (-1));
        }
        else
        {
            // A number was not passed
            // Call ParseEnglish Method
            // From: http://stackoverflow.com/questions/11278081/convert-words-string-to-int
            intTempDays = ParseEnglish(Days.Entity);
            intDays = (Convert.ToInt32(intTempDays) * (-1));
        }
        // 30 days maximum
        if (intDays > 30)
        {
            intDays = 30;
        }
    }
    #endregion
    await ShowHighScores(context, intDays);
    context.Wait(this.MessageReceived);
}
```

An Introduction to the Microsoft Bot Framework

This code will set the number of days the user is asking the *high scores* to include. It first tries to detect if a period of time was passed (in the **PeriodOfTime** entity). If it has been, the code converts a known period of time to a number of days.

If a number of days was passed (in the **Days** entity), the code tries to convert the days into a number. If it cannot, it assumes the number of days was passed as a word not a number. If this is the case, it passes the value to the **ParseEnglish** method that converts the word to a number.

Note: *You can get the **ParseEnglish** method from http://stackoverflow.com/questions/11278081/convert-words-string-to-int*

The number of days (and the current context) is then passed to the **ShowHighScores** method.

An Introduction to the Microsoft Bot Framework

As the final step, enter the following code to implement the **ShowHighScores** method into the **LUISDialogClass**:

```csharp
#region private async Task ShowHighScores(IDialogContext context, int paramDays)
private async Task ShowHighScores(IDialogContext context, int paramDays)
{
    // Get the High Scores
    Models.BotDataEntities DB = new Models.BotDataEntities();
    // Get Yesterday
    var ParamYesterday = DateTime.Now.AddDays(paramDays);
    var HighScores = (from UserLog in DB.UserLogs
                      where UserLog.CountOfTurnsToWin != null
                      where UserLog.created > ParamYesterday
                      select UserLog)
                      .OrderBy(x => x.CountOfTurnsToWin)
                      .Take(5)
                      .ToList();
    System.Text.StringBuilder sb = new System.Text.StringBuilder();
    sb.Append("High Scores:\n\n");
    foreach (var Score in HighScores)
    {
        sb.Append(String.Format("Score: {0} - {1} - ({2} {3})\n\n"
            , Score.CountOfTurnsToWin
            , Score.WinnerUserName
            , Score.created.ToLocalTime().ToShortDateString()
            , Score.created.ToLocalTime().ToShortTimeString()));
    }
    // Create a reply message
    var resultMessage = context.MakeMessage();
    resultMessage.Type = "message";
    resultMessage.Text = sb.ToString();
    // Send Message
    await context.PostAsync(resultMessage);
}
#endregion
```

An Introduction to the Microsoft Bot Framework

Chapter 8: Calling The Microsoft Bot Framework Using The Direct Line API

The sample code for this chapter can be obtained at the link "Calling The Microsoft Bot Framework Using The Direct Line API" at http://AiHelpWebsite.com/Downloads

You may need to call your **Microsoft Bot Framework Bot** directly from a custom application, a service, or a website. **The Microsoft Bot Connector Direct Line REST API** allows you to do this. In addition, it allows you to authenticate a user in your application and securely communicate with the **Bot** as that user.

An Introduction to the Microsoft Bot Framework

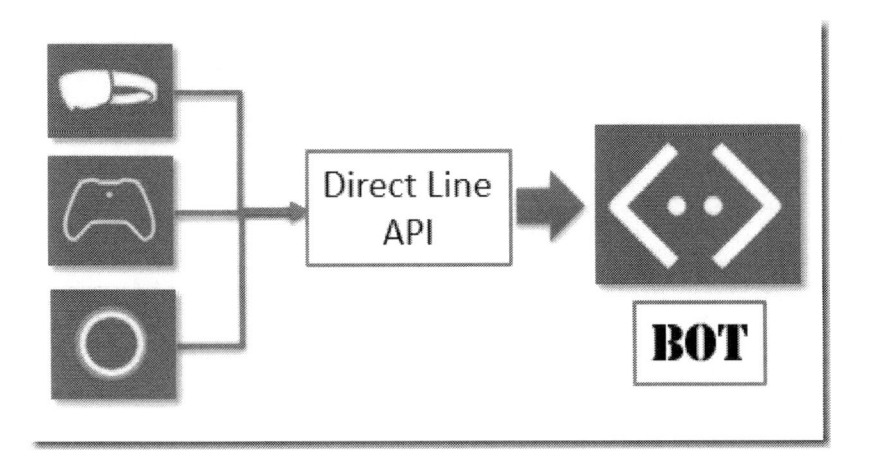

The **Direct Line API** exposes a *REST API* that allows you to communicate with a single **Bot** that has been registered with the **Microsoft Bot Connector Service**.

This API is intended for developers who want to communicate with their **Bot** from their own client applications, such as mobile apps, a service, or even a HoloLens.

An Introduction to the Microsoft Bot Framework

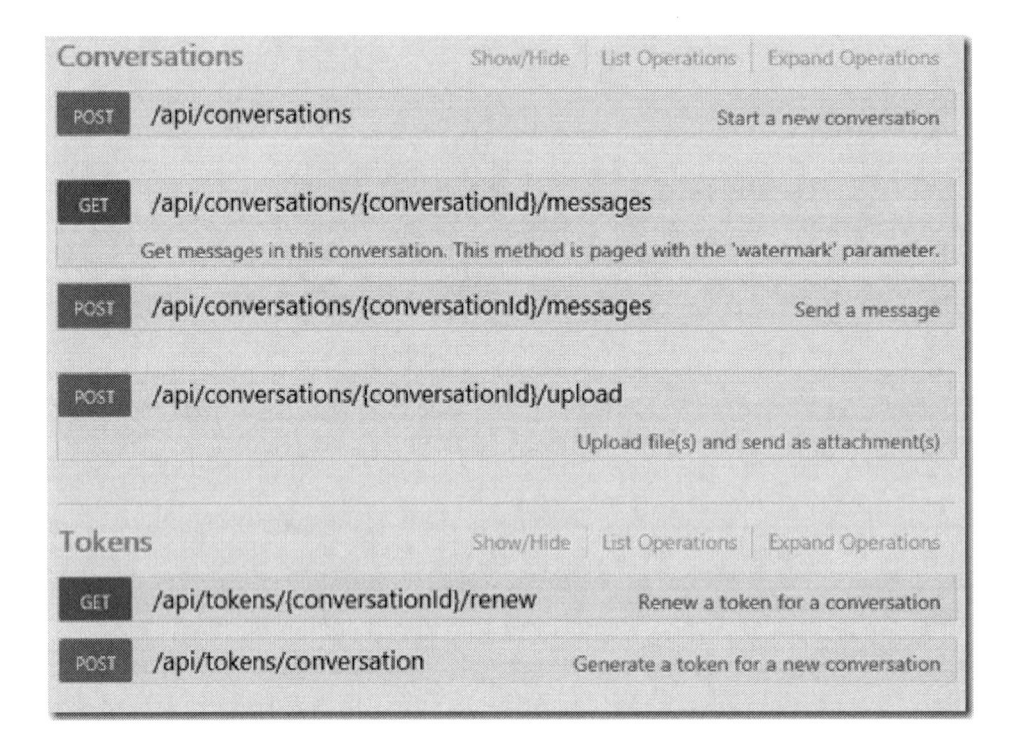

Conversations		Show/Hide · List Operations · Expand Operations
POST	/api/conversations	Start a new conversation
GET	/api/conversations/{conversationId}/messages	Get messages in this conversation. This method is paged with the 'watermark' parameter.
POST	/api/conversations/{conversationId}/messages	Send a message
POST	/api/conversations/{conversationId}/upload	Upload file(s) and send as attachment(s)
Tokens		Show/Hide · List Operations · Expand Operations
GET	/api/tokens/{conversationId}/renew	Renew a token for a conversation
POST	/api/tokens/conversation	Generate a token for a new conversation

The procedure for working with the API is:

1. Register your **Bot** with the **Bot Framework Developer Portal**
2. Configure the **Direct Line Connector**
3. Use the credentials obtained from the **Bot Framework Developer Portal** to make *REST* based calls to communicate with the **Bot**
   In our example, we will use the **Microsoft.Bot.Connector.DirectLine Nuget** package to help us make the calls.

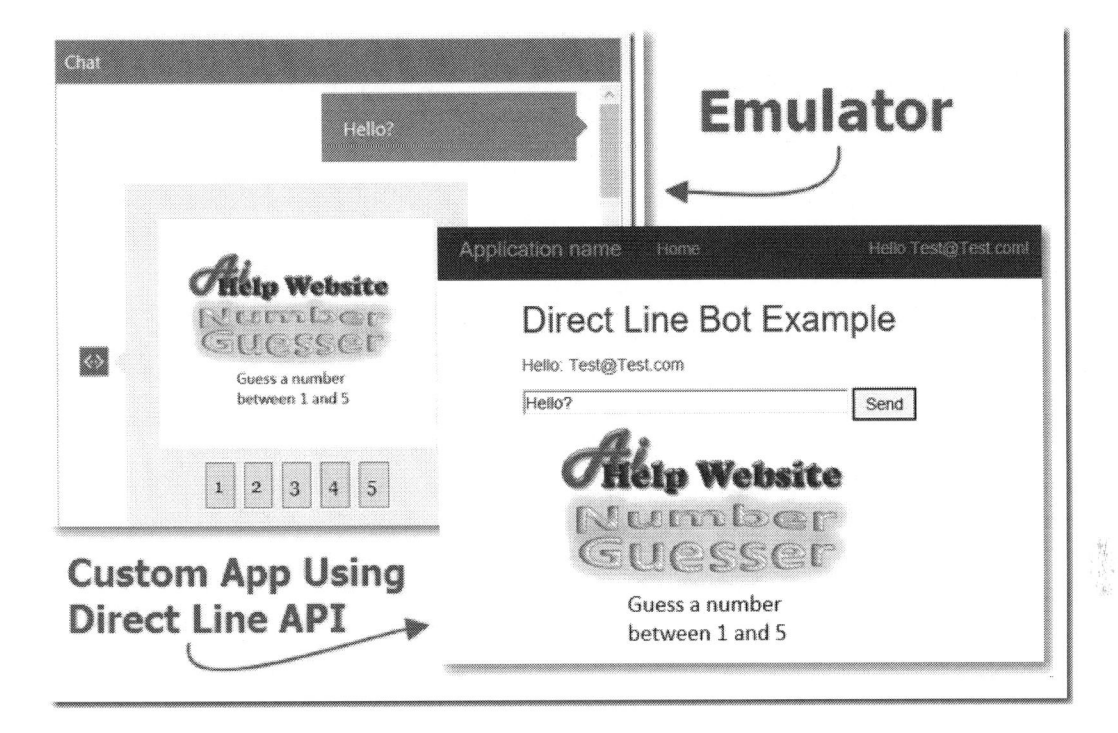

An Introduction to the Microsoft Bot Framework

Note: The rendering of the output will be the responsibility of the developer of the custom application that is calling the Direct Line API.

Media such an *images*, *cards*, and *buttons* will require custom code to render in a manner that is appropriate for the particular application.

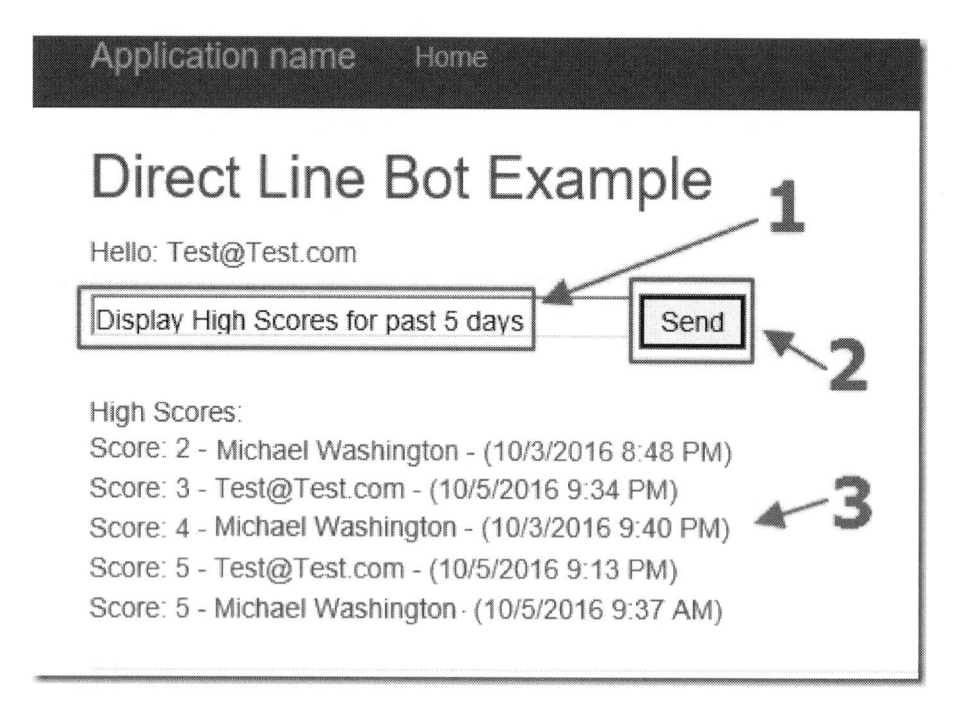

An Introduction to the Microsoft Bot Framework

The example application we will build will create a custom client that will allow a user to create an account, sign-in, and securely communicate with the **Bot** that was created in the previous chapter.

Configuring The Direct Line Connector

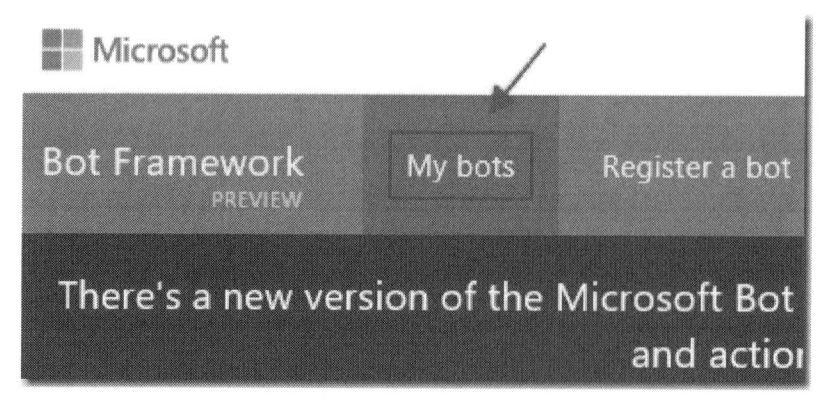

We want to configure the **Direct Line** connector for our **Bot**.

An Introduction to the Microsoft Bot Framework

Go to https://dev.botframework.com/, log in, and select **My Bots**.

Open a **Bot** that has been deployed to the **Microsoft Bot Framework Developer Portal**.

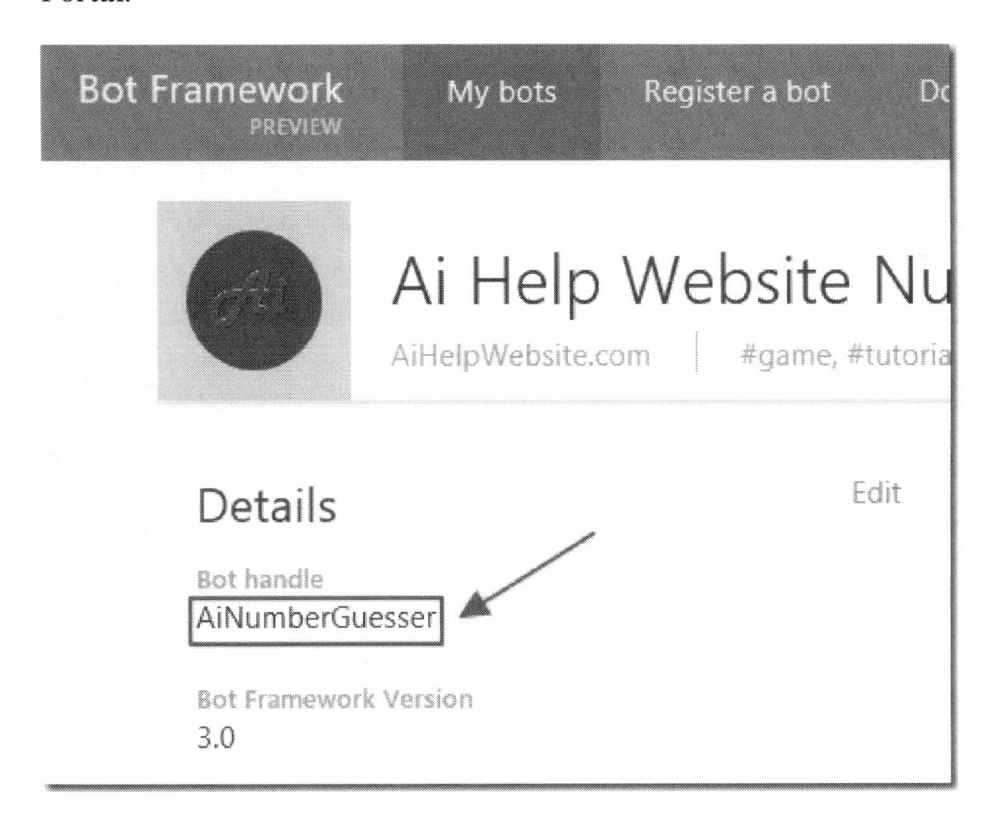

The first step is to make a note of the **Bot handle** you gave your **Bot**. You will need this later when you create the **Web Application**.

175

An Introduction to the Microsoft Bot Framework

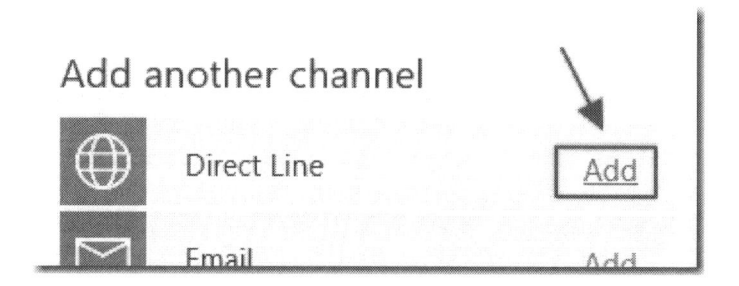

Under **Add another channel**, click the **Add** button next to **Direct Line**.

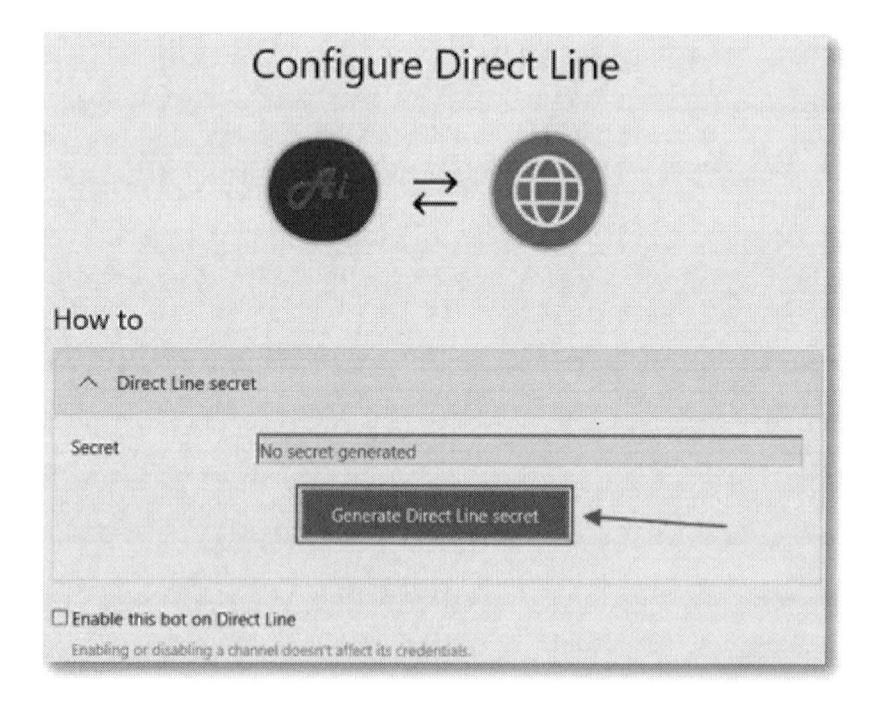

When the **Configure Direct Line** screen appears, click the **Generate Direct Line secret** button.

An Introduction to the Microsoft Bot Framework

![Configure Direct Line screen with 1) Copy arrow pointing to Secret field and 2) Click arrow pointing to I'm done configuring Direct Line button]

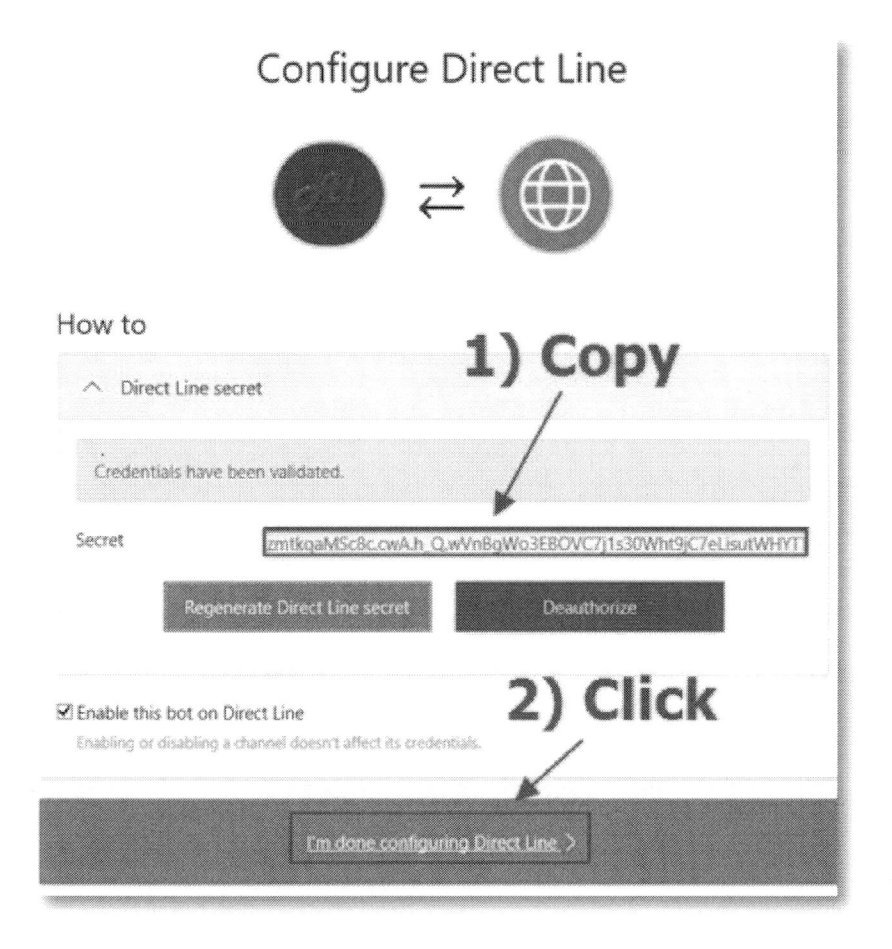

Copy the **Secret** code. You will need this later when you create the **Web Application**.

Click **I'm done configuring Direct Line** button.

The screen will close.

An Introduction to the Microsoft Bot Framework

Create The Web Application

Open **Visual Studio**.

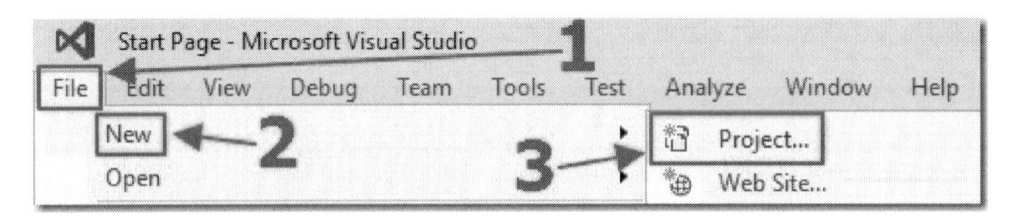

From the **toolbar** in **Visual Studio**, select **File**, then **New**, and then **Project**.

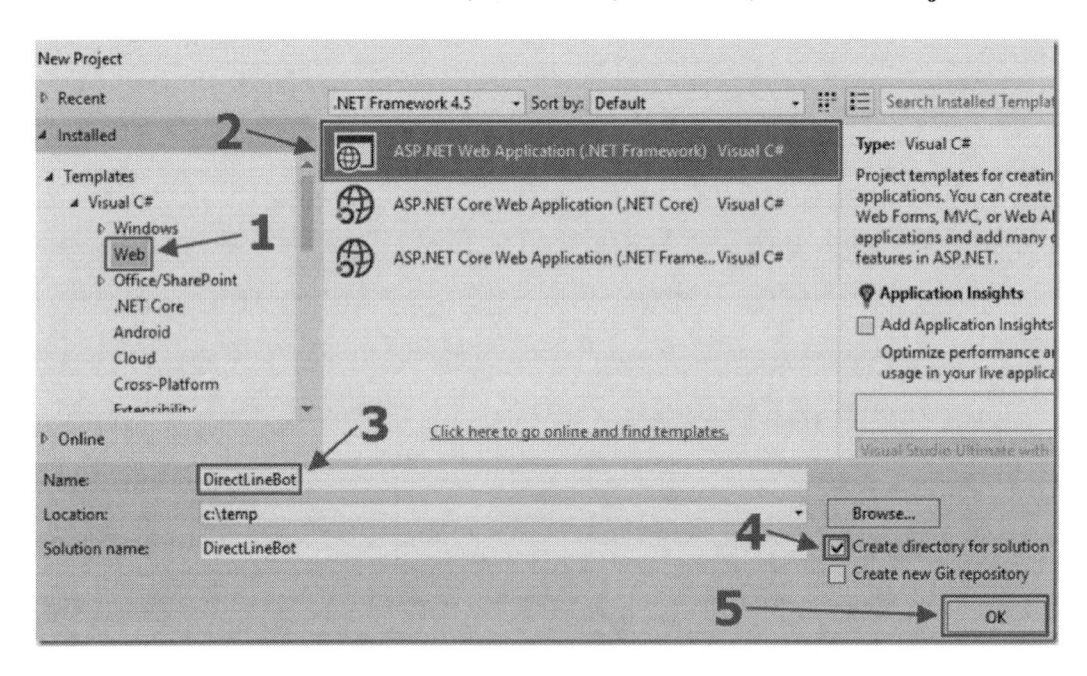

Select **Web** and then **ASP.NET Web Application (.Net Framework)**.

An Introduction to the Microsoft Bot Framework

Enter **DirectLineBot** for the **Name**.

Select the **Create directory for solution** box.

Press **OK**.

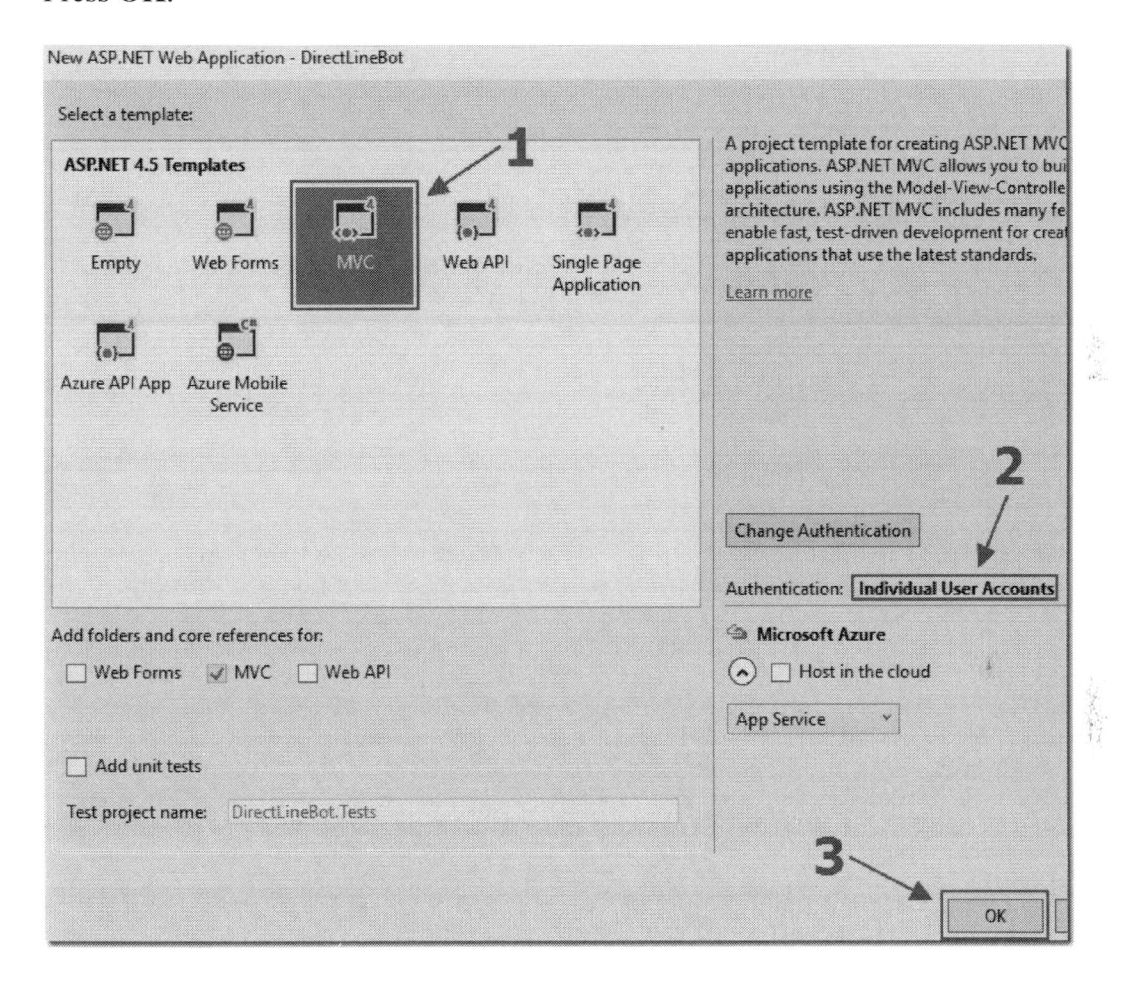

When the application configuration box appears, select the **MVC** template.

Ensure that **Individual User Accounts** is selected for **Authentication**. If not, click the **Change Authentication** button and change it.

Press **OK**.

179

An Introduction to the Microsoft Bot Framework

> Microsoft Visual Studio
>
> Creating project 'DirectLineBot'...

The application will be created.

We need to add the **Microsoft.Bot.Connector.DirectLine NuGet Package** that will allow us to easily communicate with the **DirectLine API**.

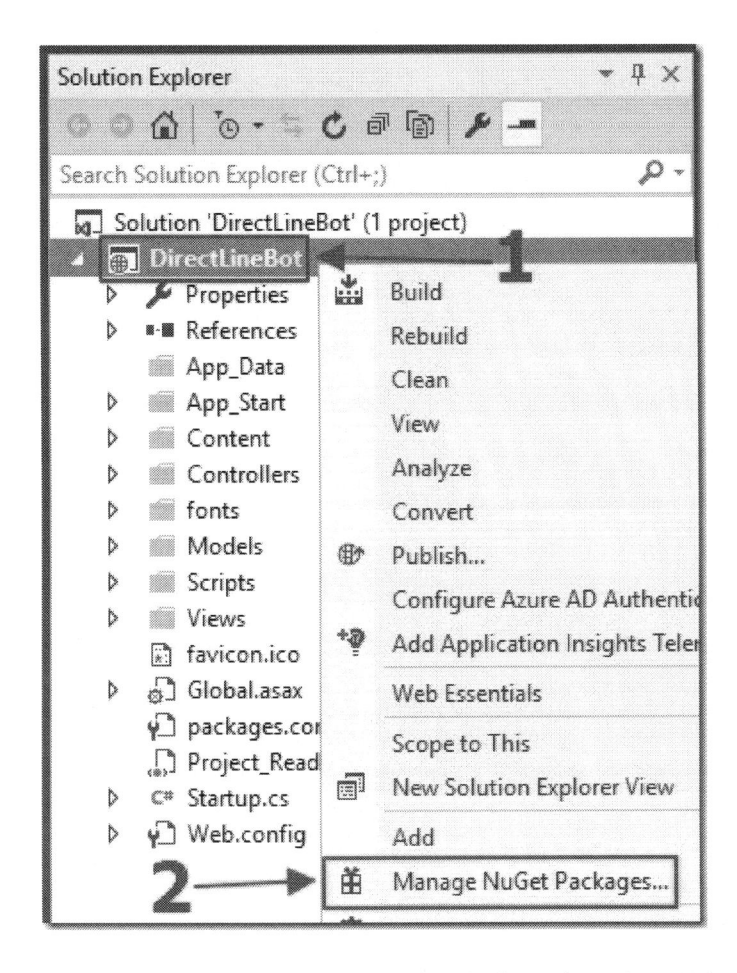

An Introduction to the Microsoft Bot Framework

In the **Solution Explorer**, *right-click* on the **DirectLineBot** project node (not the **Solution** node), and select **Manage NuGet Packages**.

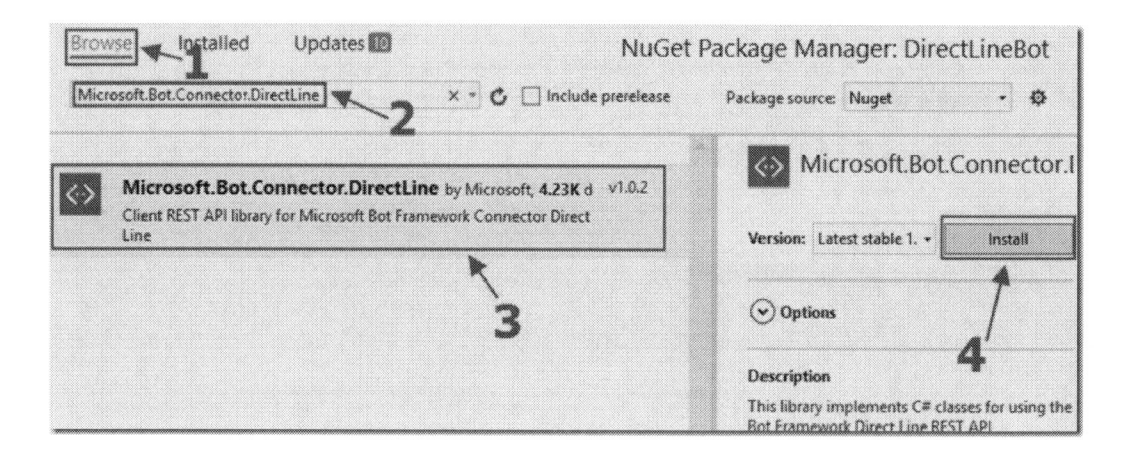

An Introduction to the Microsoft Bot Framework

When the **NuGet Package** configuration window appears, click the **Browse** button.

Enter **Microsoft.Bot.Connector.DirectLine** in the search box to conduct the search.

When the **Microsoft.Bot.Connector.DirectLine** package shows up, click on it, so its *properties* appear in the window on the right.

Click the **Install** button to install the package.

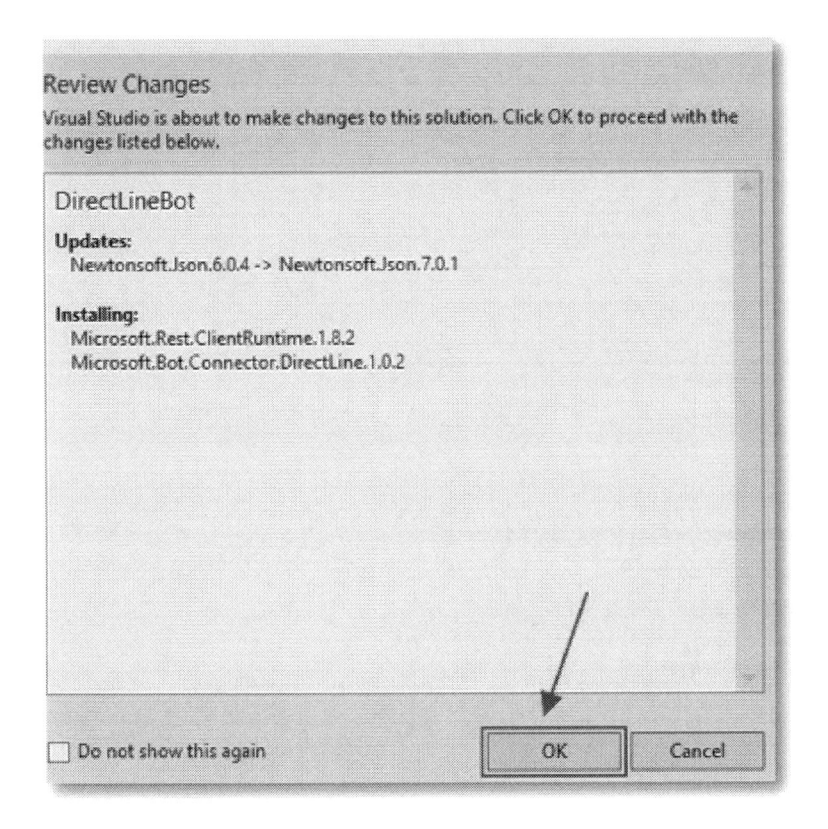

An Introduction to the Microsoft Bot Framework

Click **OK** when the **Preview** window shows.

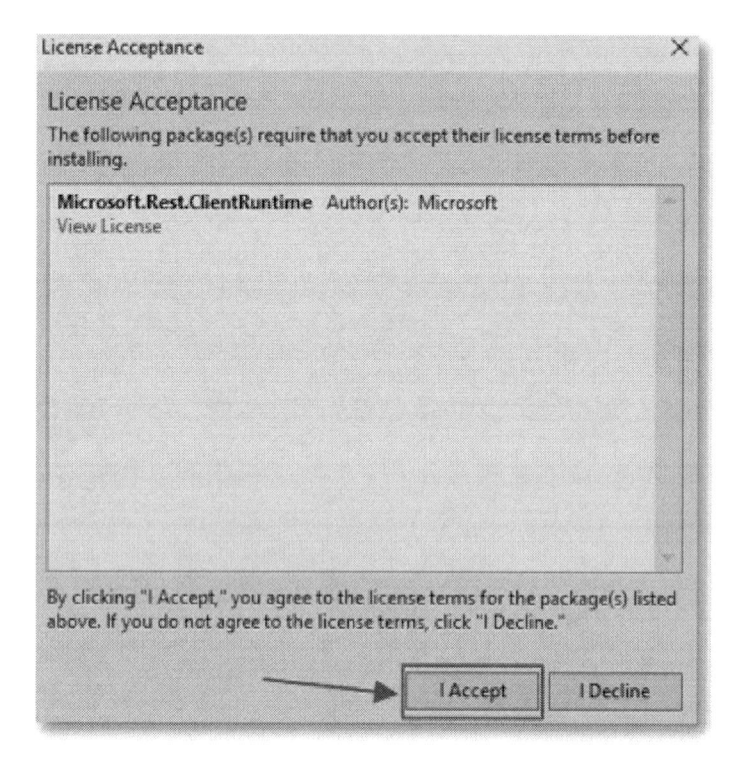

An Introduction to the Microsoft Bot Framework

Click the **I Accept** button when the **License Acceptance** window appears.

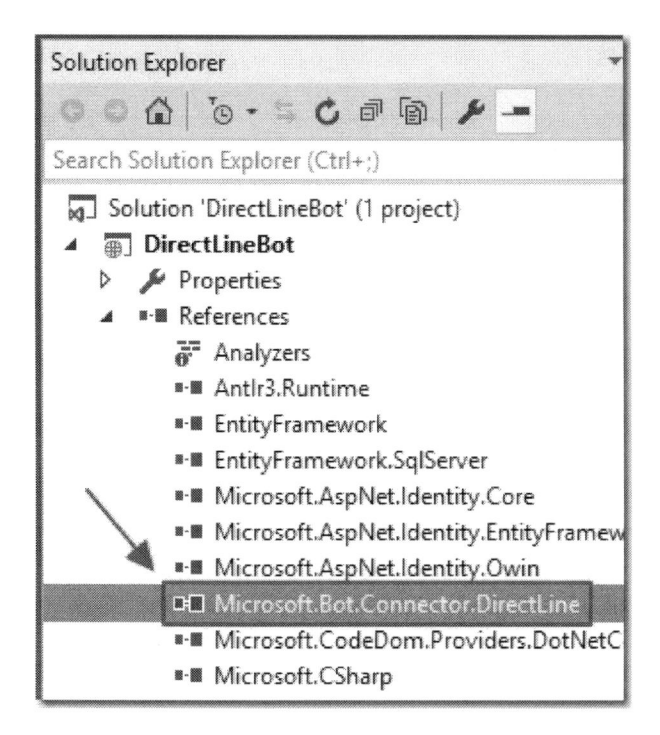

An Introduction to the Microsoft Bot Framework

The **Microsoft.Bot.Connector.DirectLine** assembly will be installed.

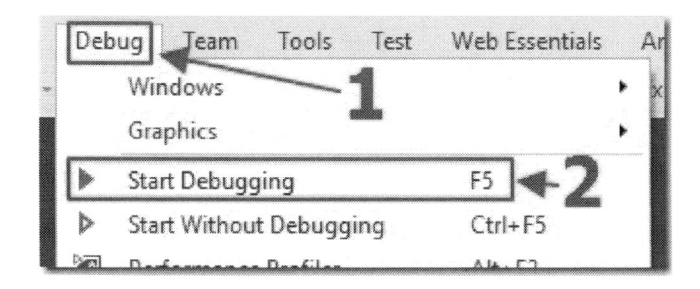

Hit **F5** to *debug* and run the application.

The application will open in the web browser.

An Introduction to the Microsoft Bot Framework

You will see the default web application created by the **MVC** template.

We can click the **Register** button to create a new account.

We can also click the **Log in** button to log in using a registered account.

An Introduction to the Microsoft Bot Framework

Complete The Web Application

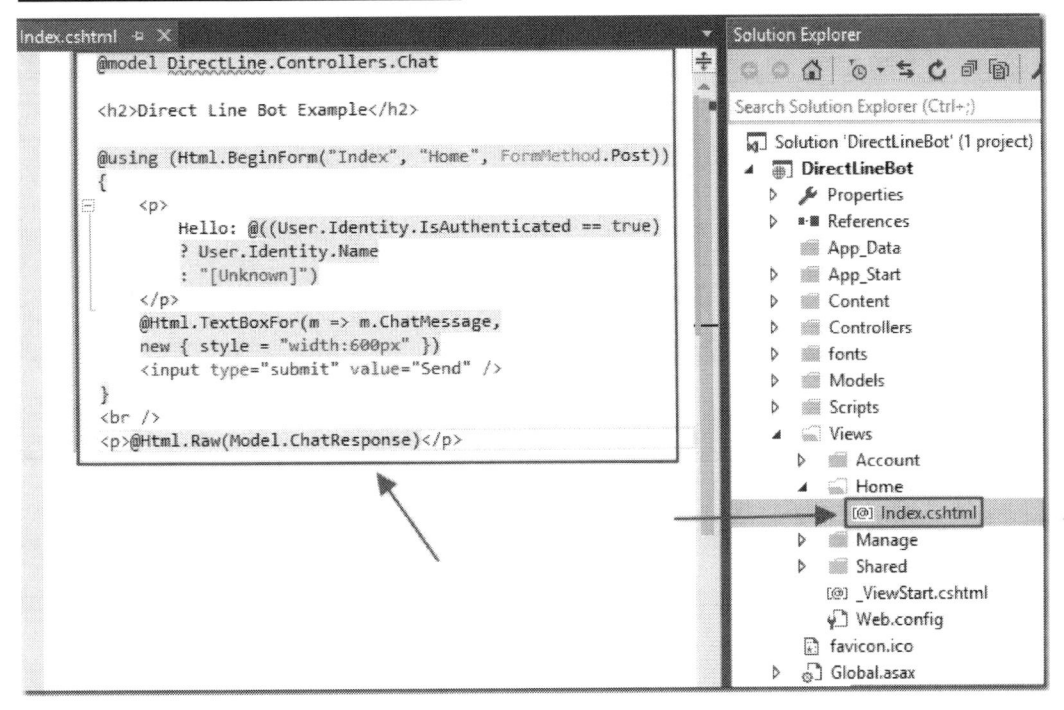

```
@model DirectLine.Controllers.Chat

<h2>Direct Line Bot Example</h2>

@using (Html.BeginForm("Index", "Home", FormMethod.Post))
{
    <p>
        Hello: @((User.Identity.IsAuthenticated == true)
        ? User.Identity.Name
        : "[Unknown]")
    </p>
    @Html.TextBoxFor(m => m.ChatMessage,
    new { style = "width:600px" })
    <input type="submit" value="Send" />
}
<br />
<p>@Html.Raw(Model.ChatResponse)</p>
```

We will update the **home** page to show the chat box and the **Bot** response only if the user has created an account and logged in.

Stop debugging the application and open the **Index.cshtml** file in the *Views/Home* folder.

Replace all of the code with the following code:

187

An Introduction to the Microsoft Bot Framework

```
@model DirectLine.Controllers.Chat
<h2>Direct Line Bot Example</h2>
@using (Html.BeginForm("Index", "Home", FormMethod.Post))
{
    <p>
        Hello: @((User.Identity.IsAuthenticated == true)
        ? User.Identity.Name
        : "[Unknown]")
    </p>
    @Html.TextBoxFor(m => m.ChatMessage,
    new { style = "width:600px" })
    <input type="submit" value="Send" />
}
<br />
<p>@Html.Raw(Model.ChatResponse)</p>
```

```
using System.Web.Mvc;

namespace DirectLine.Controllers
{
    #region public class Chat
    public class Chat
    {
        public string ChatMessage { get; set; }
        public string ChatResponse { get; set; }
        public string watermark { get; set; }
    }
    #endregion

    public class HomeController : Controller
    {
        private static string DiretlineUrl
            = @"https://directline.botframework.com";
        private static string directLineSecret =
            "** INSERT YOUR SECRET CODE HERE **";
        private static string botId =
            "** INSERT YOUR BOTID HERE **";

        #region public async Task<ActionResult> Index()
        public async Task<ActionResult> Index()
```

An Introduction to the Microsoft Bot Framework

Open the **HomeController.cs** file in the *Controllers* folder, and replace all the code with the following code:

```csharp
using Microsoft.Bot.Connector.DirectLine;
using Microsoft.Bot.Connector.DirectLine.Models;
using System;
using System.Linq;
using System.Threading.Tasks;
using System.Web.Mvc;
namespace DirectLine.Controllers
{
    #region public class Chat
    public class Chat
    {
        public string ChatMessage { get; set; }
        public string ChatResponse { get; set; }
        public string watermark { get; set; }
    }
    #endregion
    public class HomeController : Controller
    {
        private static string DiretlineUrl
            = @"https://directline.botframework.com";
        private static string directLineSecret =
            "** INSERT YOUR SECRET CODE HERE **";
        private static string botId =
            "** INSERT YOUR BOTID HERE **";
        #region public async Task<ActionResult> Index()
        public async Task<ActionResult> Index()
        {
            // Create an Instance of the Chat object
            Chat objChat = new Chat();
            // Only call Bot if logged in
            if (User.Identity.IsAuthenticated)
            {
                // Pass the message to the Bot
                // and get the response
                objChat = await TalkToTheBot("Hello");
            }
            else
            {
                objChat.ChatResponse = "Must be logged in";
            }
            // Return response
            return View(objChat);
        }
        #endregion
    }
}
```

An Introduction to the Microsoft Bot Framework

At this point the code is not complete; however, it sets up the basic framework.

Replace ** **INSERT YOUR SECRET CODE HERE** ** and ** **INSERT YOUR BOTID HERE** ** with the values from you own published **Bot**.

When a logged in user loads the page or submits text to the **Bot**, the **TalkToTheBot** method is called.

To implement it, add the following method to the **HomeController** class:

An Introduction to the Microsoft Bot Framework

```
#region private async Task<Chat> TalkToTheBot(string paramMessage)
private async Task<Chat> TalkToTheBot(string paramMessage)
{
    // Connect to the DirectLine service
    DirectLineClient client = new DirectLineClient(directLineSecret);
    // Try to get the existing Conversation
    Conversation conversation =
        System.Web.HttpContext.Current.Session["conversation"] as Conversation;
    // Try to get an existing watermark
    // the watermark marks the last message we received
    string watermark =
        System.Web.HttpContext.Current.Session["watermark"] as string;
    if (conversation == null)
    {
        // There is no existing conversation
        // start a new one
        conversation = client.Conversations.NewConversation();
    }
    // Use the text passed to the method (by the user)
    // to create a new message
    Message message = new Message
    {
        FromProperty = User.Identity.Name,
        Text = paramMessage
    };
    // Post the message to the Bot
    await client.Conversations.PostMessageAsync(conversation.ConversationId, message);
    // Get the response as a Chat object
    Chat objChat =
        await ReadBotMessagesAsync(client, conversation.ConversationId, watermark);
    // Save values
    System.Web.HttpContext.Current.Session["conversation"] = conversation;
    System.Web.HttpContext.Current.Session["watermark"] = objChat.watermark;
    // Return the response as a Chat object
    return objChat;
}
#endregion
```

The **TalkToTheBot** method calls the **ReadBotMessagesAsync** method to read the response from the **Bot**.

To implement it, add the following method to the **HomeController** class:

An Introduction to the Microsoft Bot Framework

```
private async Task<Chat> ReadBotMessagesAsync(
    DirectLineClient client, string conversationId, string watermark)
{
    // Create an Instance of the Chat object
    Chat objChat = new Chat();
    // We want to keep waiting until a message is received
    bool messageReceived = false;
    while (!messageReceived)
    {
        // Get any messages related to the conversation since the last watermark
        var messages =
            await client.Conversations.GetMessagesAsync(conversationId, watermark);
        // Set the watermark to the message received
        watermark = messages?.Watermark;
        // Get all the messages
        var messagesFromBotText = from message in messages.Messages
                                  where message.FromProperty == botId
                                  select message;
        // Loop through each message
        foreach (Message message in messagesFromBotText)
        {
            // We have Text
            if (message.Text != null)
            {
                // Set the text response
                // to the message text
                objChat.ChatResponse
                    += " "
                    + message.Text.Replace("\n\n", "<br />");
            }
            // We have an Image
            if (message.Images.Count > 0)
            {
                // Set the text response as an HTML link
                // to the image
                objChat.ChatResponse
                    += " "
                    + RenderImageHTML(message.Images[0]);
            }
        }
        // Mark messageReceived so we can break
        // out of the loop
        messageReceived = true;
    }
    // Set watermark on the Chat object that will be
    // returned
    objChat.watermark = watermark;
    // Return a response as a Chat object
    return objChat;
}
```

An Introduction to the Microsoft Bot Framework

When there is an image that is returned by the **Bot**, the **ReadBotMessagesAsync** method calls the **RenderImageHTML** method.

To implement it, add the following method to the **HomeController** class:

```
#region private static string RenderImageHTML(string ImageLocation)
private static string RenderImageHTML(string ImageLocation)
{
    // Construct a URL to the image
    string strReturnHTML =
        String.Format(@"<img src='{0}/{1}'><br />",
        DiretlineUrl,
        ImageLocation);
    return strReturnHTML;
}
#endregion
```

Run The Application

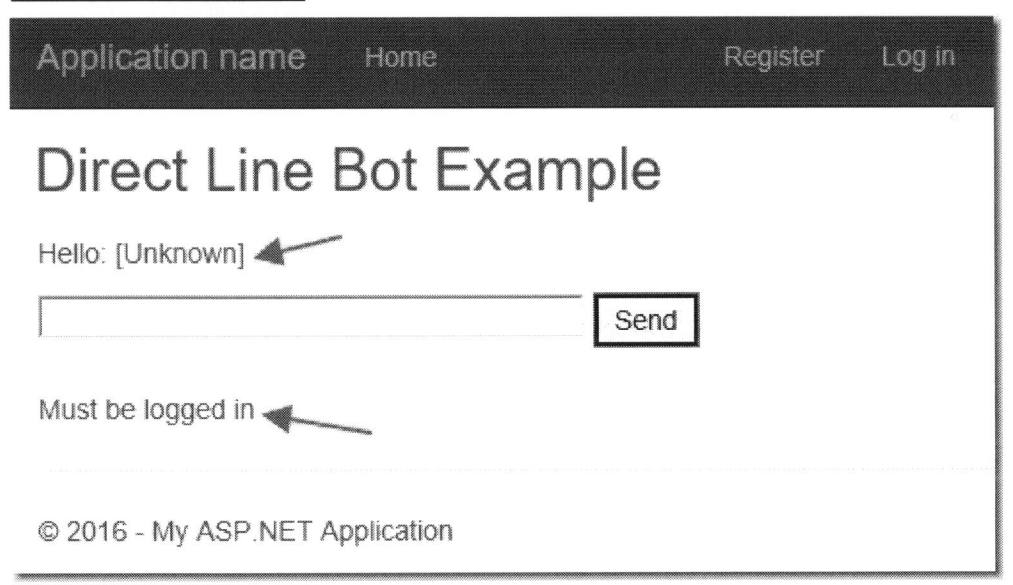

Hit **F5** to run the application.

193

An Introduction to the Microsoft Bot Framework

The application will open in the web browser. Initially, we are not logged in, so we will be unable to communicate with the **Bot**.

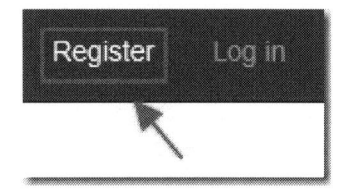

Click the **Register** button to create an account.

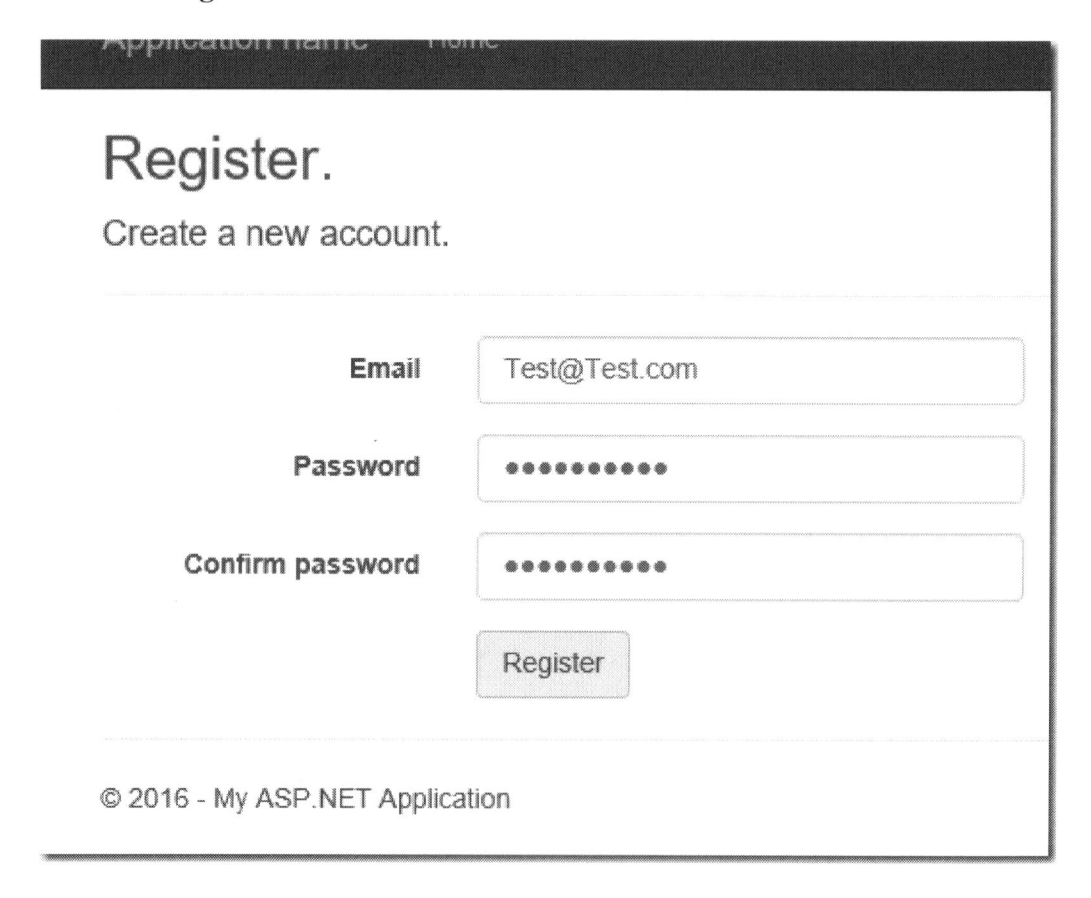

Fill in the required information and click the **Register** button.

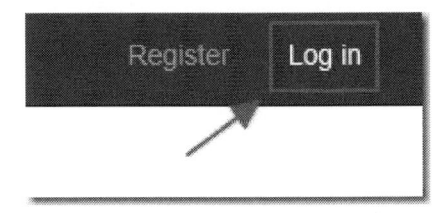

An Introduction to the Microsoft Bot Framework

After you have created an account, you can click the **Log in** button to log in (if you are not already logged in).

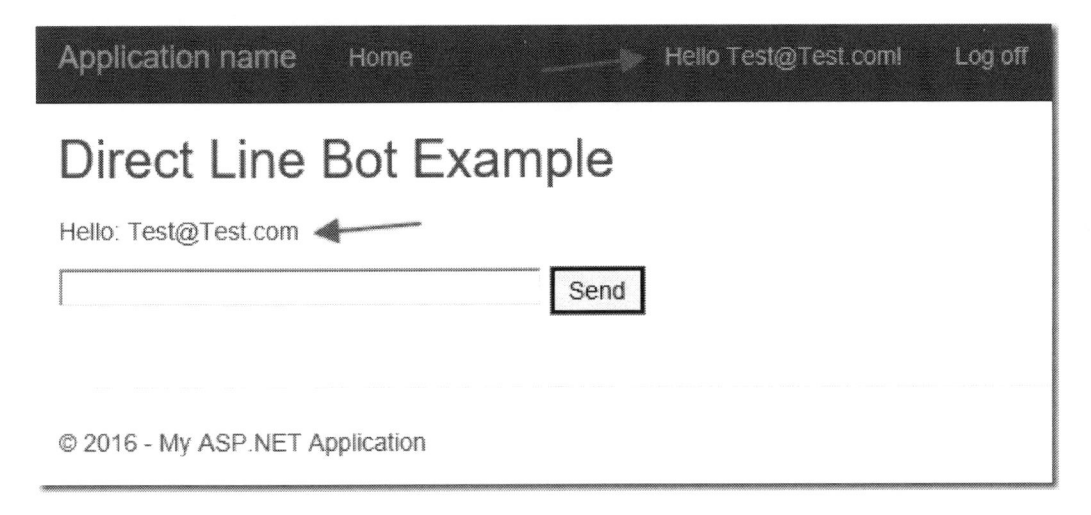

You will know you are logged in when you see your email address in the menu bar and on the **Home** page.

An Introduction to the Microsoft Bot Framework

Direct Line Bot Example

Hello: Test@Test.com

| 1 | × | Send |

Help Website Number Guesser

Guess a number between 1 and 5

You can now communicate with the **Bot** and run the same code that was created in the previous chapter.

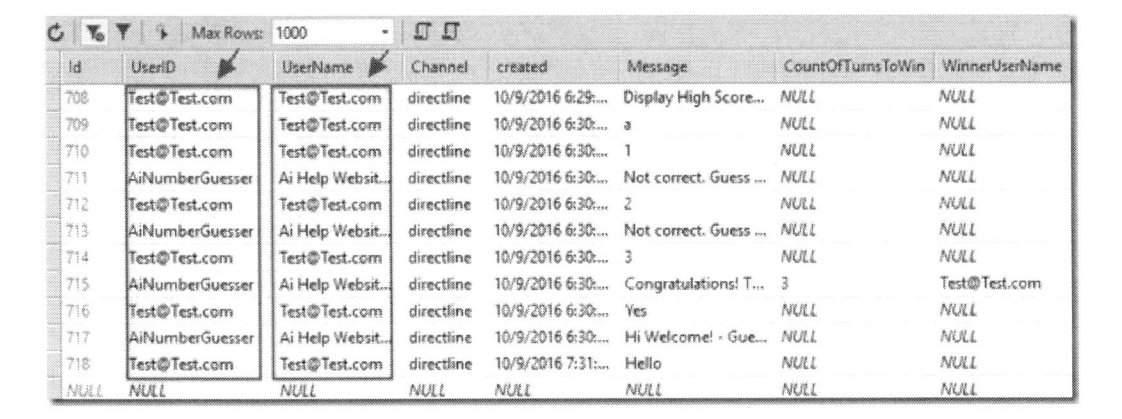

An Introduction to the Microsoft Bot Framework

Id	UserID	UserName	Channel	created	Message	CountOfTurnsToWin	WinnerUserName
708	Test@Test.com	Test@Test.com	directline	10/9/2016 6:29:...	Display High Score...	NULL	NULL
709	Test@Test.com	Test@Test.com	directline	10/9/2016 6:30:...	a	NULL	NULL
710	Test@Test.com	Test@Test.com	directline	10/9/2016 6:30:...	1	NULL	NULL
711	AiNumberGuesser	Ai Help Websit...	directline	10/9/2016 6:30:...	Not correct. Guess ...	NULL	NULL
712	Test@Test.com	Test@Test.com	directline	10/9/2016 6:30:...	2	NULL	NULL
713	AiNumberGuesser	Ai Help Websit...	directline	10/9/2016 6:30:...	Not correct. Guess ...	NULL	NULL
714	Test@Test.com	Test@Test.com	directline	10/9/2016 6:30:...	3	NULL	NULL
715	AiNumberGuesser	Ai Help Websit...	directline	10/9/2016 6:30:...	Congratulations! T...	3	Test@Test.com
716	Test@Test.com	Test@Test.com	directline	10/9/2016 6:30:...	Yes	NULL	NULL
717	AiNumberGuesser	Ai Help Websit...	directline	10/9/2016 6:30:...	Hi Welcome! - Gue...	NULL	NULL
718	Test@Test.com	Test@Test.com	directline	10/9/2016 7:31:...	Hello	NULL	NULL
NULL	NULL	NULL	NULL	NULL	NULL	NULL	NULL

When we look at the data in the database on **Azure**, we see the **UserID** and **UserName** for messages posted to the **Bot** are completely under the control of the following custom code:

```
// Use the text passed to the method (by the user)
// to create a new message
Message message = new Message
{
    FromProperty = User.Identity.Name,
    Text = paramMessage
};
// Post the message to the Bot
await client.Conversations.PostMessageAsync(conversation.ConversationId, message);
```

An Introduction to the Microsoft Bot Framework

Chapter 9: Using Application Insights To Monitor Your Bot

The sample code for this chapter can be obtained at the link "Using Application Insights With Microsoft Bot Framework" at
http://AiHelpWebsite.com/Downloads

With **Application Insights**, you can insert a few lines of code in your **Bot** to find out what your users are doing.

When you install **Application Insights**, you are installing a small instrumentation package in your application. Next, you set up an **Application Insights** resource in the **Microsoft Azure** portal.

An Introduction to the Microsoft Bot Framework

The instrumentation you install monitors your app and sends *telemetry* data to the **Microsoft Azure** portal. The **Microsoft Azure** portal shows statistical charts and has powerful search tools to help you monitor your application and diagnose any problems.

To demonstrate this, we will start with the **Bot** created in **Chapter Six**.

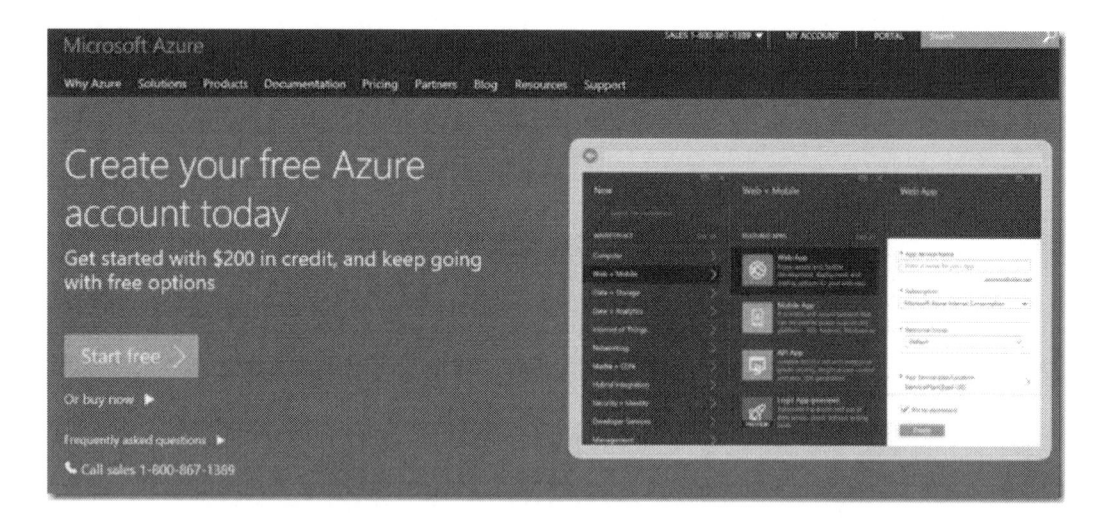

An Introduction to the Microsoft Bot Framework

This will require using **Microsoft Azure**. If you do not have a **Microsoft Azure** account, go to https://azure.microsoft.com and create an account and a subscription.

An Introduction to the Microsoft Bot Framework

Enable Application Insights

Open the **AiNumberGuesserBot** project in **Visual Studio**.

In the **Solution Explorer**, *right-click* on the **Project** (not the **Solution**), and select **Add Application Insights Telemetry**.

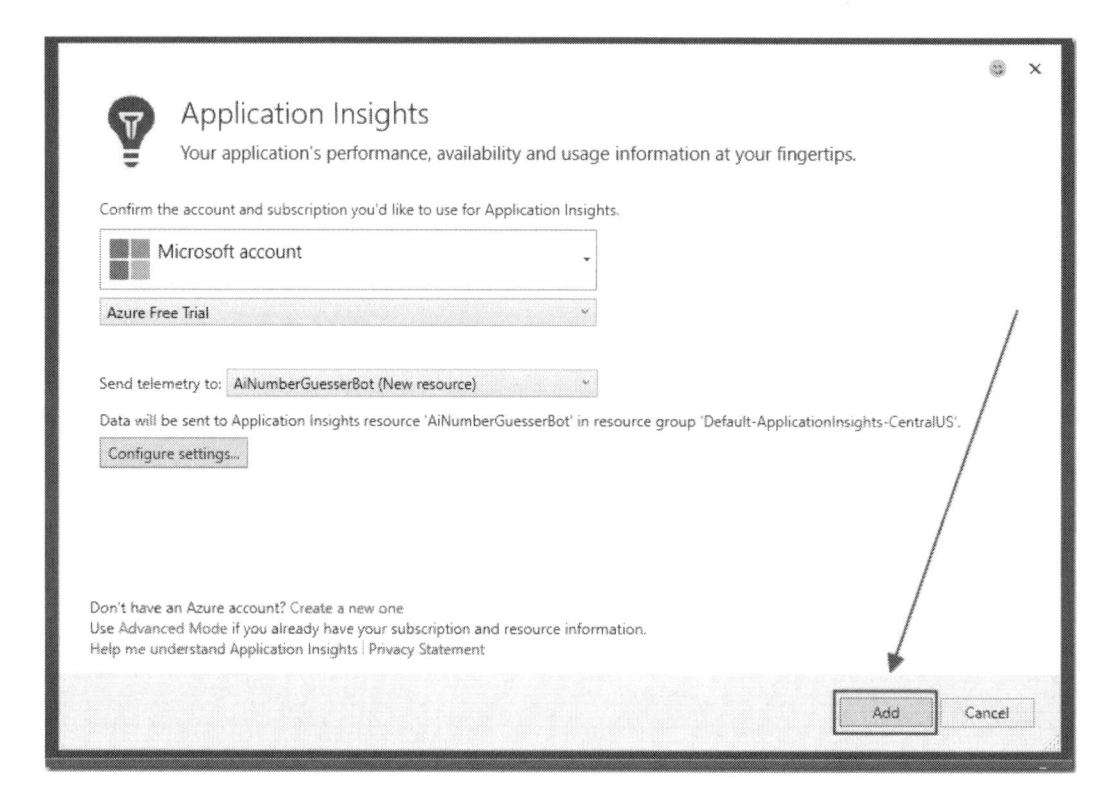

An Introduction to the Microsoft Bot Framework

First, you will be required to log into your **Microsoft Azure Account**.

After doing so, you will be presented with a form to *create* an **Application Insights** resource (by choosing the *New resource* option in the *Send telemetry to* dropdown) or *connect* to an existing **Application Insights** resource (by selecting it in the *Send telemetry to* dropdown).

After selecting the configuration options, click the **Add** button to proceed.

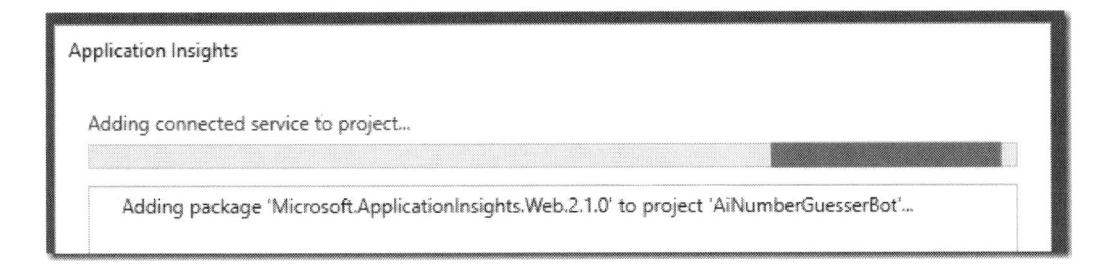

An Introduction to the Microsoft Bot Framework

```
Application Insights

Adding connected service to project...

Adding package 'Microsoft.ApplicationInsights.Web.2.1.0' to project 'AiNumberGuesserBot'...
```

Application Insights assemblies will be added to the project.

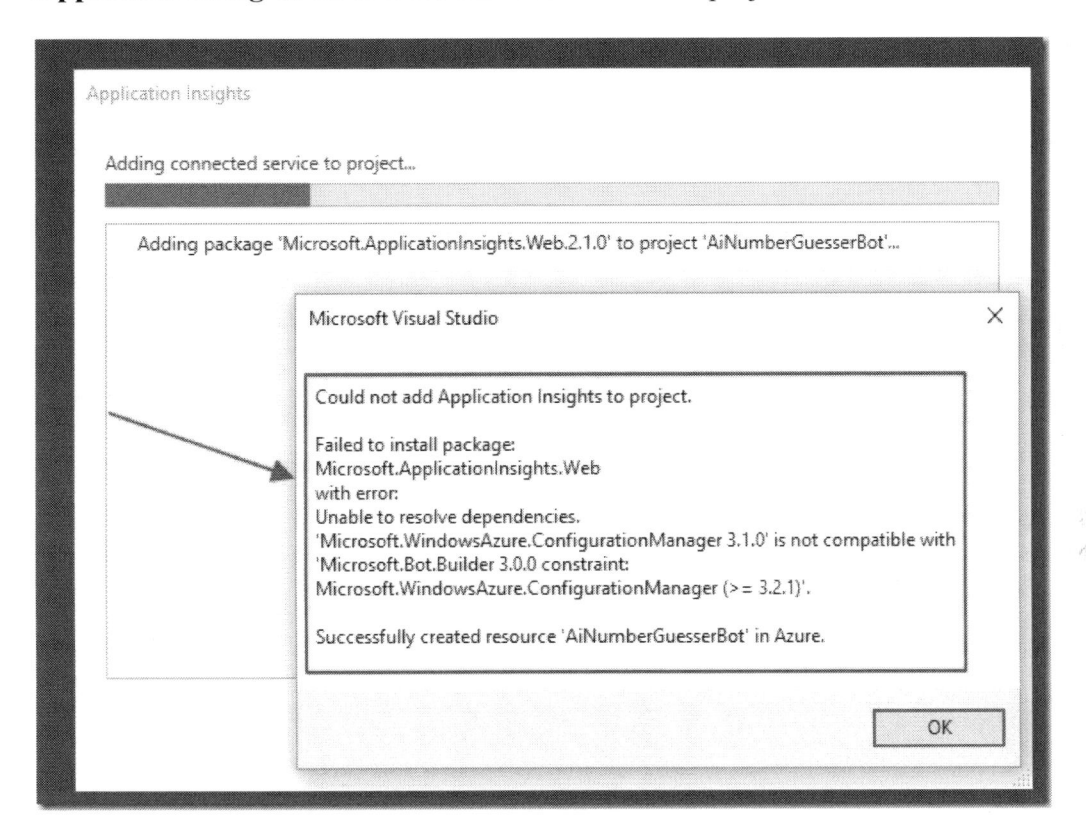

```
Application Insights

Adding connected service to project...

Adding package 'Microsoft.ApplicationInsights.Web.2.1.0' to project 'AiNumberGuesserBot'...

Microsoft Visual Studio                                    ×

Could not add Application Insights to project.

Failed to install package:
Microsoft.ApplicationInsights.Web
with error:
Unable to resolve dependencies.
'Microsoft.WindowsAzure.ConfigurationManager 3.1.0' is not compatible with
'Microsoft.Bot.Builder 3.0.0 constraint:
Microsoft.WindowsAzure.ConfigurationManager (>= 3.2.1)'.

Successfully created resource 'AiNumberGuesserBot' in Azure.

                                                          OK
```

If you get an error, most likely you have components that need to be updated.

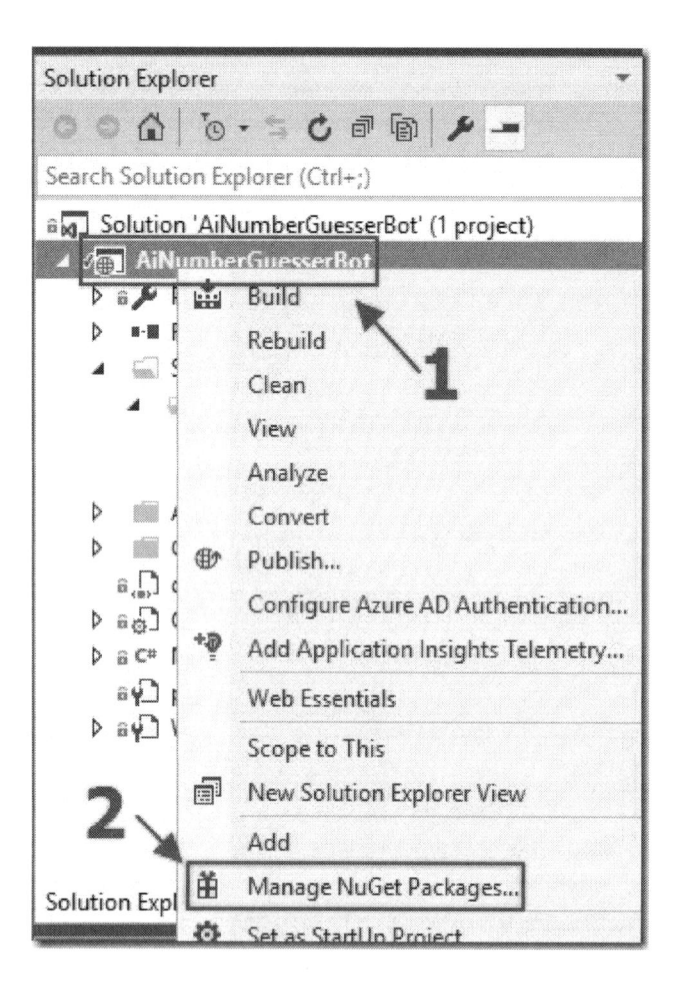

An Introduction to the Microsoft Bot Framework

In the **Solution Explorer** in **Visual Studio**, *right-click* on the **Project** (not the **Solution**), and select **Manage NuGet Packages**.

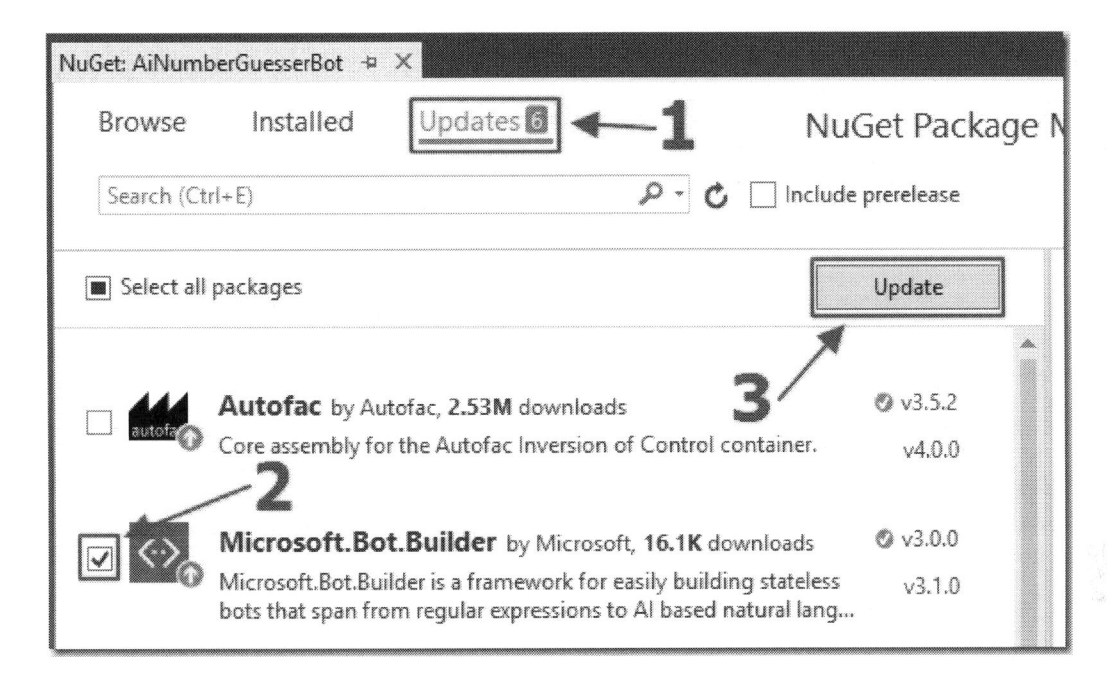

An Introduction to the Microsoft Bot Framework

Select **Updates**, select the components that the error message indicates need to be updated, and click the **Update** button.

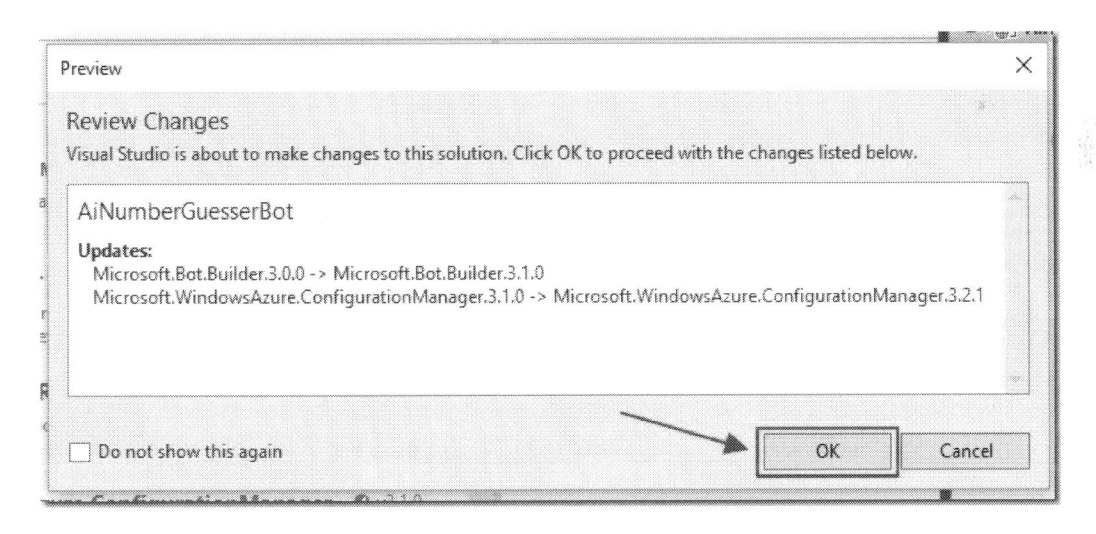

When the **Review Changes** box shows, click the **OK** button.

An Introduction to the Microsoft Bot Framework

Next, *right-click* on the **Project** and select **Add Application Insights Telemetry** again to re-start the process.

The **Application Insights** components should now install successfully.

Debug The Application

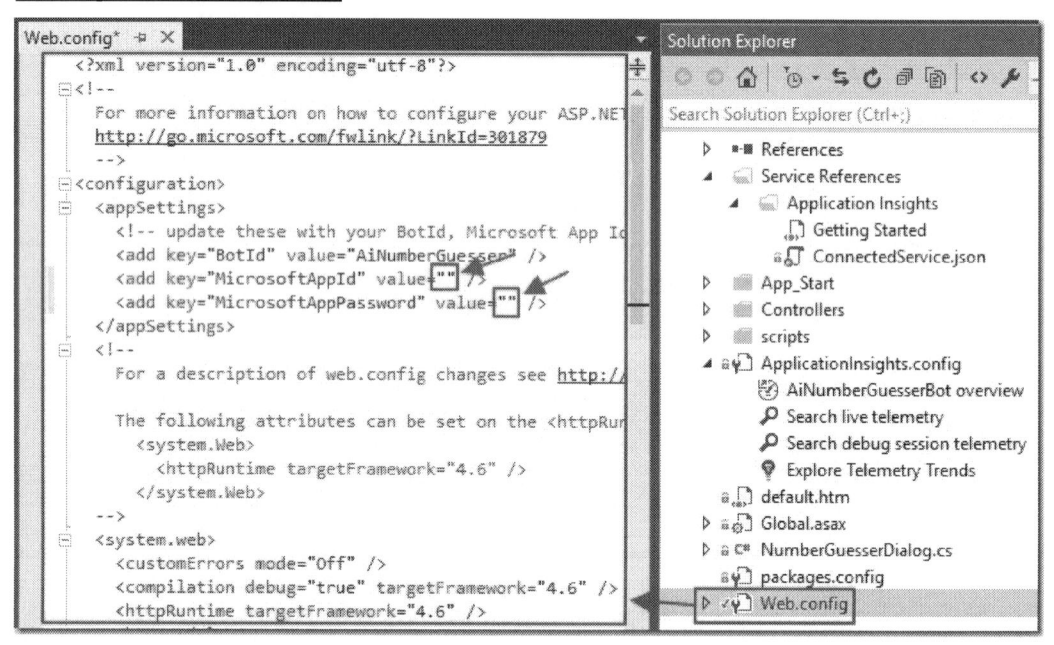

Before you try to debug, clear any **MicrosoftAppId** and **MicrosoftAppPassword** settings there may be in the **Web.config** file and then save the file.

This is required, so you can easily debug locally.

Remember to replace any settings if you need to re-publish the application.

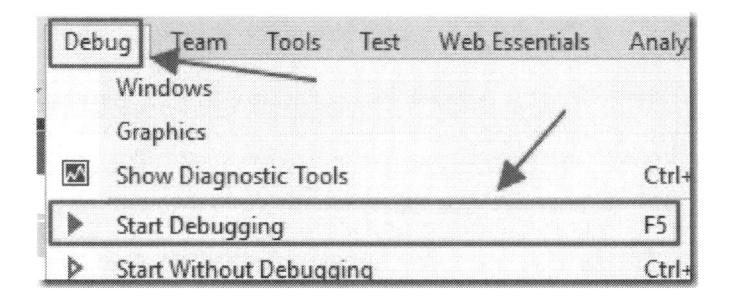

An Introduction to the Microsoft Bot Framework

Hit **F5** to run the project.

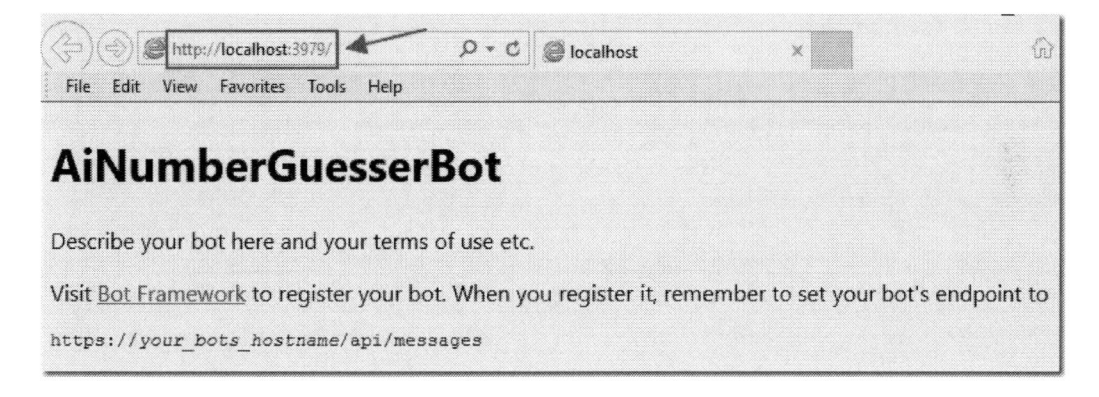

The application will open in the web browser.

Note the web address, as you will need it in the next step.

Using The Bot Emulator

Open and run the **Microsoft Bot Framework Emulator**.

An Introduction to the Microsoft Bot Framework

When the emulator starts, connect to the **Bot** by setting the address to the one indicted in the web browser; however, add **/api/messages** to the end.

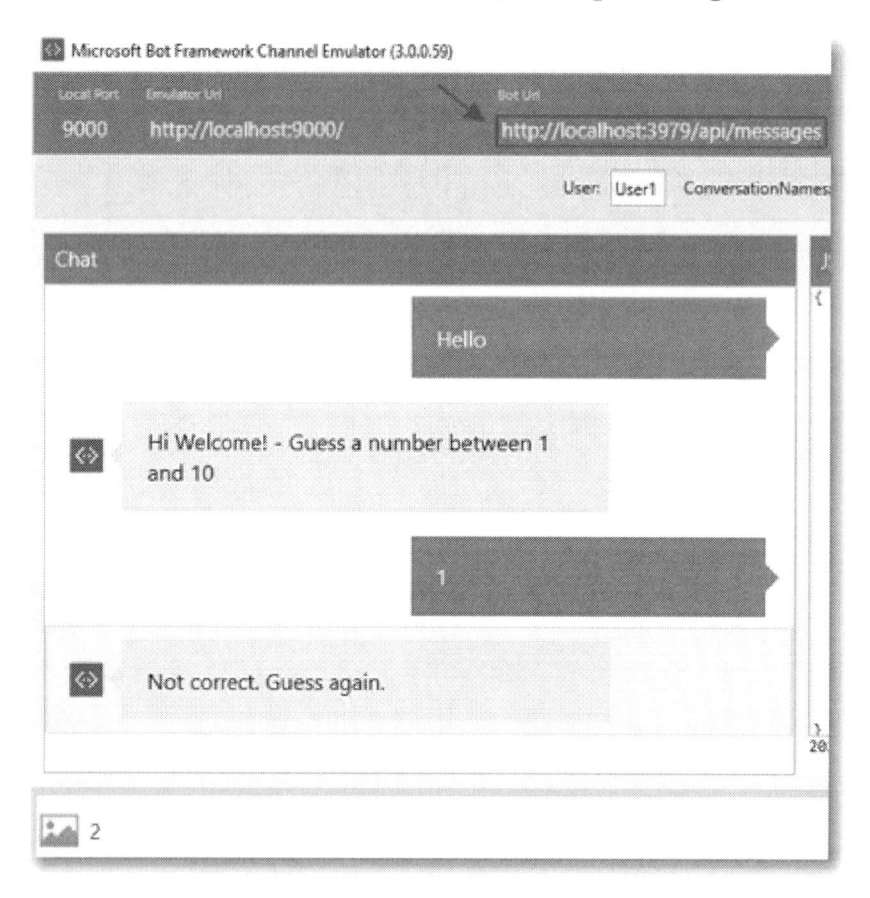

In the **Bot Emulator**, enter **Hello** in the text box and click the send key (or press enter).

You will see the response in the **Chat** window and the **JSON** contents of the response in the **JSON** window.

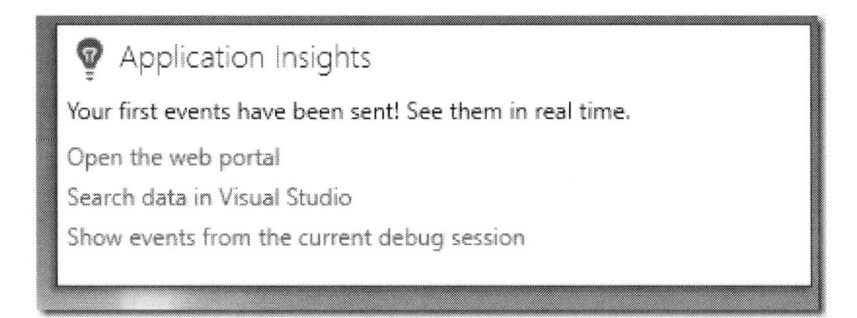

An Introduction to the Microsoft Bot Framework

> **Application Insights**
>
> Your first events have been sent! See them in real time.
>
> Open the web portal
> Search data in Visual Studio
> Show events from the current debug session

You should see a window pop up that provides links to the telemetry data.

An Introduction to the Microsoft Bot Framework

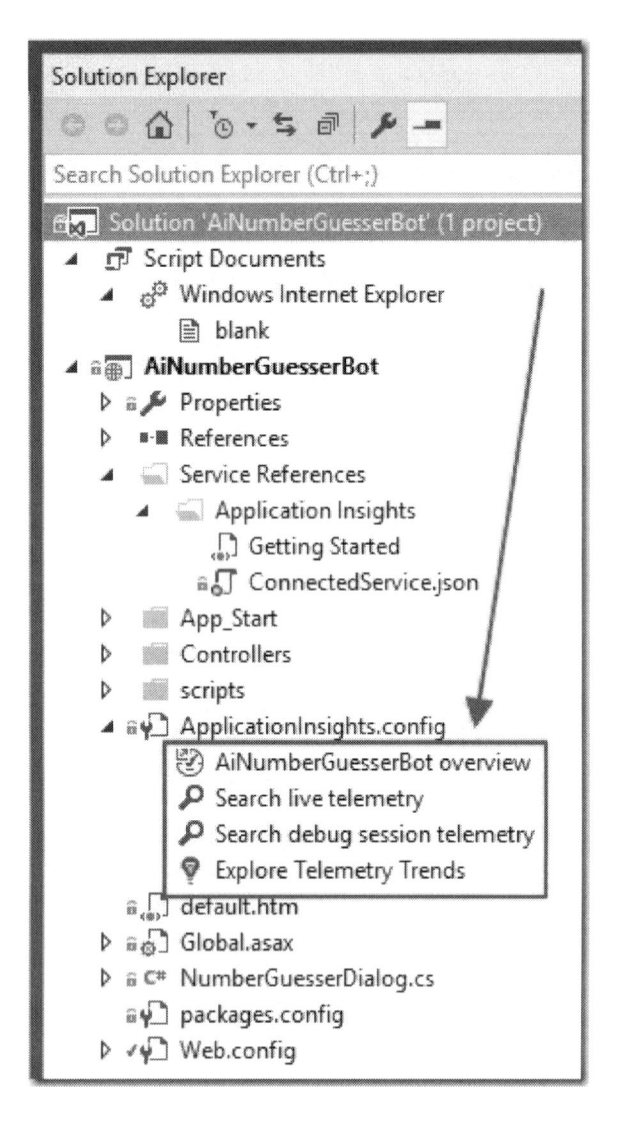

You can also access the data by clicking on the links in the **ApplicationInsight.config** section in the **Solution Explorer** of **Visual Studio** while the application is running.

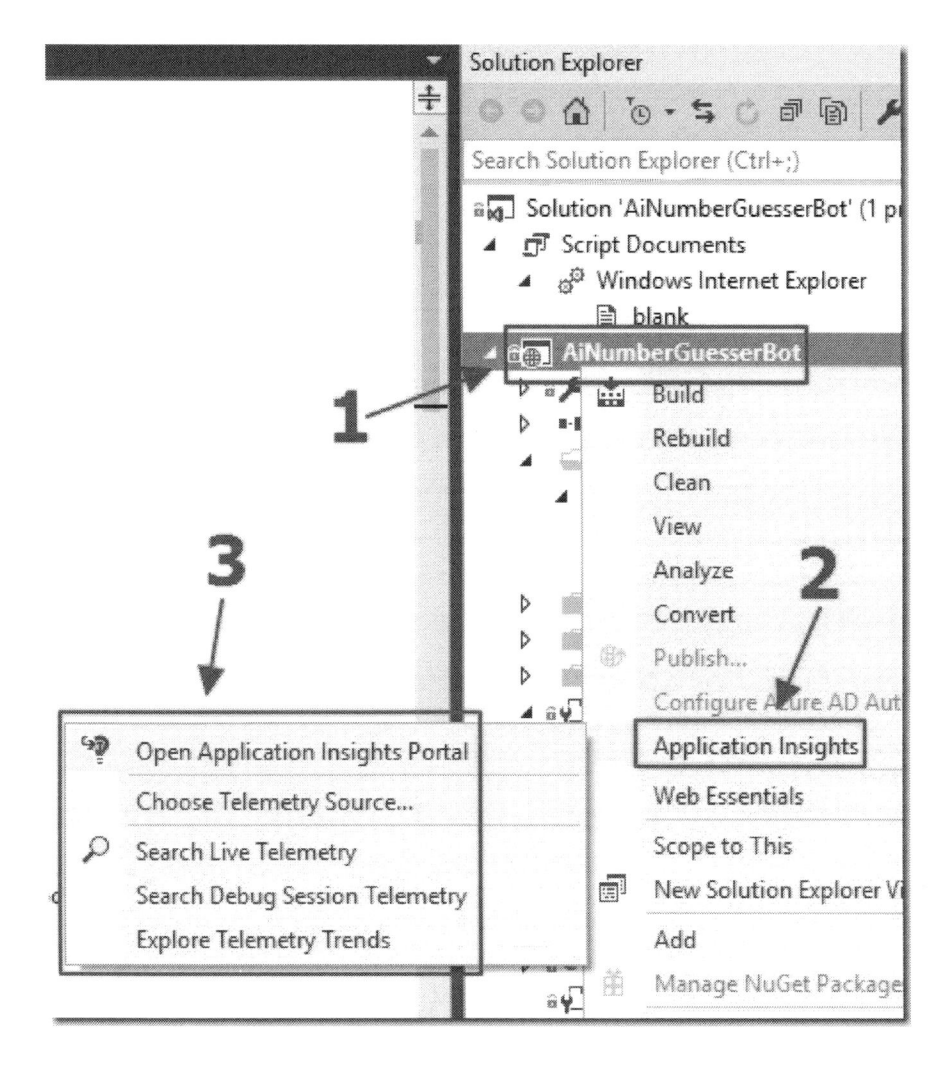

An Introduction to the Microsoft Bot Framework

Also, you can *right-click* on the **Project** and select **Application Insights** to show the menu that will provide all the options.

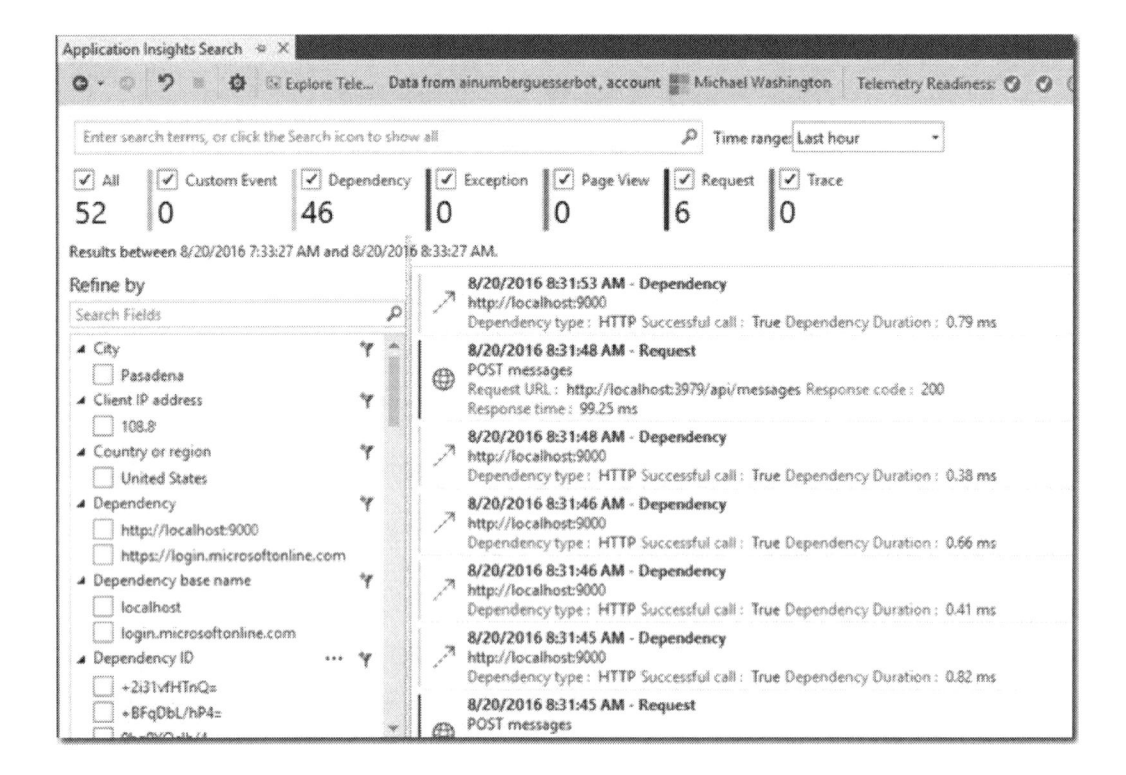

An Introduction to the Microsoft Bot Framework

Selecting **Search Live Telemetry** or **Search Debug Session Telemetry** will open a window in **Visual Studio** that will display telemetry data.

*Note: See **Learn more about Application Insights tools in Visual Studio** at https://azure.microsoft.com/en-us/documentation/articles/app-insights-visual-studio/ for more information on using these windows.*

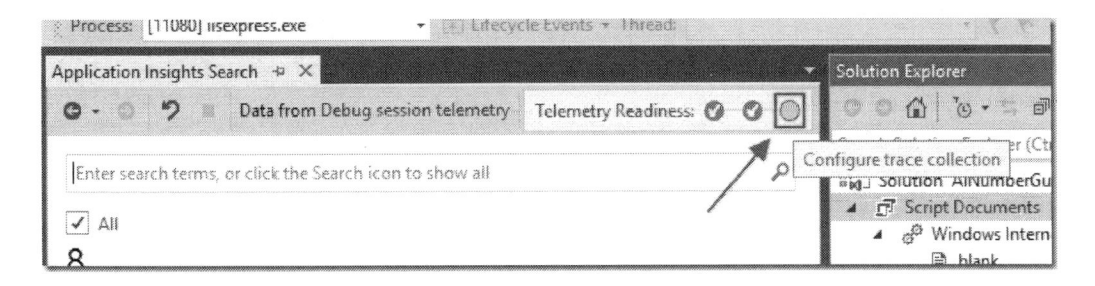

An Introduction to the Microsoft Bot Framework

For full **Telemetry Readiness**, ensure all the green dots are checked. If any aren't, click on them.

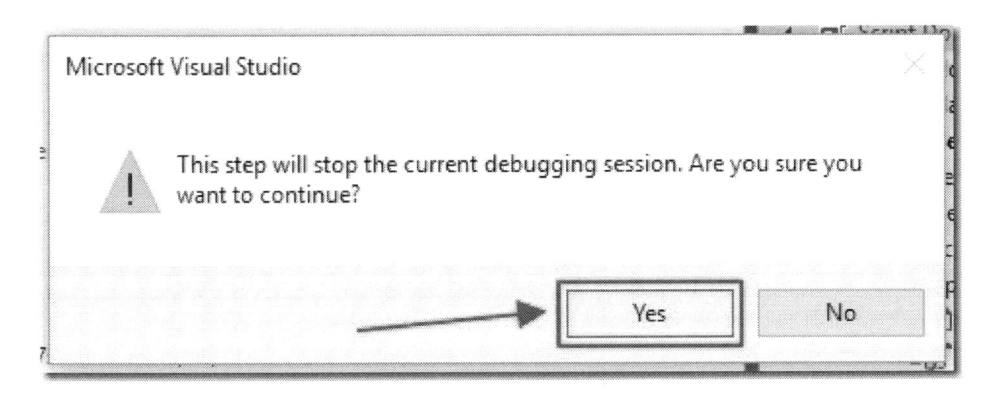

It will stop debugging to add components.

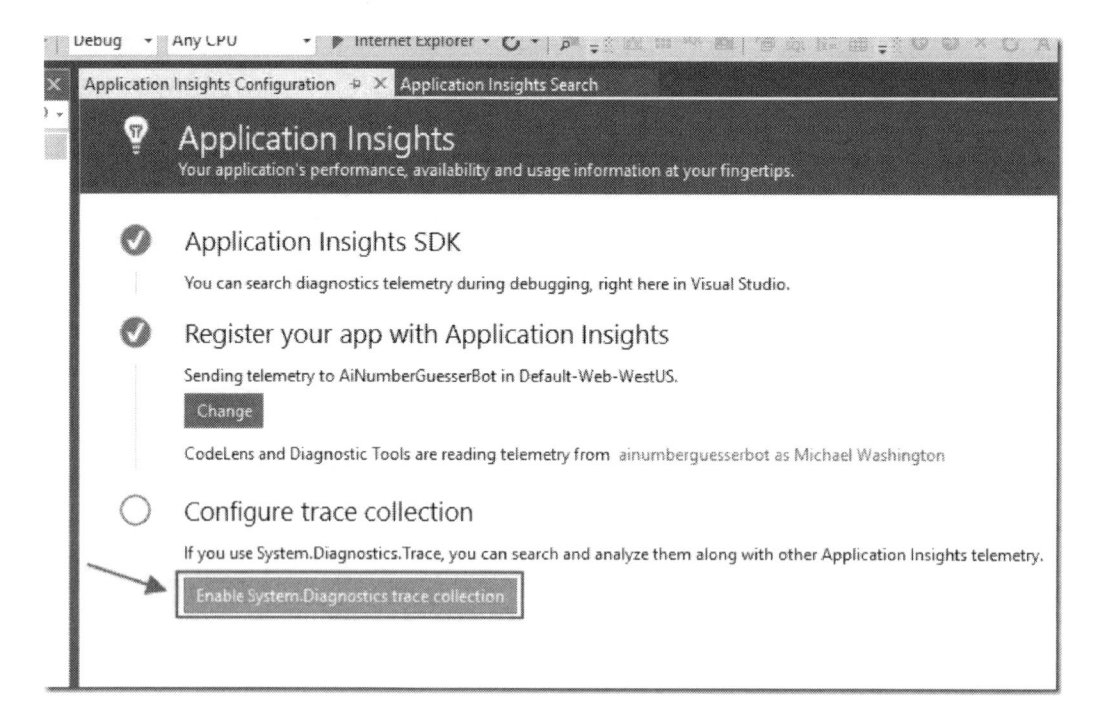

An Introduction to the Microsoft Bot Framework

You will be able to click a button to **add** or **configure** the components.

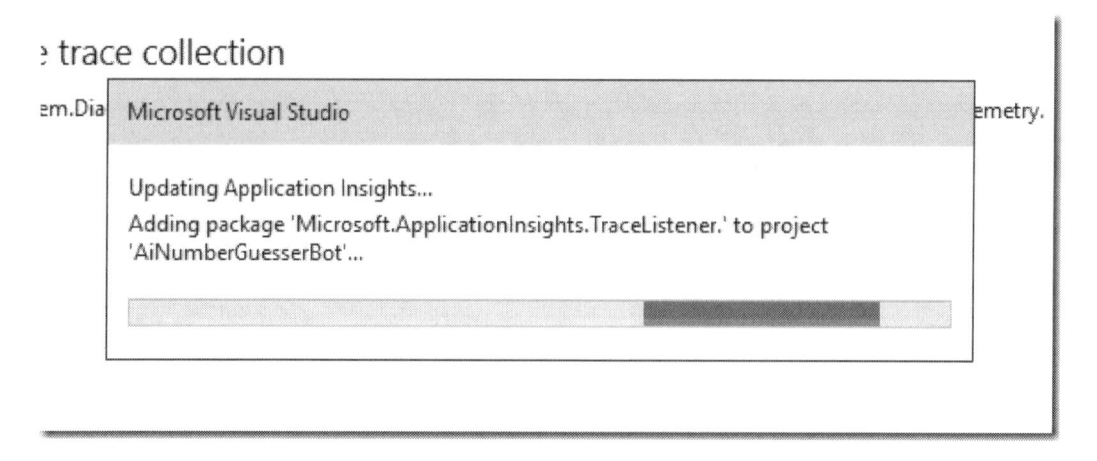

The components will be added.

An Introduction to the Microsoft Bot Framework

✓ **Configure trace collection**

Your app is configured to send traces from System.Diagnostics.Trace to Application Insights.

▲ Use System.Diagnostics.Traces to log information from your app at runtime:

```
System.Diagnostics.Trace.TraceInformation("Information");
System.Diagnostics.Trace.TraceWarning("Warning");
System.Diagnostics.Trace.TraceError("Error");
```

The result will be displayed.

Custom Telemetry

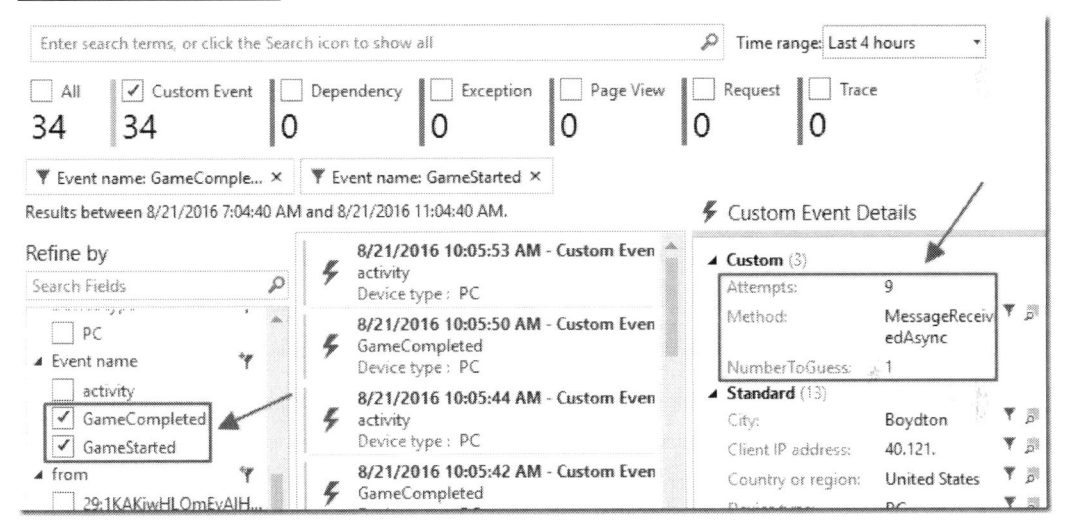

One of the most powerful features of **Application Insights** is being able to use it to track your own **custom telemetry**.

We will now demonstrate using it to track when a game is started, completed, what number a user needed to guess, and how many attempts they required.

An Introduction to the Microsoft Bot Framework

In the **AiNumberGuesserBot** project, open the **NumberGuesserDialog.cs** file and add the following using statements:

```
using Microsoft.ApplicationInsights;
using System.Collections.Generic;
```

Next, add the following line to the class:

```
// TelemetryClient is not Serializable but is in a class
// marked [Serializable] so it must be marked as [NonSerialized]
[NonSerialized()]
private TelemetryClient telemetry = new TelemetryClient();
```

Finally, add the following lines to the **StartAsync** method:

```
// Set up some properties and metrics:
// Properties - String values that you can use to filter
// your telemetry in the usage reports.
// Metrics - Numeric values that can be presented graphically
var properties = new Dictionary<string, string>
{ {"Method", "StartAsync"}};
var metrics = new Dictionary<string, double>
{ {"NumberToGuess", this.intNumberToGuess}};
// Send the event:
telemetry.TrackEvent("GameStarted", properties, metrics);
```

This will track a game being started and the number the user needs to guess.

An Introduction to the Microsoft Bot Framework

Also, add the following code to track the game completed:

```
// Because telemetry client is not serialized we have to
// instantiate it each time we use it
telemetry = new TelemetryClient();
var properties = new Dictionary<string, string>
{ {"Method", "MessageReceivedAsync"}};
var metrics = new Dictionary<string, double>
{
    { "NumberToGuess", this.intNumberToGuess},
    { "Attempts", this.intAttempts}
};
// Send the event:
telemetry.TrackEvent("GameCompleted", properties, metrics);
```

There are a number of API calls we can use to track custom events as the following table illustrates:

Application Insights API summary

From: *https://azure.microsoft.com/en-us/documentation/articles/app-insights-api-custom-events-metrics/*

Method	Used for
TrackPageView	Pages, screens, blades, or forms
TrackEvent	User actions and other events. Used to track user behavior or to monitor performance.
TrackMetric	Performance measurements such as queue lengths not related to specific events
TrackException	Log exceptions for diagnosis. Trace where they occur in relation to other events and examine stack traces.
TrackRequest	Log the frequency and duration of server requests for performance analysis.
TrackTrace	Diagnostic log messages. You can also capture 3rd-party logs.
TrackDependency	Log the duration and frequency of calls to external components on which your app depends.

An Introduction to the Microsoft Bot Framework

You can attach properties and metrics to most of these telemetry calls.

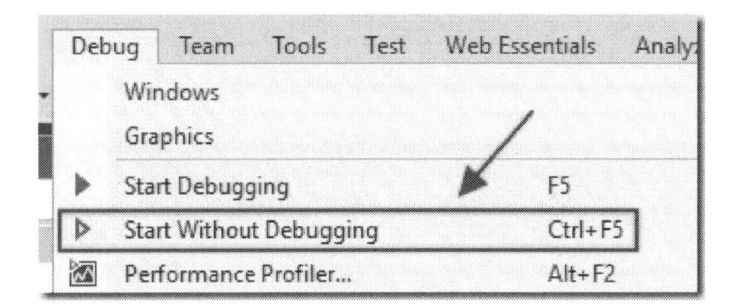

Run the application and enter some sample data.

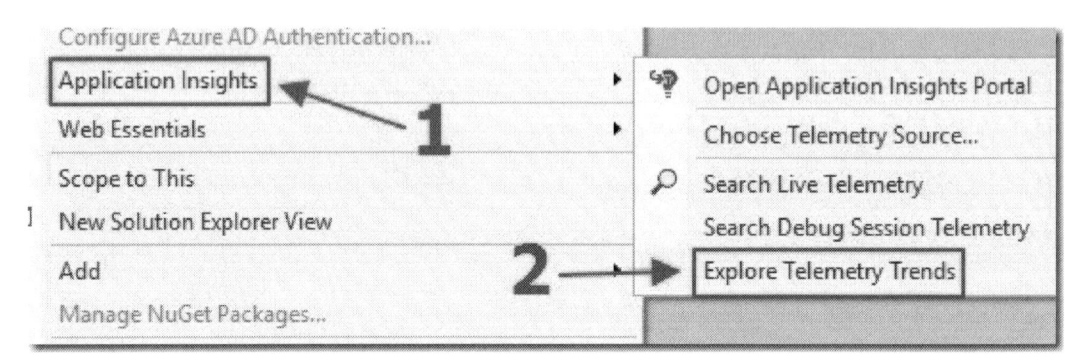

When you select the **Application Insights** menu in **Visual Studio** and select **Explore Telemetry Trends**…

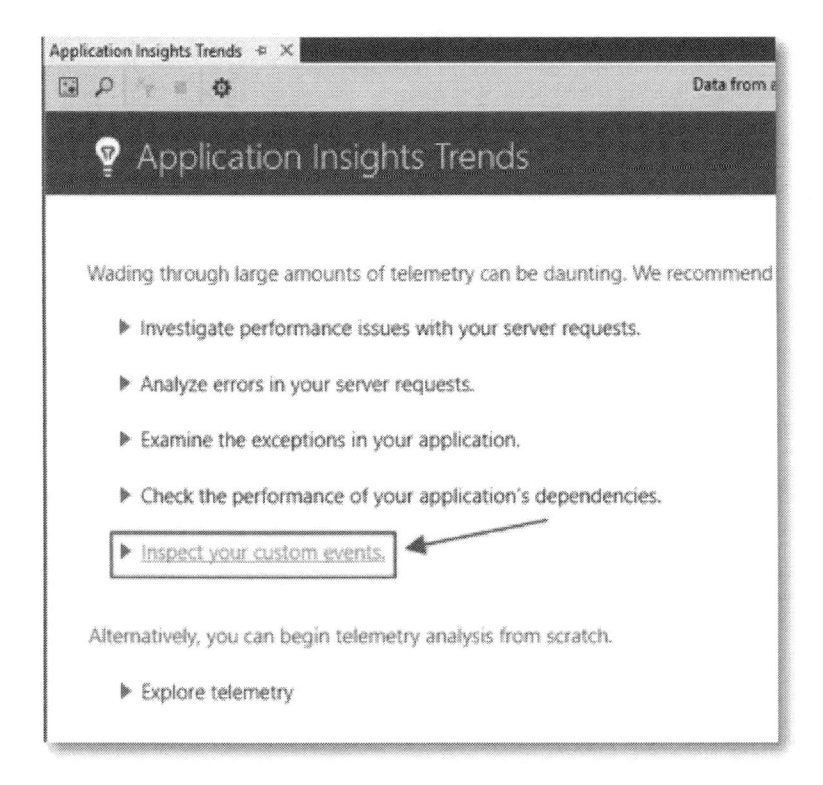

An Introduction to the Microsoft Bot Framework

...you can then select **Inspect your custom events**.

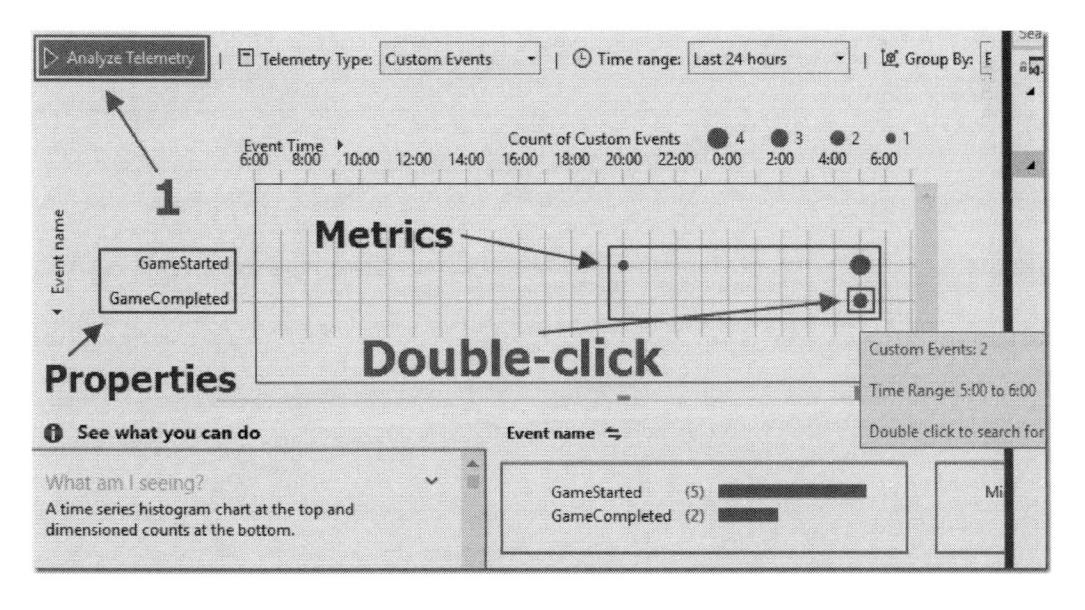

An Introduction to the Microsoft Bot Framework

Click the **Analyze Telemetry** button to process the latest data. You will see where the **Properties** and **Metrics** have been tracked.

Note: It will take a few minutes for your custom events to show.

You can *double-click* on a trend to drill into the data.

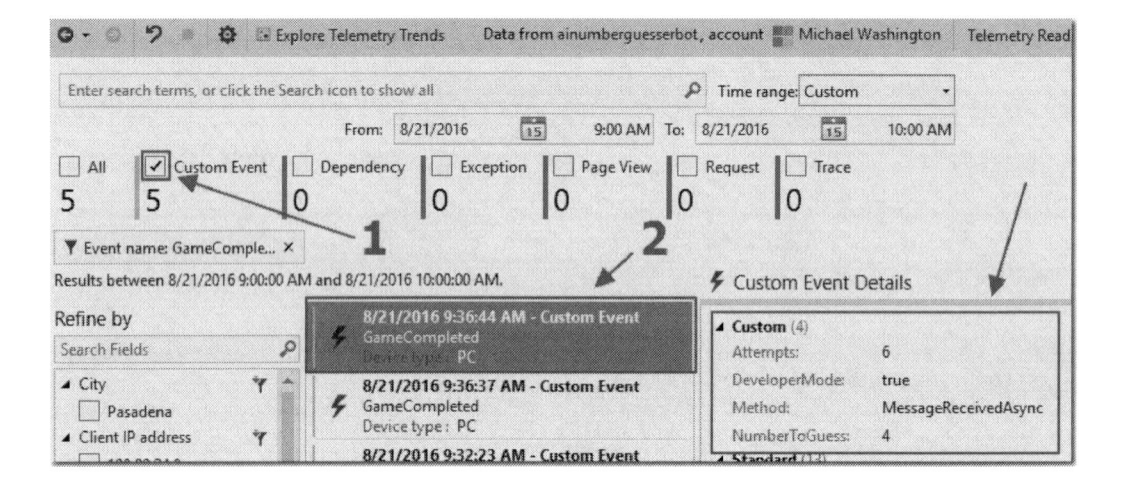

This will take you to the search screen where you can filter further and view the details of each individual event.

220

An Introduction to the Microsoft Bot Framework

Application Insights Portal

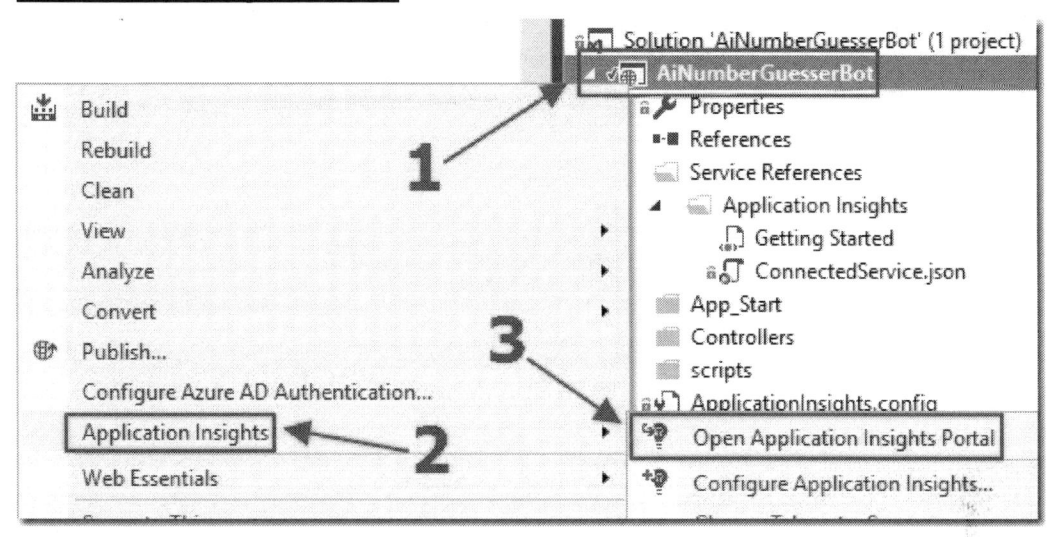

You can access the **Application Insights Portal** on the **Microsoft Azure** site by selecting it from the menu in **Visual Studio**.

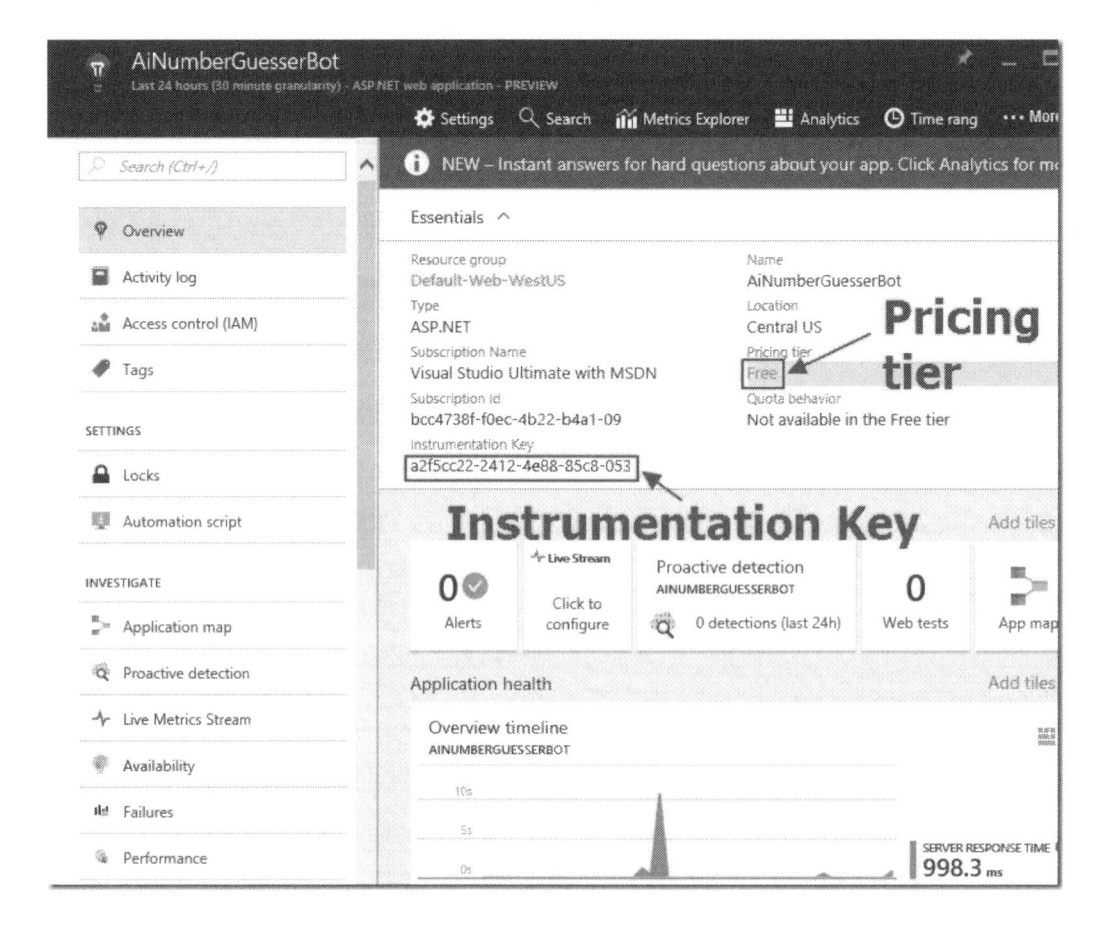

An Introduction to the Microsoft Bot Framework

It is there you can see and change your **Pricing tier**.

You can also obtain your **Instrumentation Key**.

An Introduction to the Microsoft Bot Framework

Monitoring A Published Application

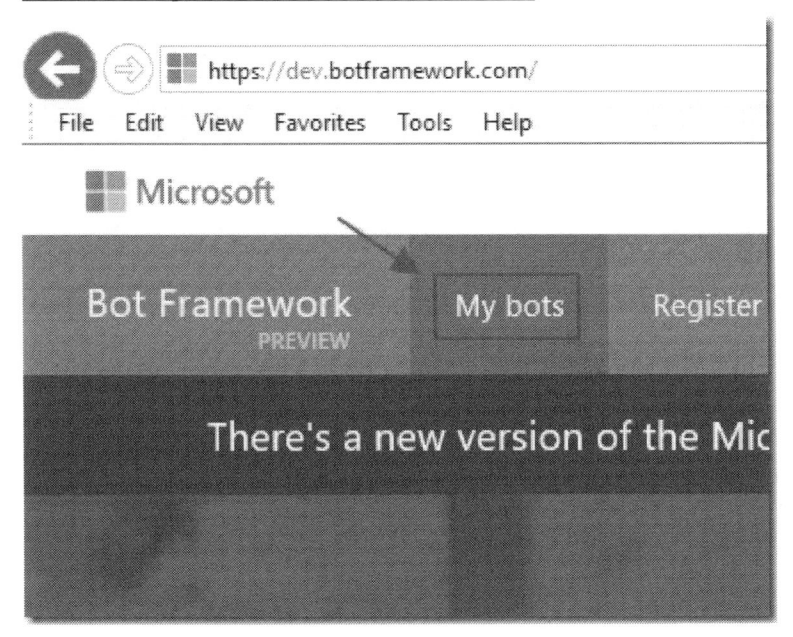

You can monitor your published **Bot**.

Publish your **Bot**. (See **Chapter 2** for directions on this.) After your **Bot** is published on the https://dev.botframework.com/ site, select **My bots**.

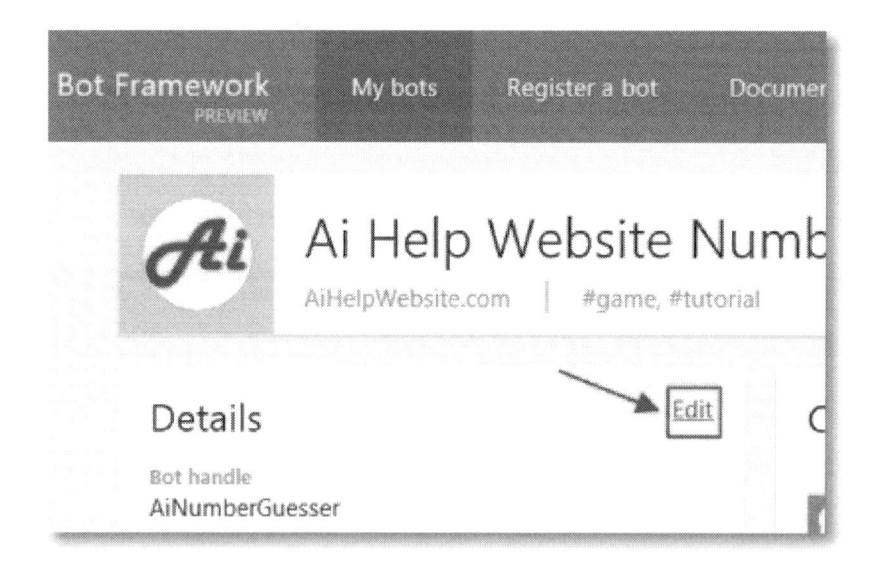

An Introduction to the Microsoft Bot Framework

Edit the **Bot** configuration.

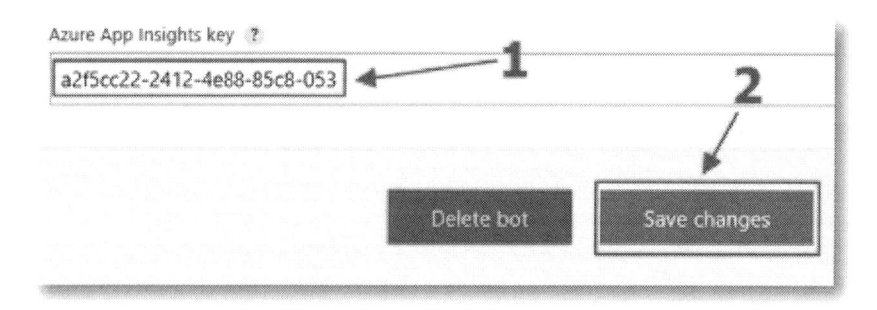

Enter the **Instrumentation Key** (from the **Microsoft Azure** site) and click **Save changes**.

This will enable additional **properties** and **metrics** to track.

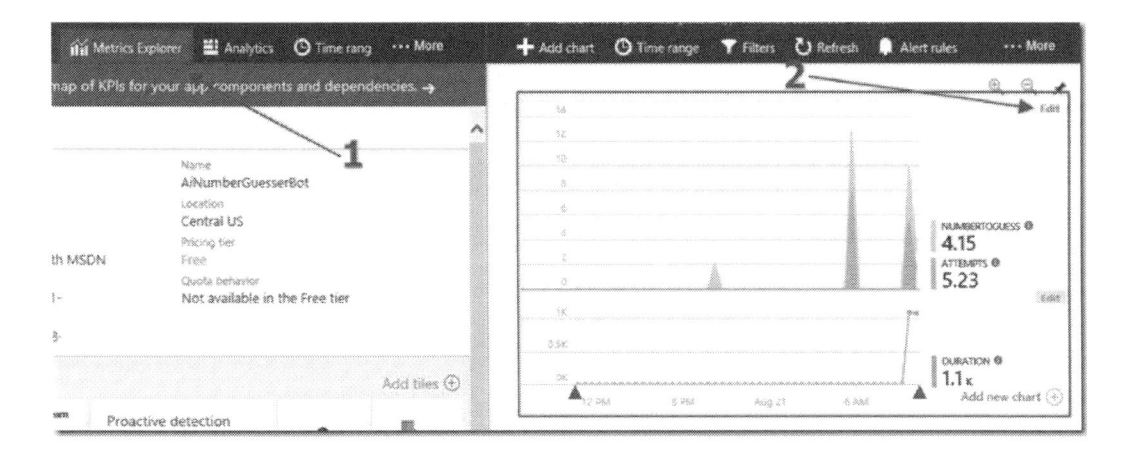

An Introduction to the Microsoft Bot Framework

Return to the **Application Insights** resource on the **Microsoft Azure** site.

You can now monitor your published application and create custom charts using default tracking data and your custom **properties** and **metrics**.

An Introduction to the Microsoft Bot Framework

Chapter 10: Creating a Skype Bot

The sample code for this chapter can be obtained at the link "Creating a Skype Bot Using The Microsoft Bot Framework" at http://AiHelpWebsite.com/Downloads

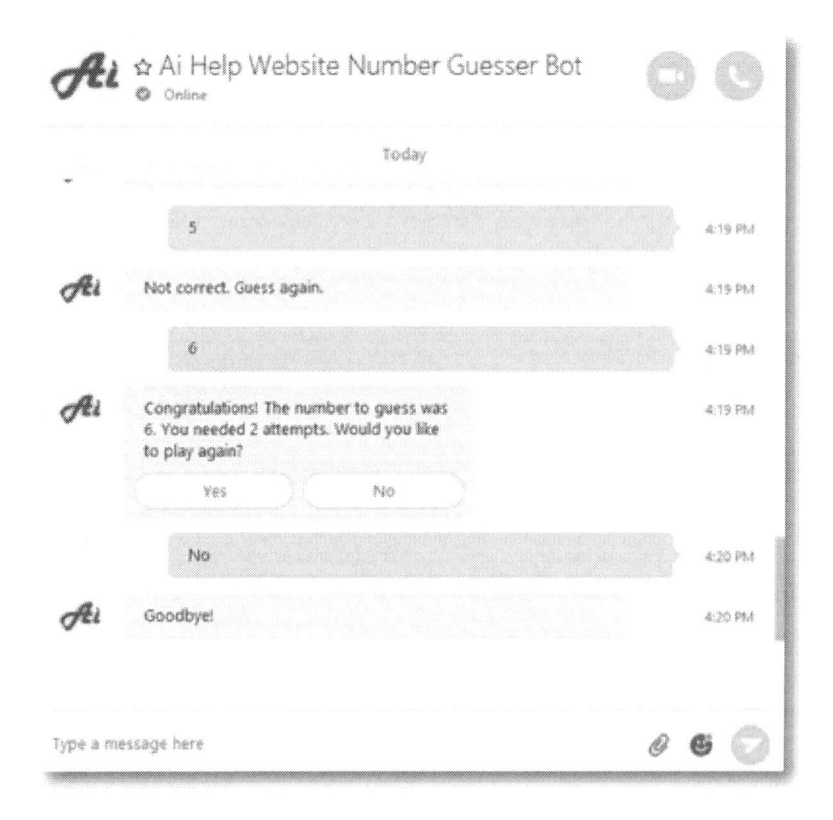

You can easily create a **Skype Bot** and deploy it to **Skype**.

An Introduction to the Microsoft Bot Framework

To demonstrate this, we will start with the **Bot** created in **Chapter Six**.

Note: *If you have not previously deployed your **Bot**, skip down to the section labeled "Register Skype".*

An Introduction to the Microsoft Bot Framework

Publishing The Bot

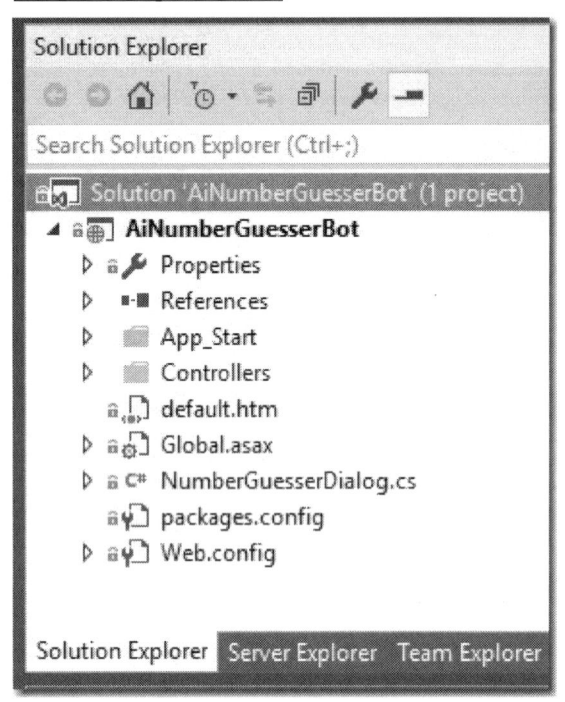

The first step is to connect the **AiNumberGuesserBot** to the **Microsoft Bot Framework Developer Portal**.

To do this, we need to publish it in a *publically accessible location*. This can be any server; however, publishing to **Azure** is recommended because publishing to it has built-in support in **Visual Studio**.

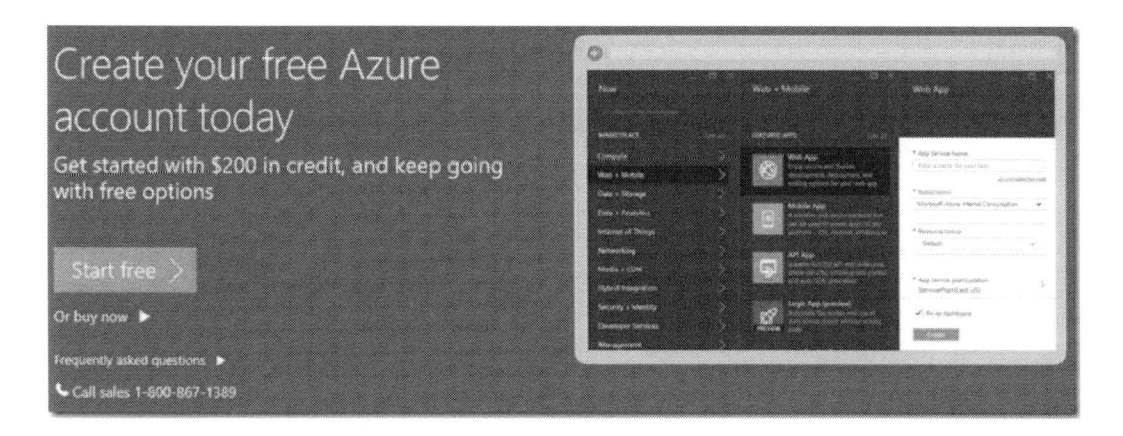

An Introduction to the Microsoft Bot Framework

First, go to https://azure.microsoft.com and create an account and a subscription (if you don't already have one).

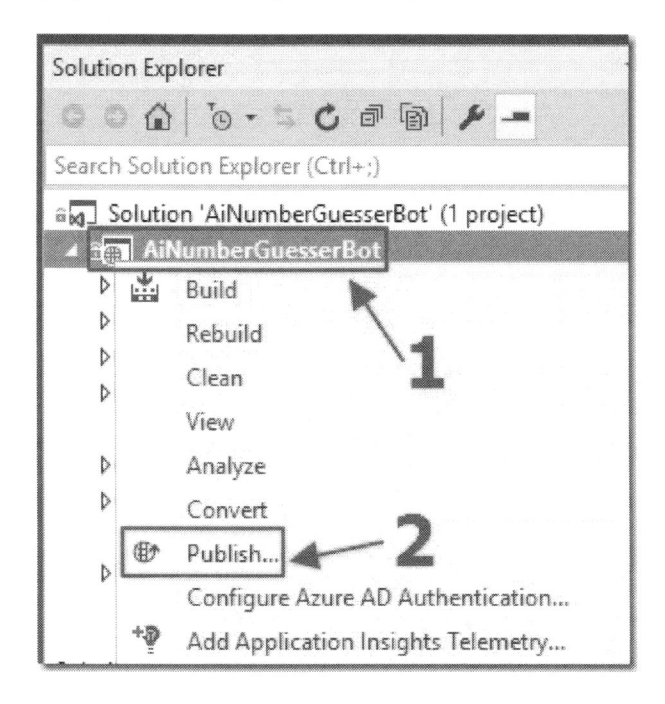

Next, open the **AiNumberGuesserBot** project in **Visual Studio** and r*ight-click* on the **Project** node (not the **Solution** node), and select **Publish**.

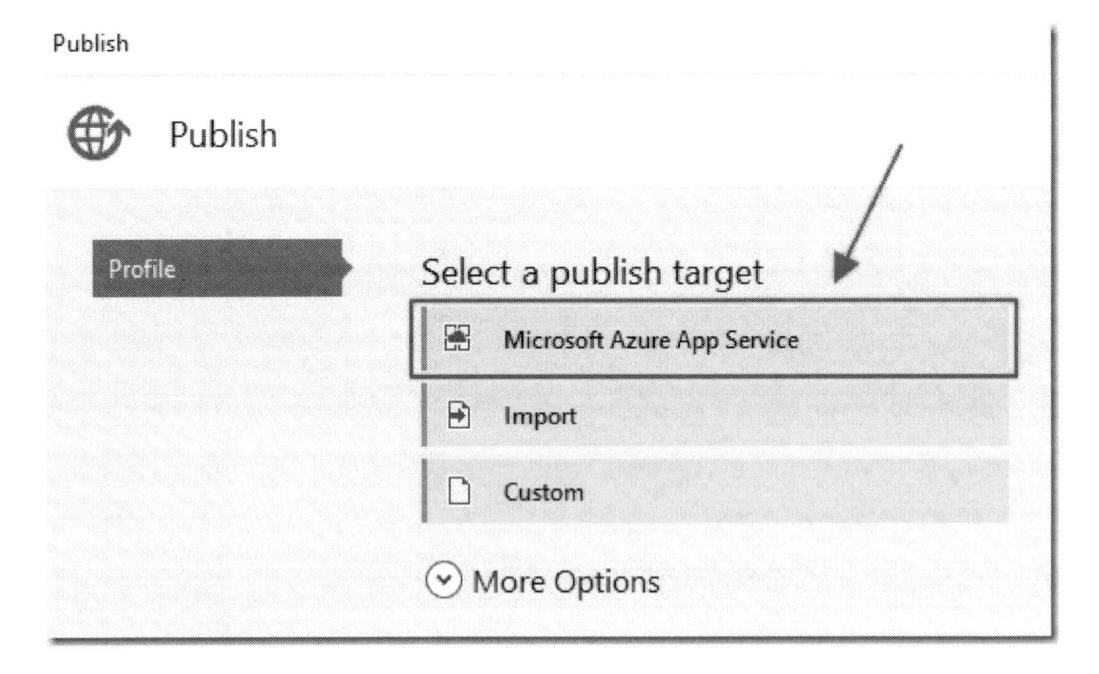

An Introduction to the Microsoft Bot Framework

Publish

Select **Microsoft Azure App Service**.

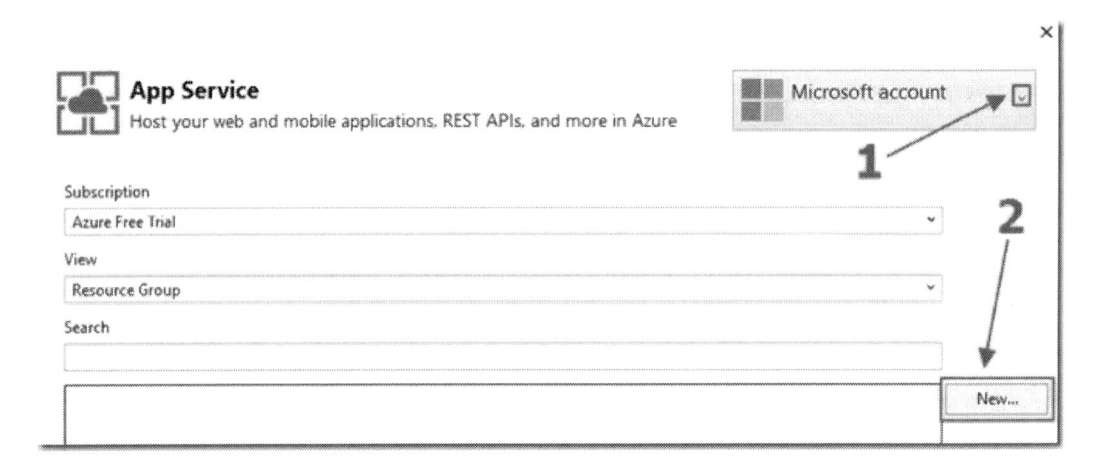

Sign into your **Azure** account and then click the **New** button.

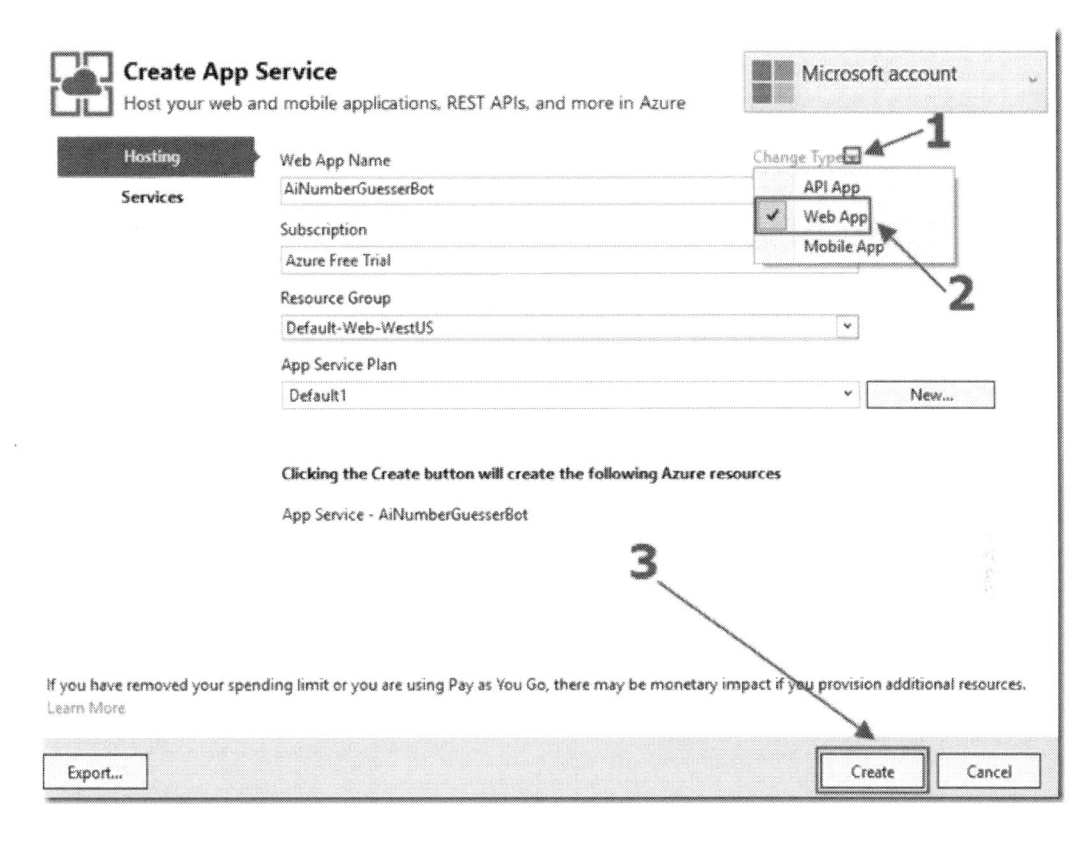

An Introduction to the Microsoft Bot Framework

Ensure the type is **Web App**.

Enter a unique **Web App name**, select your **subscription**, select or create a **service plan** and **resource group** and click the **Create** button.

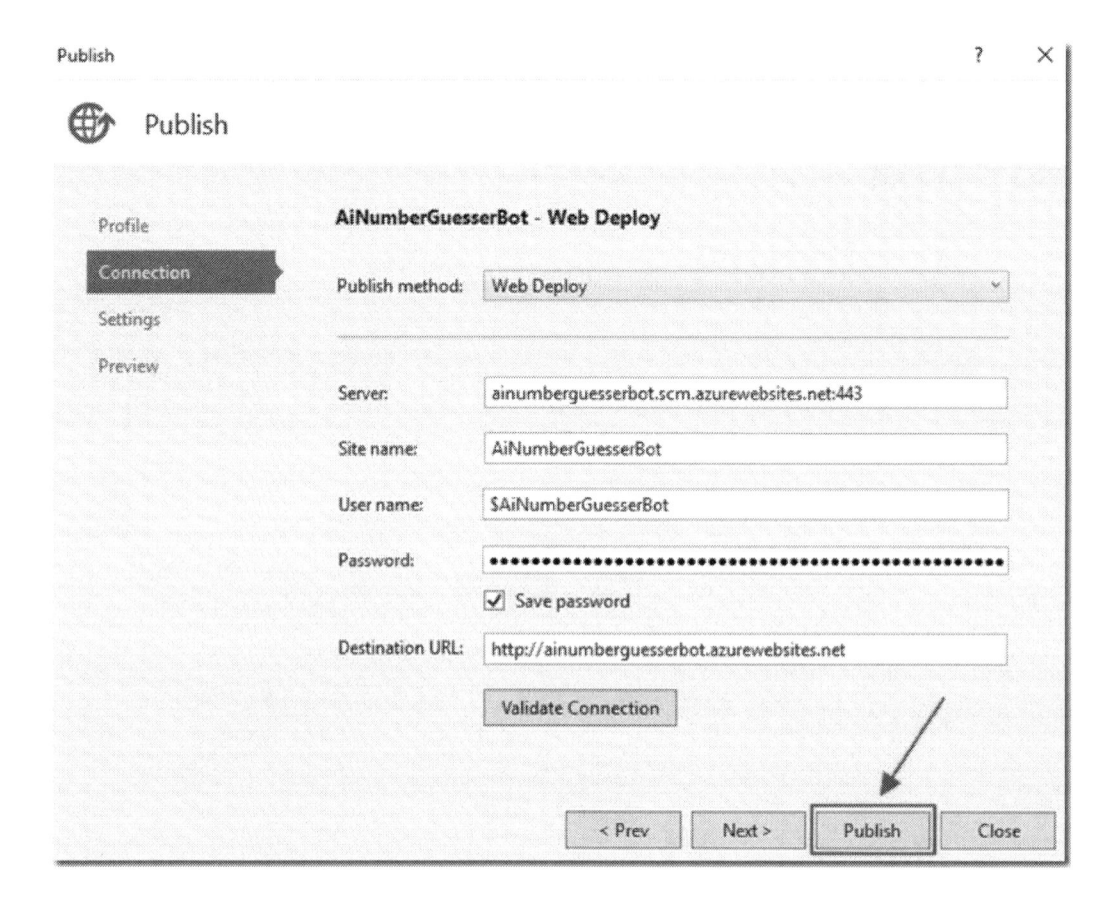

An Introduction to the Microsoft Bot Framework

After the **web app** has been created, click the **Publish** button.

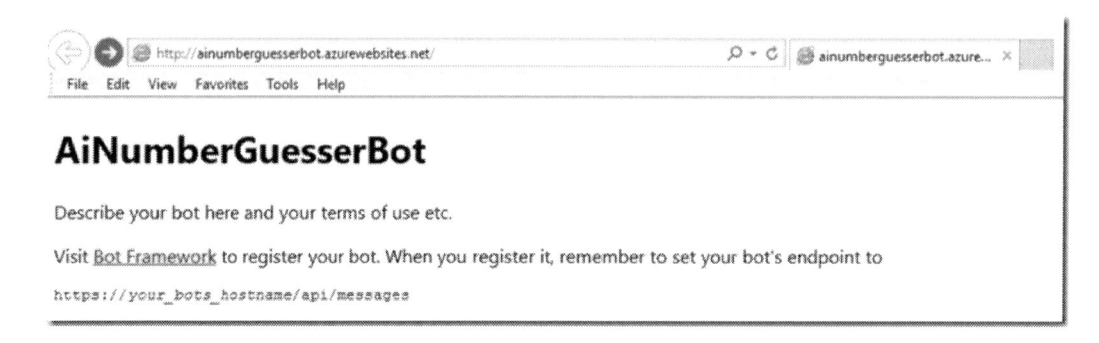

The web app will open in the web browser.

An Introduction to the Microsoft Bot Framework

Note the web address as you will need it in a later step.

Registering The Bot With The Bot Connector

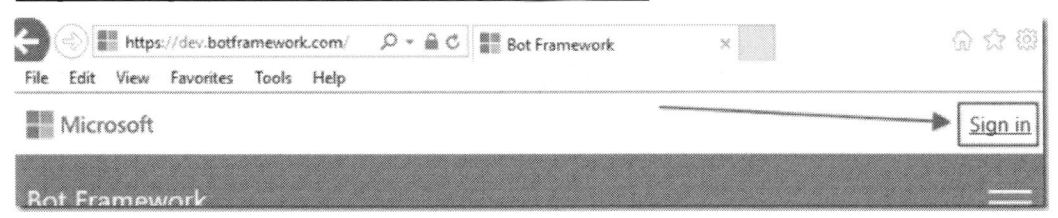

Go to the **Microsoft Bot Framework** portal at http://dev.botframework.com and sign in with your **Microsoft Account**.

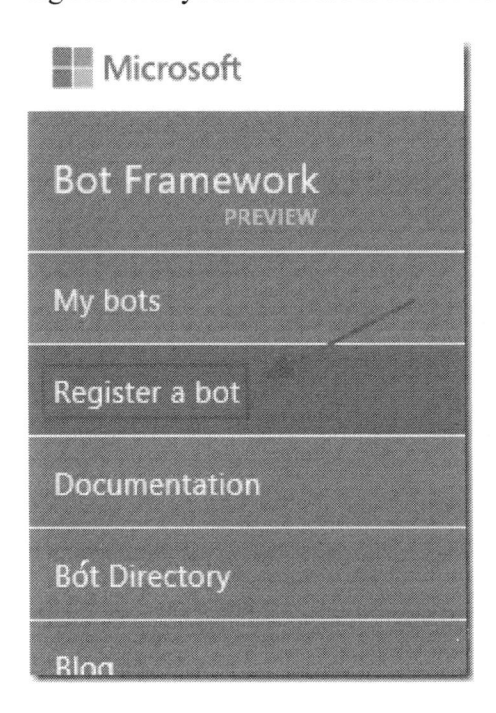

Select **Register a bot**.

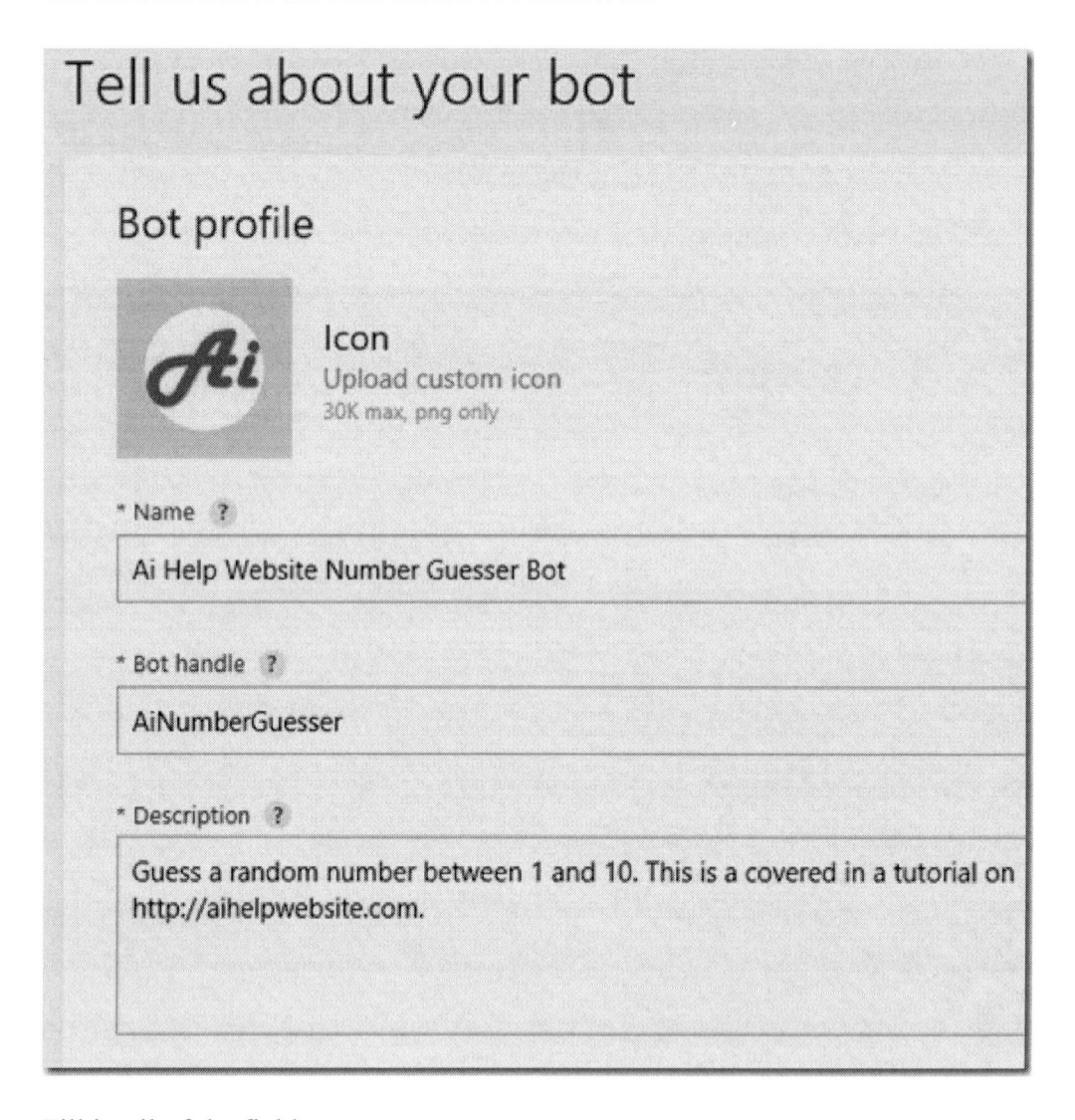

An Introduction to the Microsoft Bot Framework

Tell us about your bot

Bot profile

Icon
Upload custom icon
30K max, png only

* Name

Ai Help Website Number Guesser Bot

* Bot handle

AiNumberGuesser

* Description

Guess a random number between 1 and 10. This is a covered in a tutorial on http://aihelpwebsite.com.

Fill in all of the fields.

An Introduction to the Microsoft Bot Framework

Configuration
Messaging endpoint
https://ainumberguesserbot.azurewebsites.net/api/messages

Note: The end point web address is what you saw when the web browser opened in the previous step.

However, you have to add */api/messages* to the end of the address and use *https://* rather than *http://*.

Create Microsoft App ID and password

At one point in the form, you will see a link you will click to go to https://apps.dev.microsoft.com

It is there that you will get an **Application ID** and a **password**.

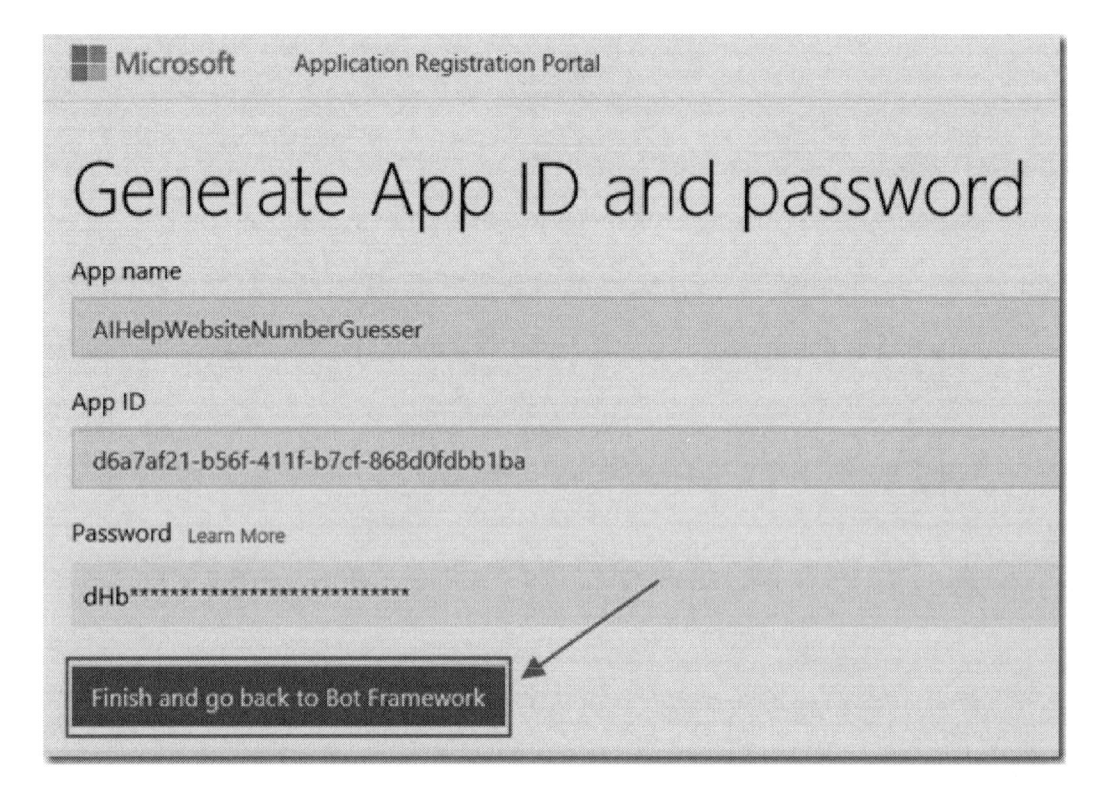

An Introduction to the Microsoft Bot Framework

Make a note of them because you will need to use them to update the **web.config** file in the **Visual Studio** project later.

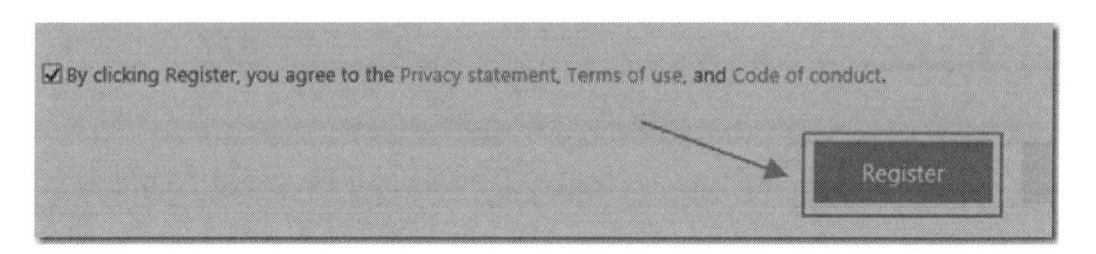

Click the **Register** button.

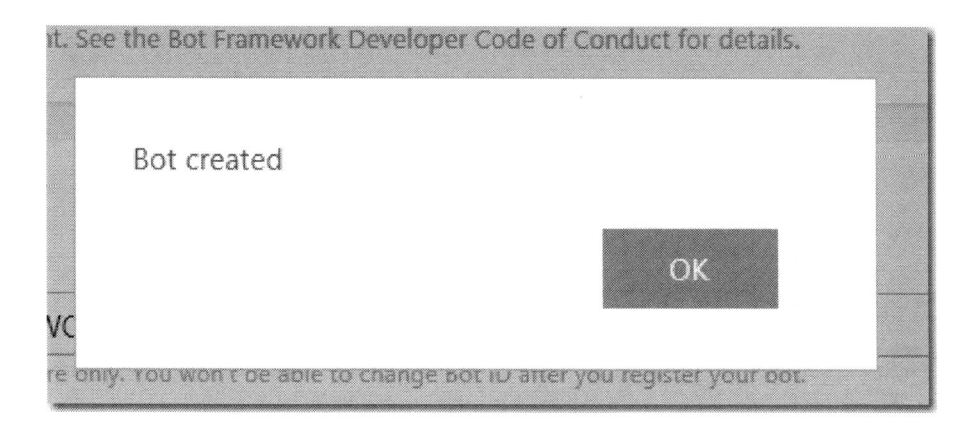

An Introduction to the Microsoft Bot Framework

The **Bot** registration will be created.

When you return to the http://dev.botframework.com page, you will see the **Microsoft App ID** from the https://apps.dev.microsoft.com site has been entered into your **Bot**'s configuration.

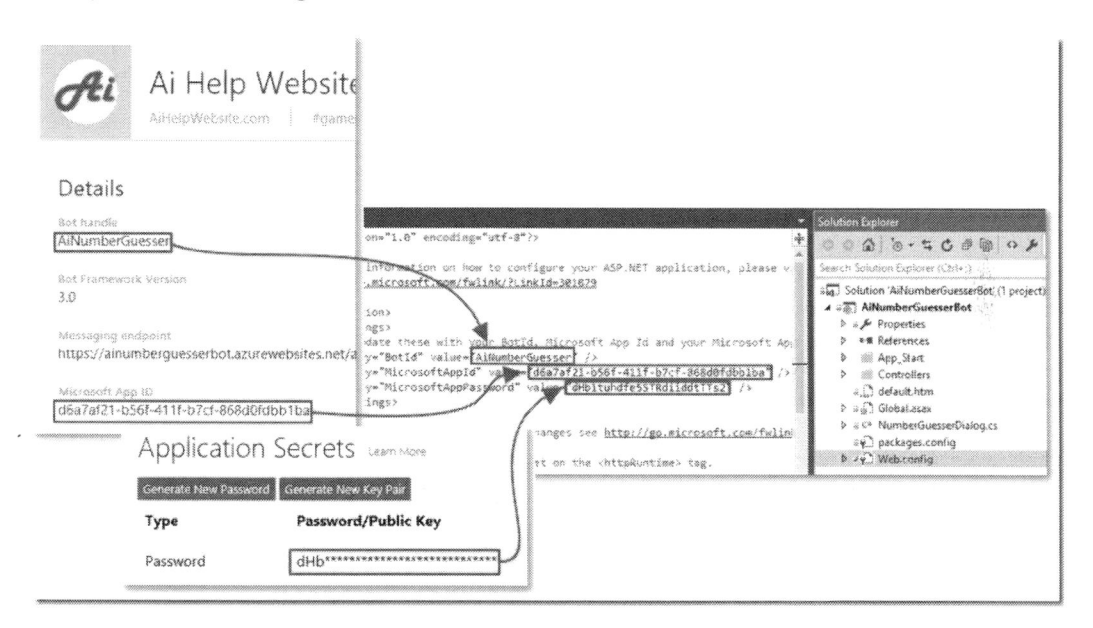

Copy the **Bot ID (Bot handle)** and **MicrosoftAppId** and **MicrosoftAppPassword** from http://dev.botframework.com and https://apps.dev.microsoft.com to the **web.config** of the **Bot** in **Visual Studio**.

An Introduction to the Microsoft Bot Framework

Note: If you forgot to note the **MicrosoftAppPassword** in the earlier step, you can click the **Generate New Password** button at https://apps.dev.microsoft.com to create another one.

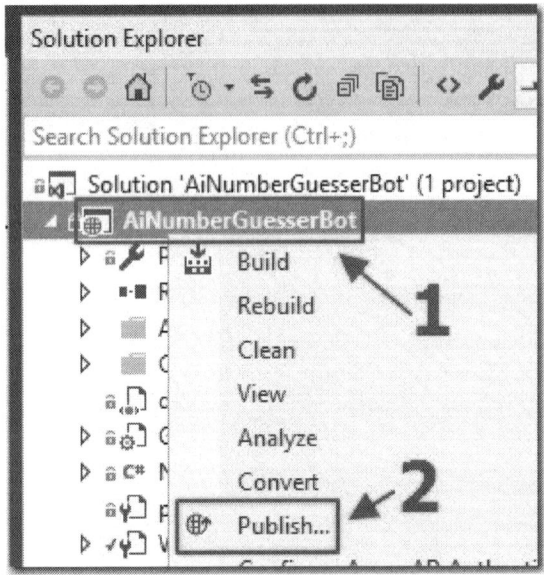

In **Visual Studio**, **Publish** the **Bot** again.

You are doing this because the **Bot Connector** will pass the **Bot ID** and **MicrosoftAppId** and **MicrosoftAppPassword** when it communicates with it.

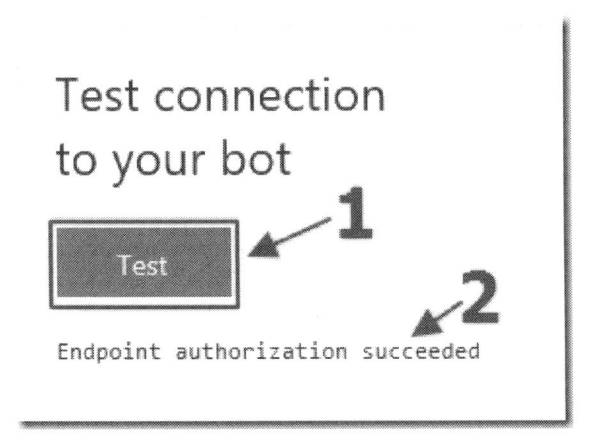

An Introduction to the Microsoft Bot Framework

Return to the **Bot** configuration page at http://dev.botframework.com.

You can now click the **Test** button on that page to test the connection to your **Bot**.

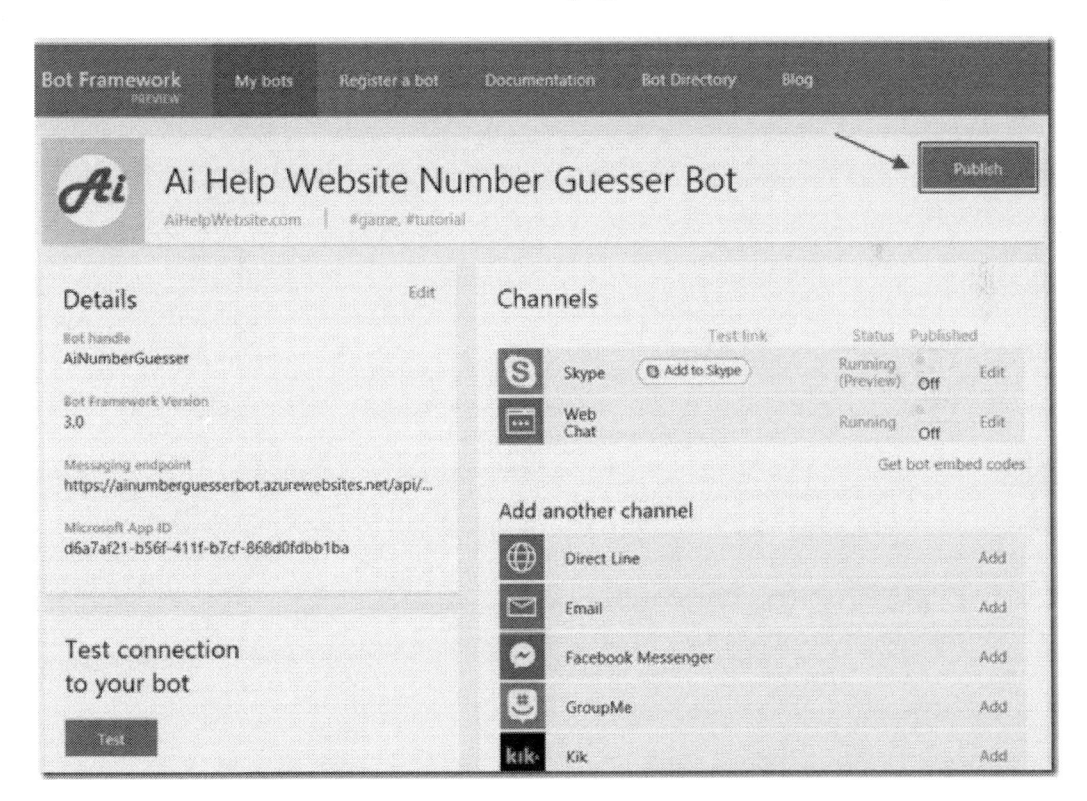

An Introduction to the Microsoft Bot Framework

You can now configure channels to your **Bot**.

When you have configured channels, if you desire, you can click the **Publish** button to submit your bot to the **Bot Directory**.

Even if you do not publish it to the **Bot Directory**, you can still call it from your own applications and through any channels you configure.

Configure Skype

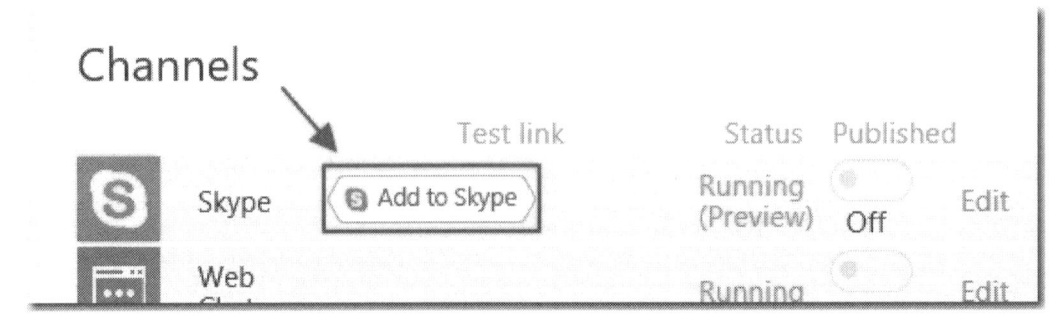

To add the **Bot** to **Skype**, click the **Add to Skype** button on the **Bot** configuration page at http://dev.botframework.com.

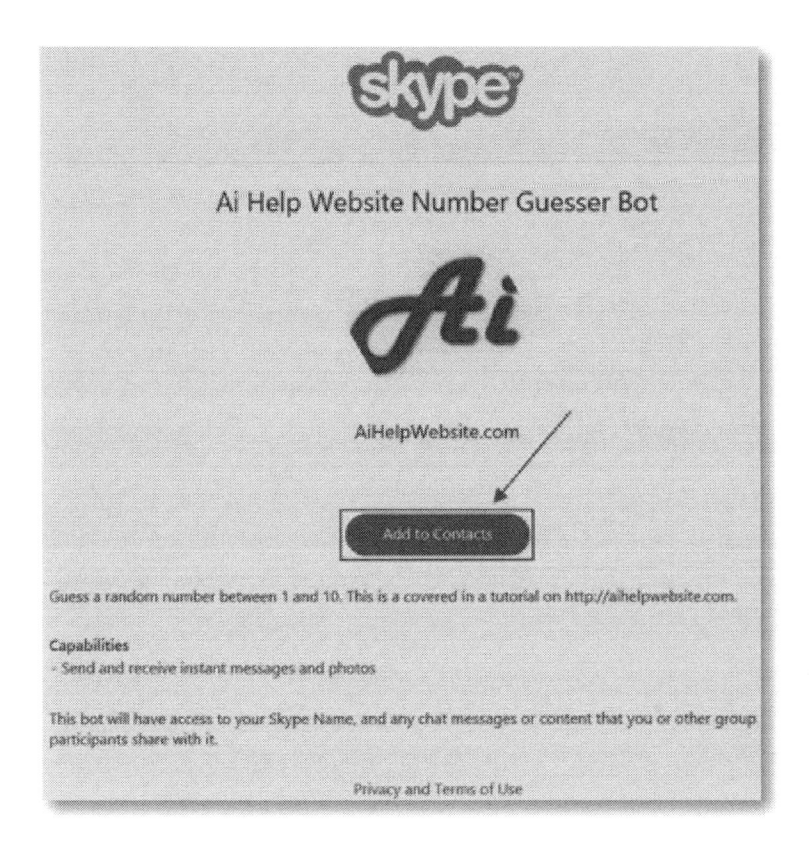

An Introduction to the Microsoft Bot Framework

You will be directed to a **Skype** configuration page for the **Bot**. Click the button to **Add to Contacts**.

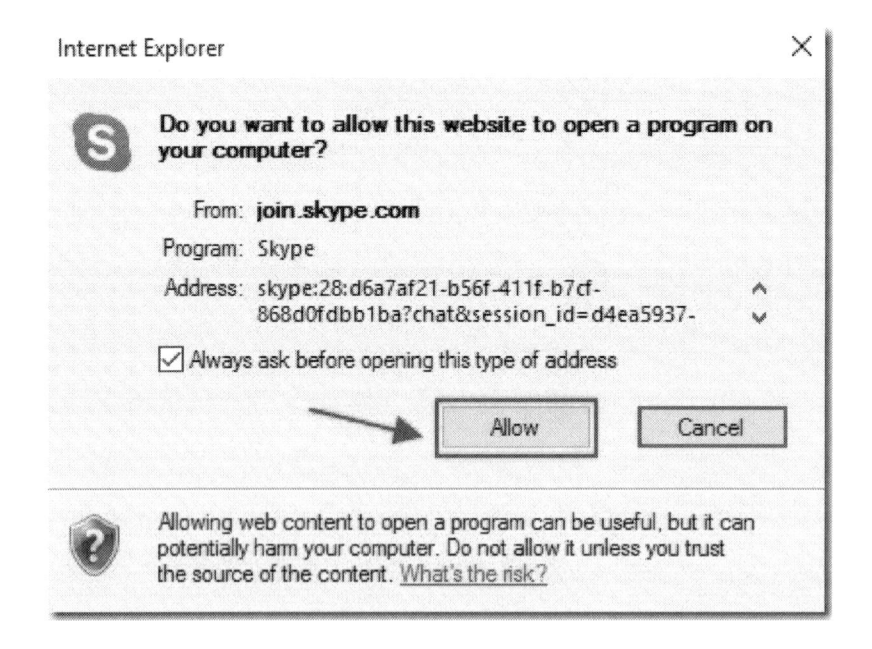

An Introduction to the Microsoft Bot Framework

Click **Allow** in the popup box.

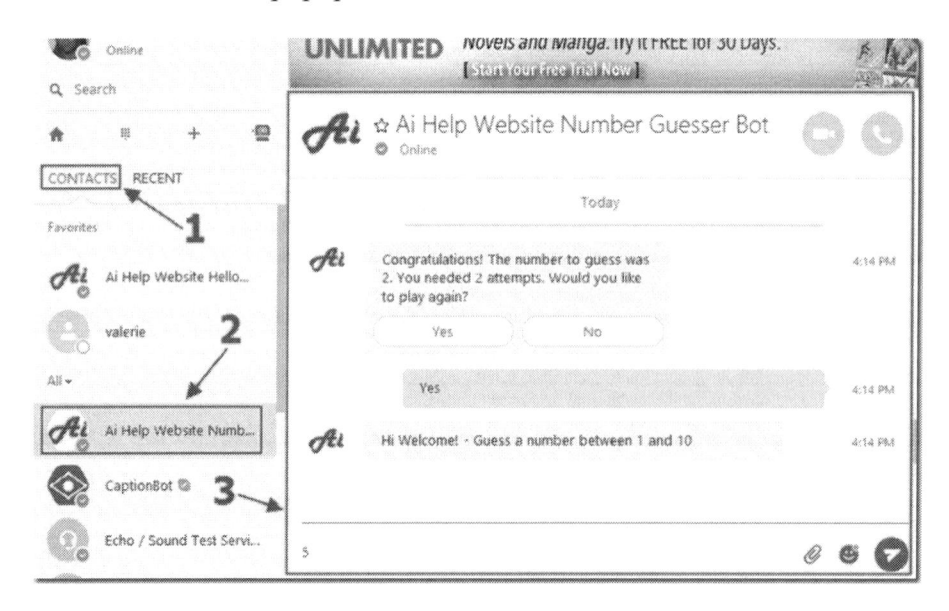

Skype will open, and you can select the **Bot** from your contacts and converse with it.

An Introduction to the Microsoft Bot Framework

Chapter 11: Creating A Facebook Messenger Bot

The sample code for this chapter can be obtained at the link "Creating A Facebook Bot Using Microsoft Bot Framework" at http://AiHelpWebsite.com/Downloads

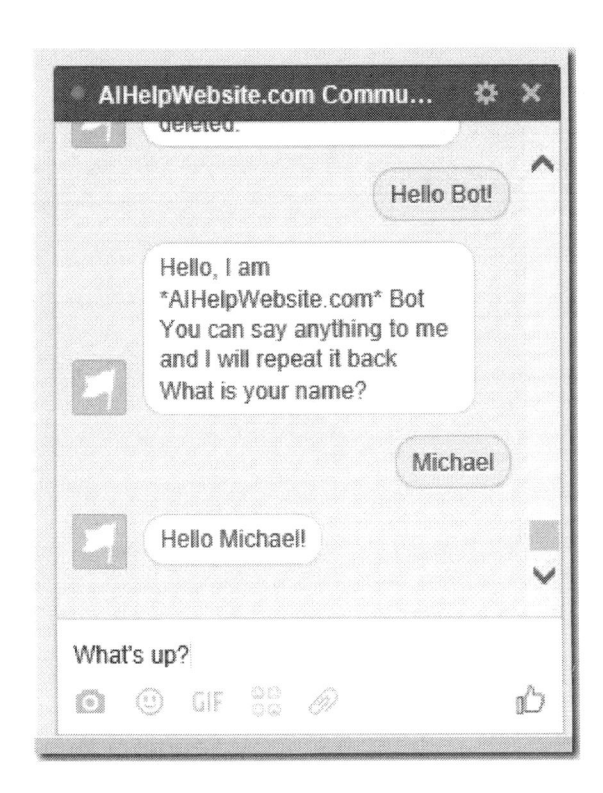

You can easily create a **Bot** and deploy it on **Facebook**.

An Introduction to the Microsoft Bot Framework

To demonstrate this, we will start with the **Bot** created in **Chapter Two**.

An Introduction to the Microsoft Bot Framework

Set-Up Facebook

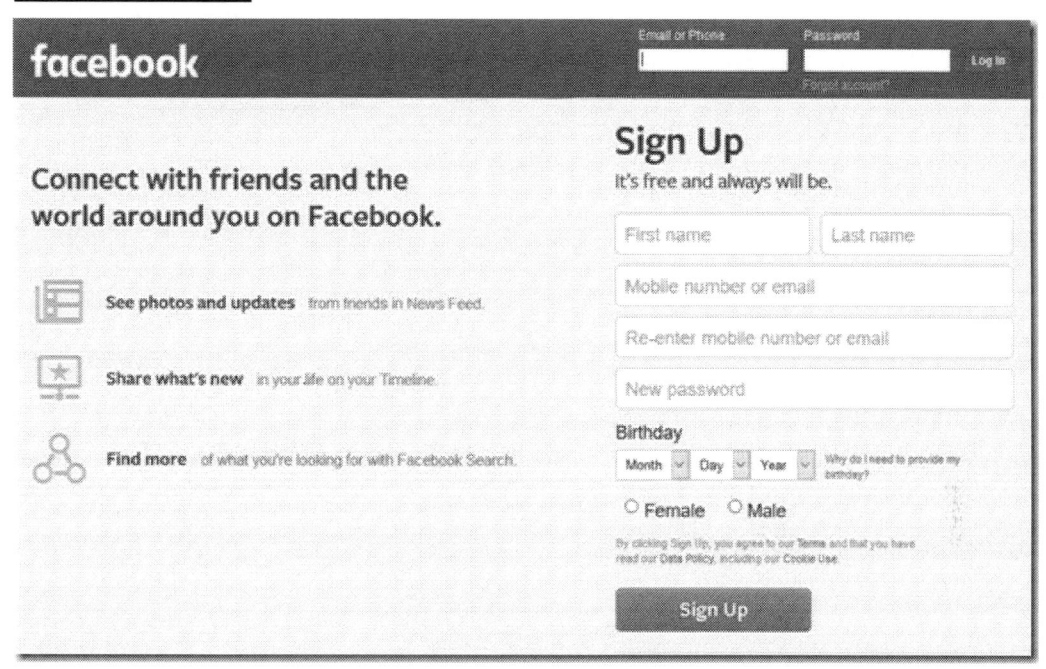

The first step is to log into your **Facebook.com** account (or create one).

Select **Create Page**.

An Introduction to the Microsoft Bot Framework

Select a template, fill in the required information, and click **Get Started**.

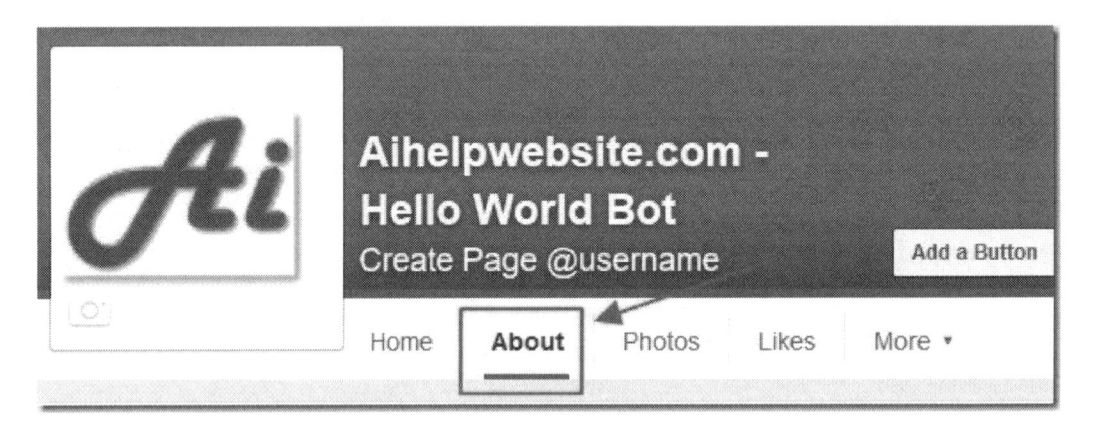

To get the **Facebook Page ID**, which you will need later, click on the **About** tab.

An Introduction to the Microsoft Bot Framework

Locate the **Facebook Page ID**.

Create A Facebook Developer Account

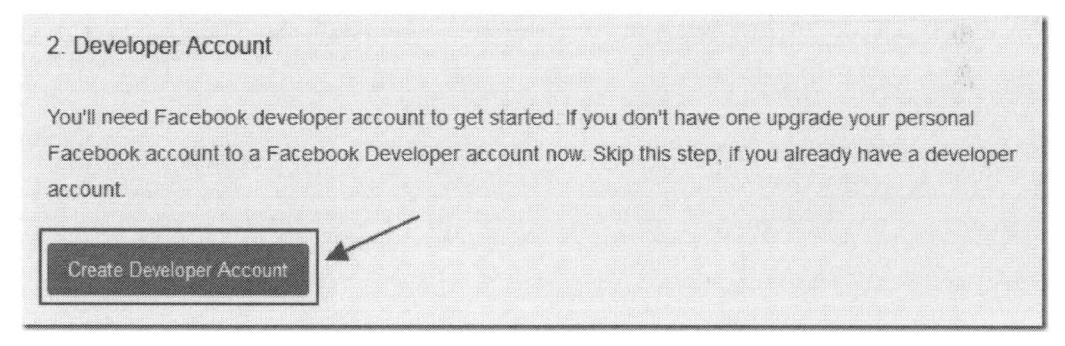

Go to https://developers.facebook.com/docs/apps/register and click the button to create a **Facebook Developer Account**.

An Introduction to the Microsoft Bot Framework

Click the slider to **Yes** to accept the policies and click **Register**.

Create A Facebook App

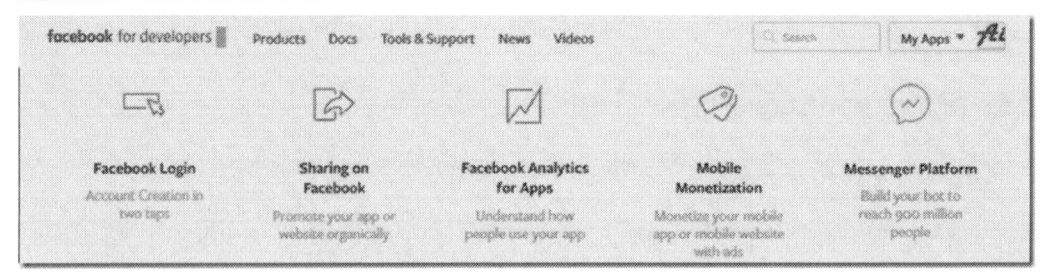

Next, go to https://developers.facebook.com/ and log in again if needed.

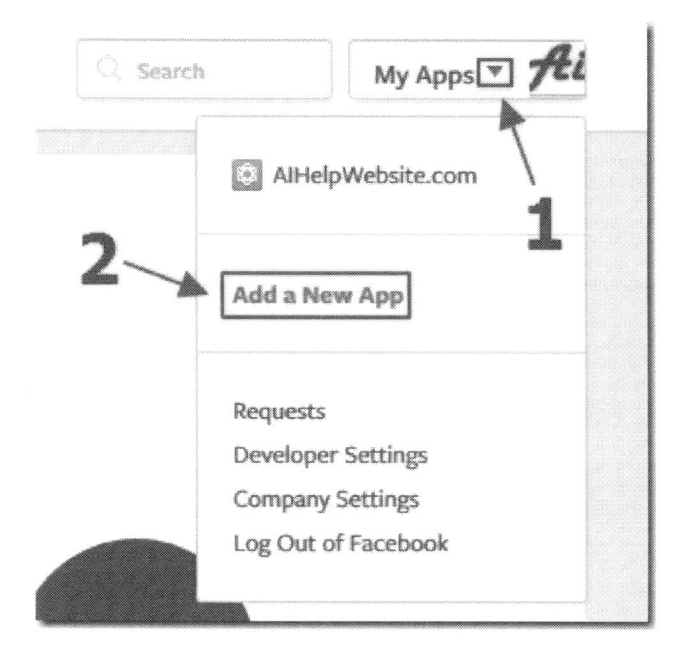

An Introduction to the Microsoft Bot Framework

Select **Add a New App**.

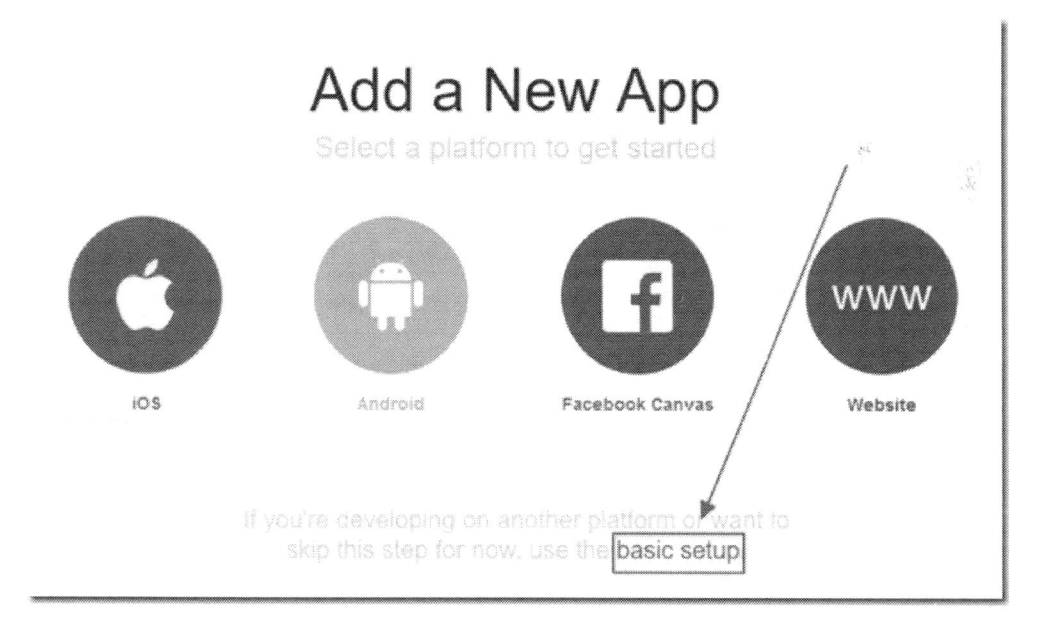

Select **basic setup**.

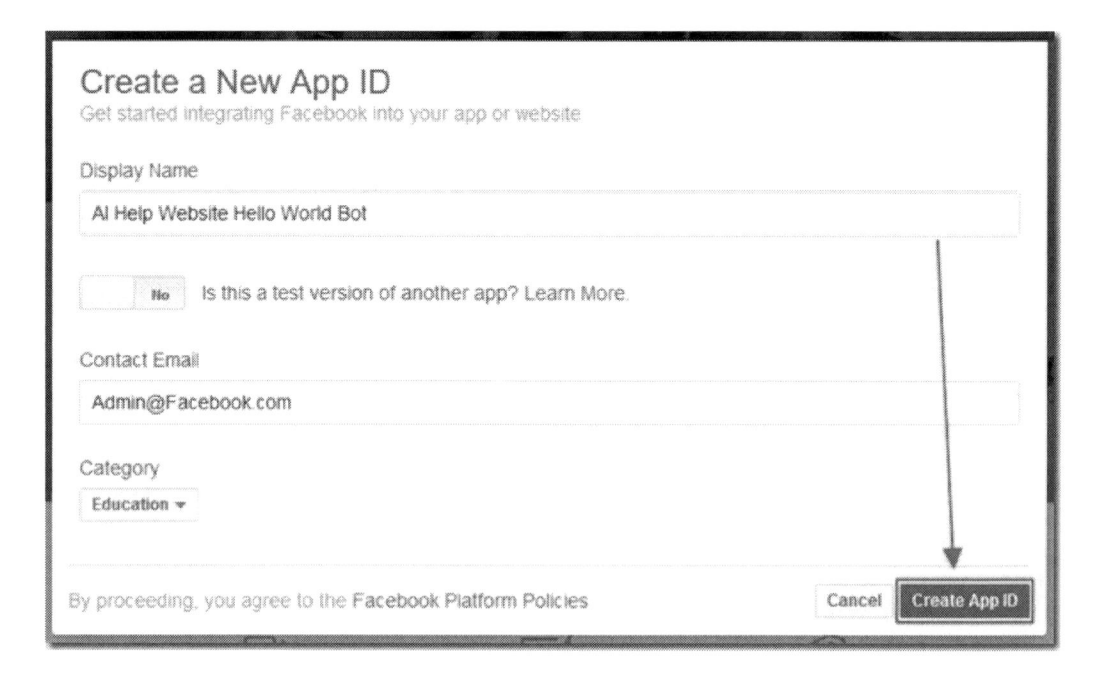

An Introduction to the Microsoft Bot Framework

Fill in the information and click **Create App ID**.

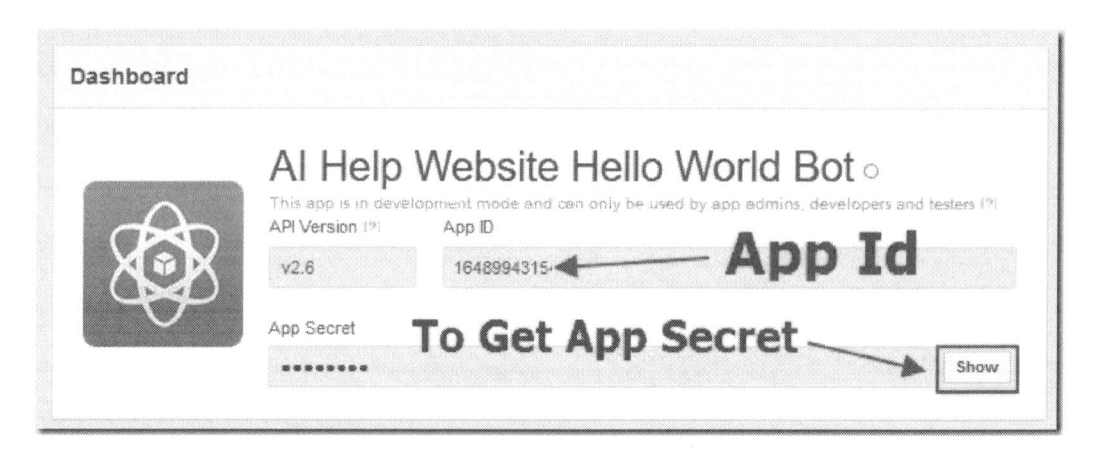

Make a note of the **App ID** as you will need it in a later step.

Click the **Show** button to display the **App Secret**. Make a note of it as you will need it in a later step.

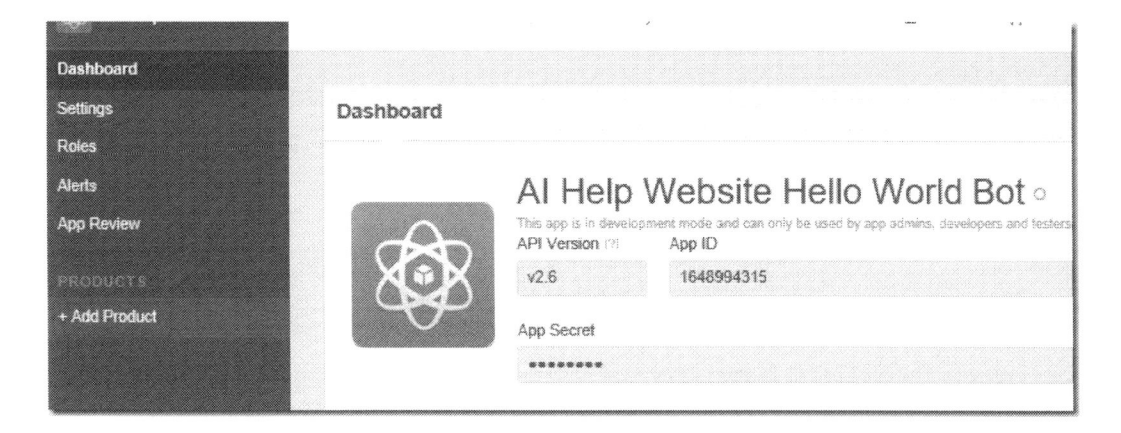

An Introduction to the Microsoft Bot Framework

Now that the **App** is created, you need to configure it to use **Facebook Messenger**.

Click **Add Product**.

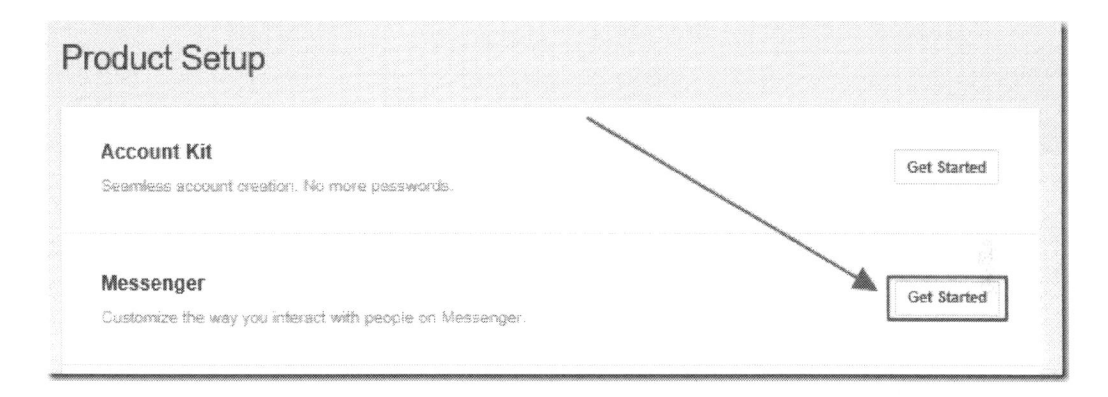

Select **Messenger**.

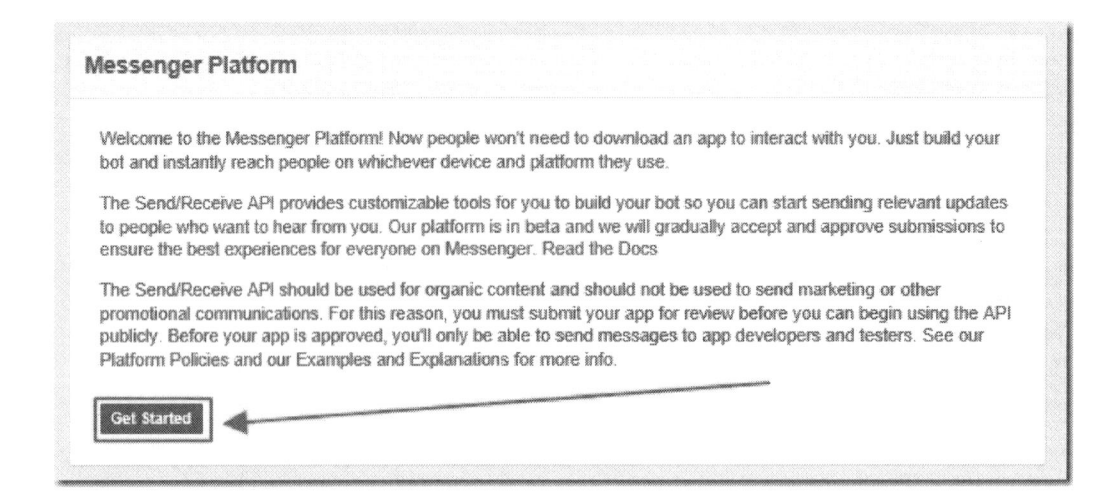

An Introduction to the Microsoft Bot Framework

Select **Get Started**.

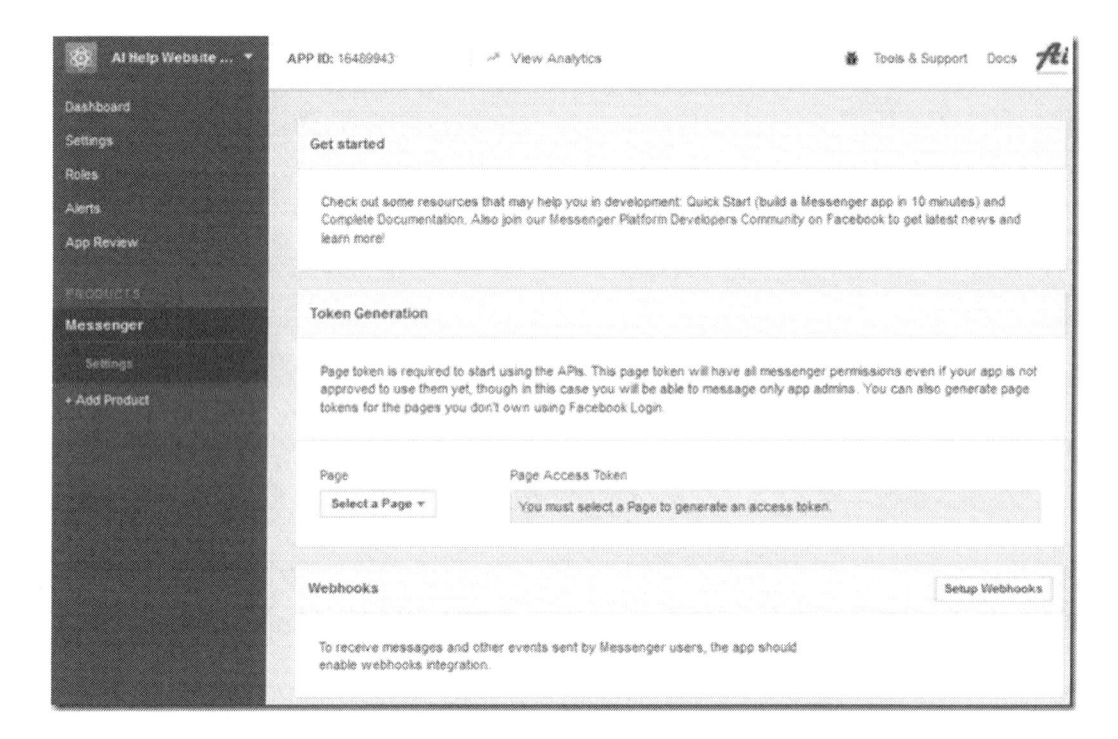

Facebook Messenger has been added.

Get Page Token

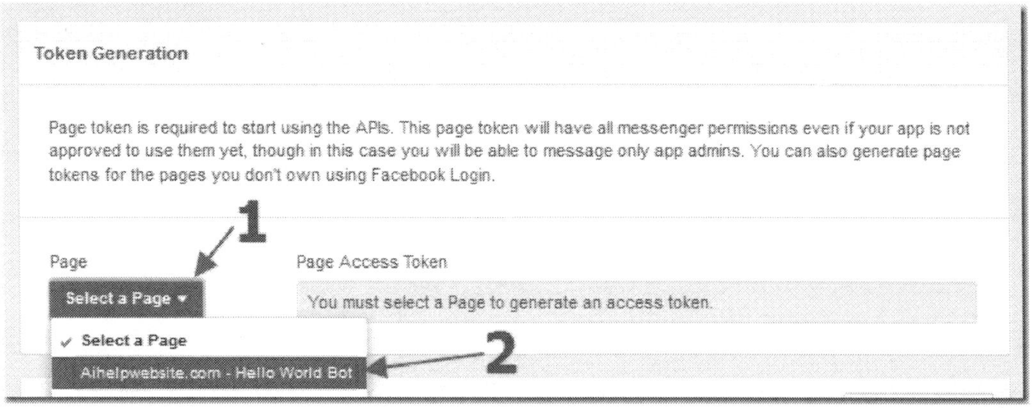

In the **Token Generation** section, select the page that you previously created.

A **Page Access Token** will be created.

Copy the **Page Access Token**.

You now need to configure it to talk to the **Microsoft Bot Connector**.

An Introduction to the Microsoft Bot Framework

Configure The Callback URL and Verify Token

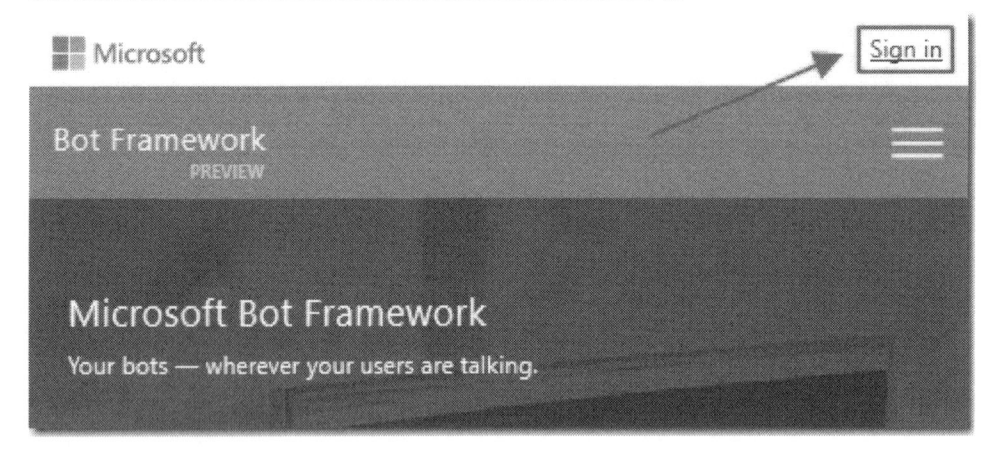

Go to htttps://dev.botframework.com/ and **Sign in**.

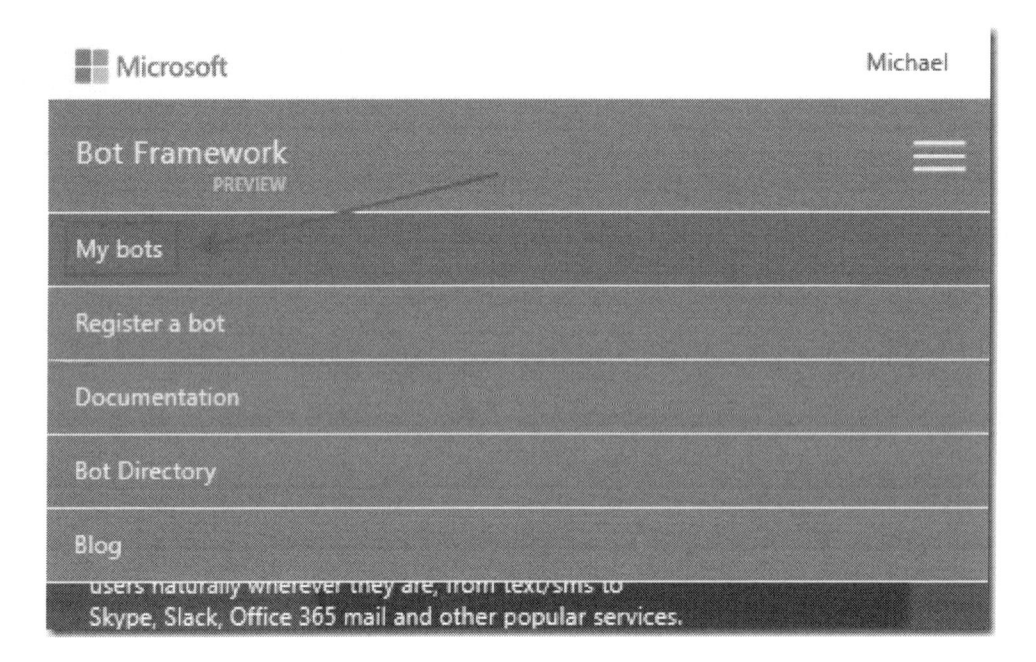

Select **My bots**.

An Introduction to the Microsoft Bot Framework

My bots

AI Help Website Hello World
AIHelpWebsite.com

Select a published bot. (See **Chapter Two** for directions on how to do this.)

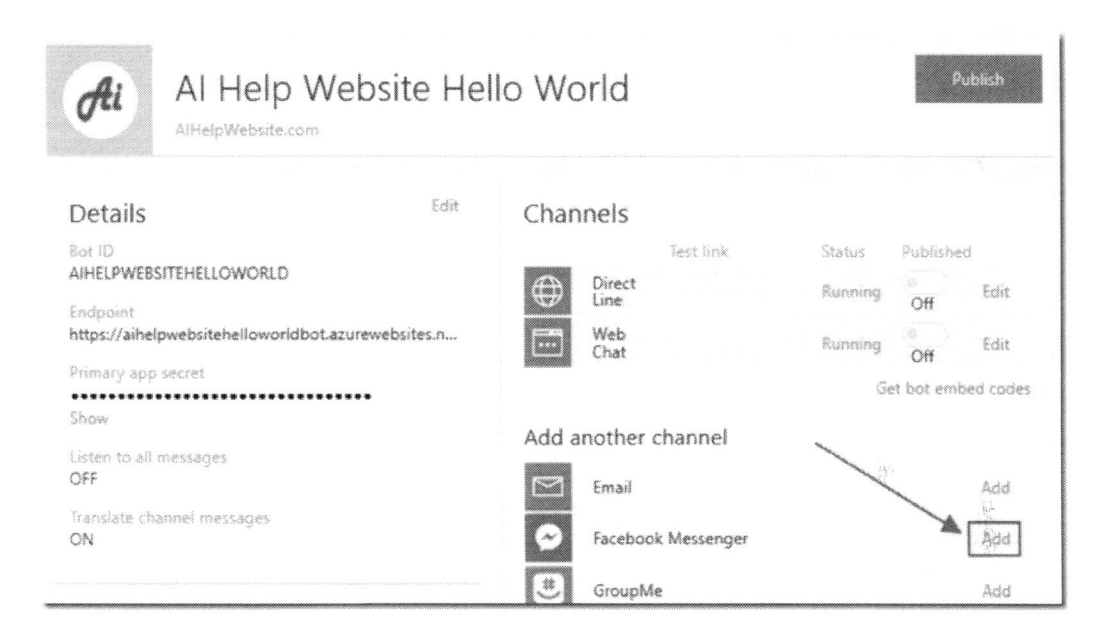

AI Help Website Hello World
AIHelpWebsite.com

Details

Bot ID
AIHELPWEBSITEHELLOWORLD

Endpoint
https://aihelpwebsitehelloworldbot.azurewebsites.n...

Primary app secret
••••••••••••••••••••••••••••••••••
Show

Listen to all messages
OFF

Translate channel messages
ON

Channels

	Test link	Status	Published	
Direct Line		Running	Off	Edit
Web Chat		Running	Off	Edit

Get bot embed codes

Add another channel

Email		Add
Facebook Messenger		Add
GroupMe		Add

Click the **Add** button next to the **Facebook Messenger** channel.

255

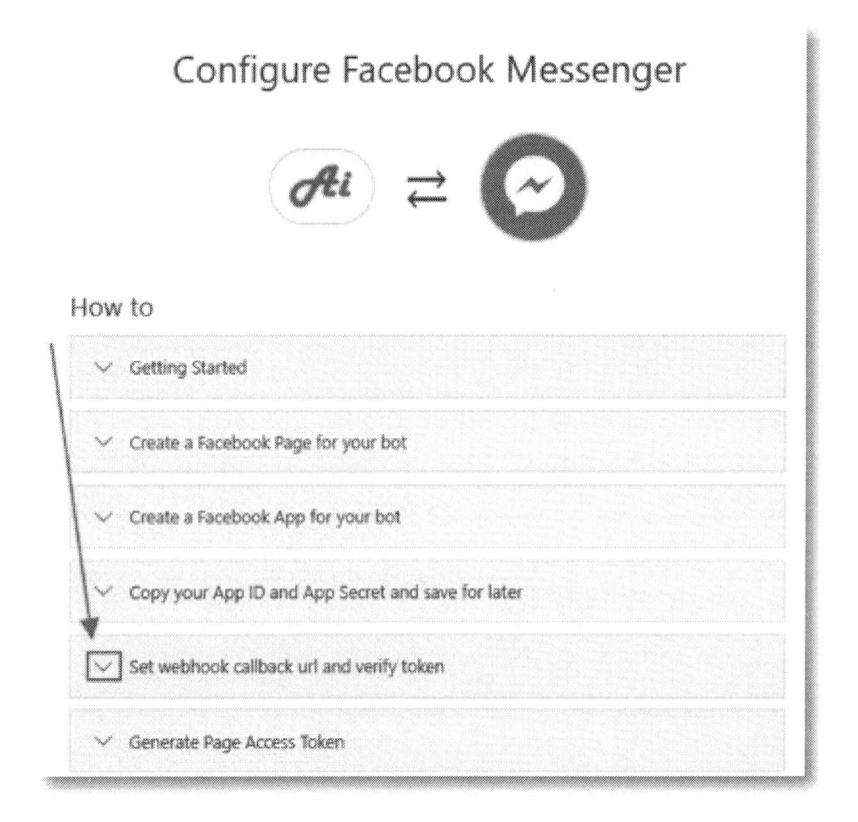

An Introduction to the Microsoft Bot Framework

Click the expander next to **Set webhook callback url and verify token**.

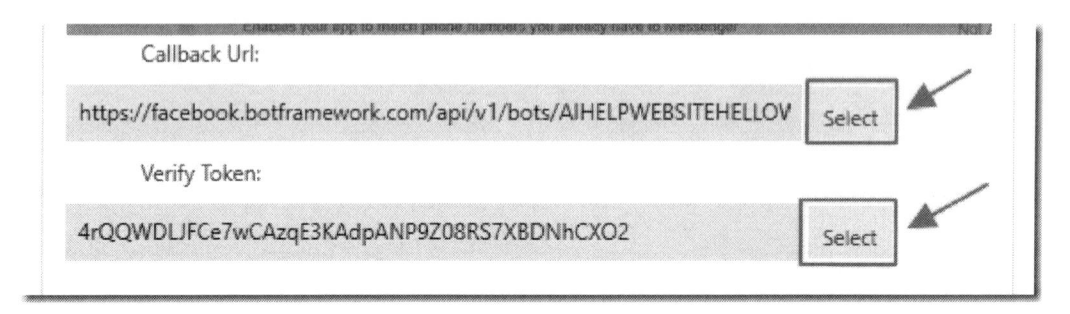

Use the **Select** buttons to individually select and copy the **Callback Url** and **Verify Token**.

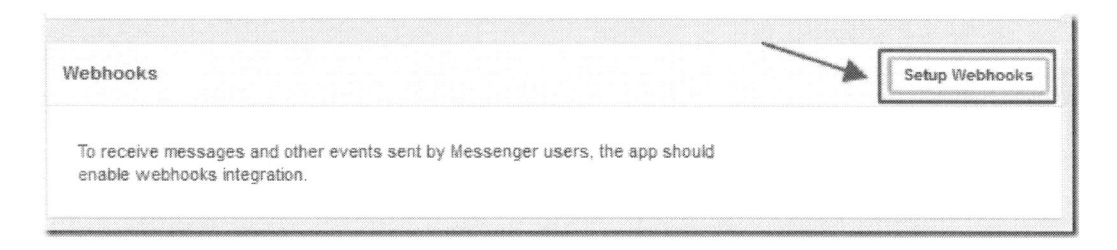

An Introduction to the Microsoft Bot Framework

Return to https://developers.facebook.com, select your application, and in the settings for **Messenger**, click the **Setup Webhooks** button.

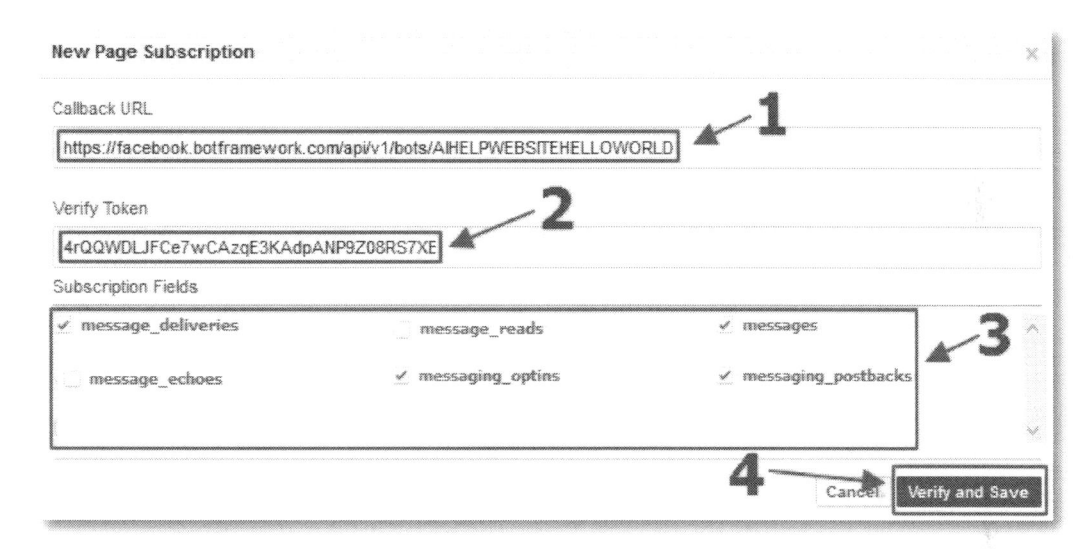

Enter the **Callback URL** and **Verify Token** you copied, check the **Subscription Fields** indicated in the image above, and click the **Verify and Save** button.

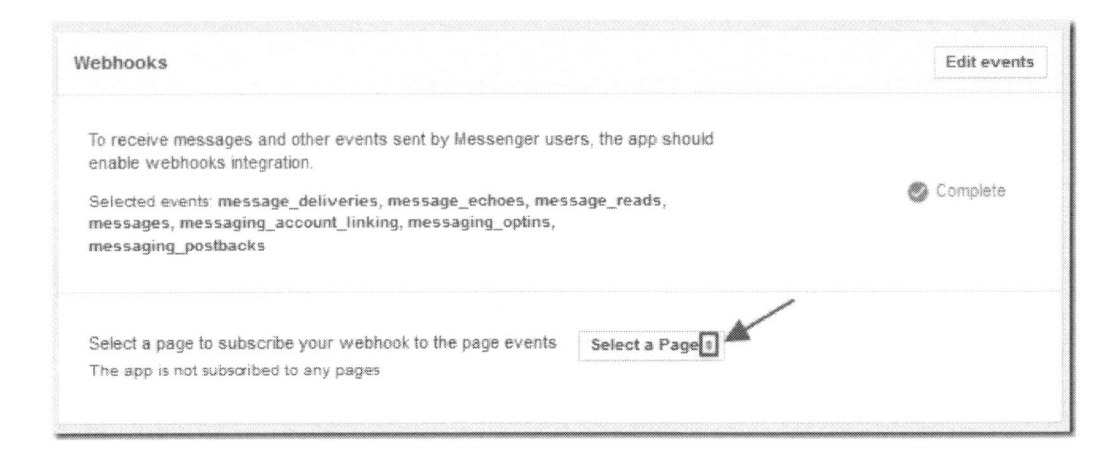

An Introduction to the Microsoft Bot Framework

After the **Webhooks** have been set, click the dropdown next to **Select a Page**.

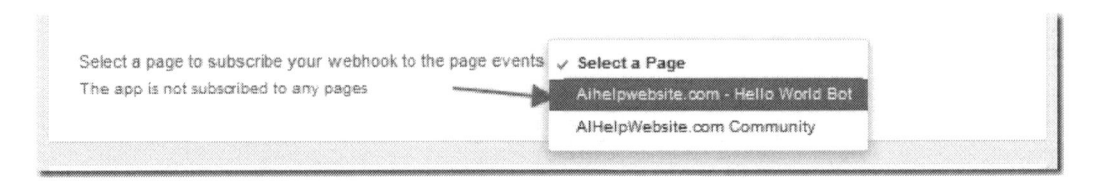

Select the **Facebook** page you created earlier.

Next, click the **Subscribe** button.

An Introduction to the Microsoft Bot Framework

Configure The Microsoft Bot Connector

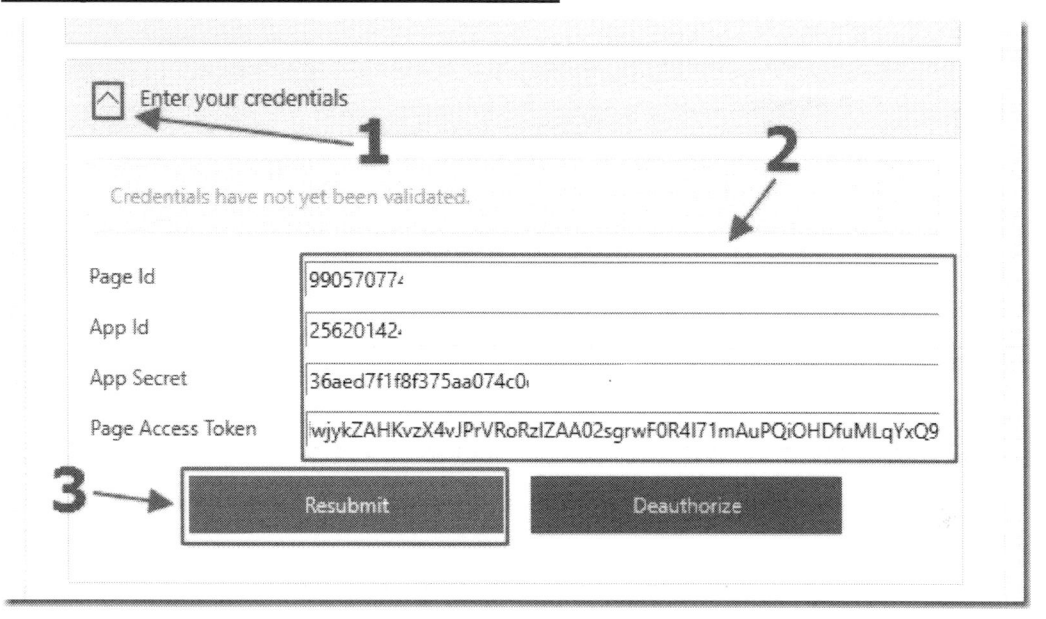

Return to https://dev.botframework.com/ and select your **Bot** again. Then click the **Edit** button next to the **Facebook Messenger** channel.

Click the expander next to **Enter your credentials**.

Enter the information you gathered in the earlier steps and click the **Resubmit** button.

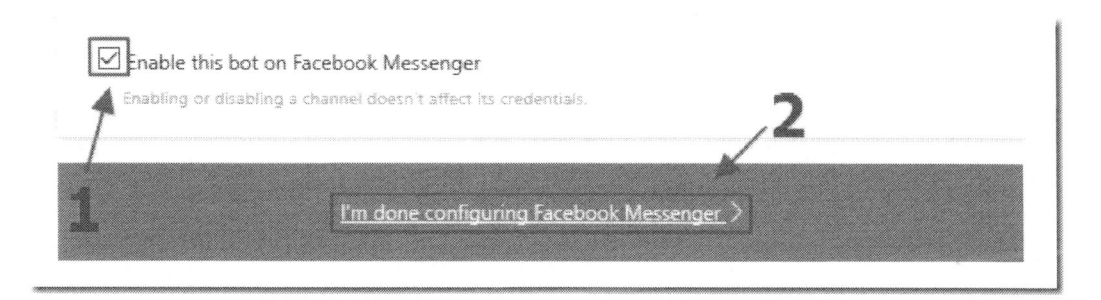

Check the box next to **Enable this bot on Facebook Messenger**.

An Introduction to the Microsoft Bot Framework

Click **I'm done configuring Facebook Messenger** button.

Talking To Your Bot

You can now talk to your **Bot** by navigating to
https://www.messenger.com/t/{Your Page ID}/

This will take you to **Facebook Messenger**, and after logging in with your **Facebook ID**, it will allow you to converse with your **Bot**.

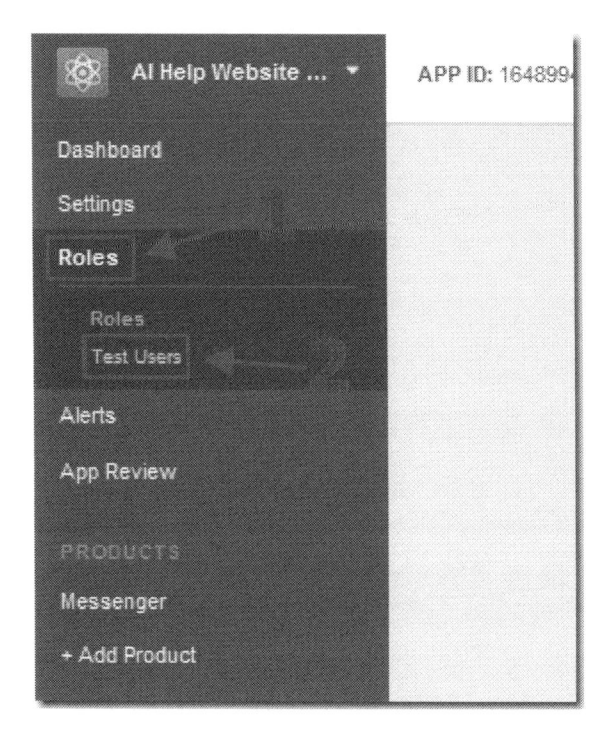

An Introduction to the Microsoft Bot Framework

Until your **App** is approved and made public, only you can chat with your **Bot**.

To create accounts to test it, go to https://developers.facebook.com/.

Select the **App** and then select **Roles** and then **Test Users**.

Fill in the form that displays to create test users.

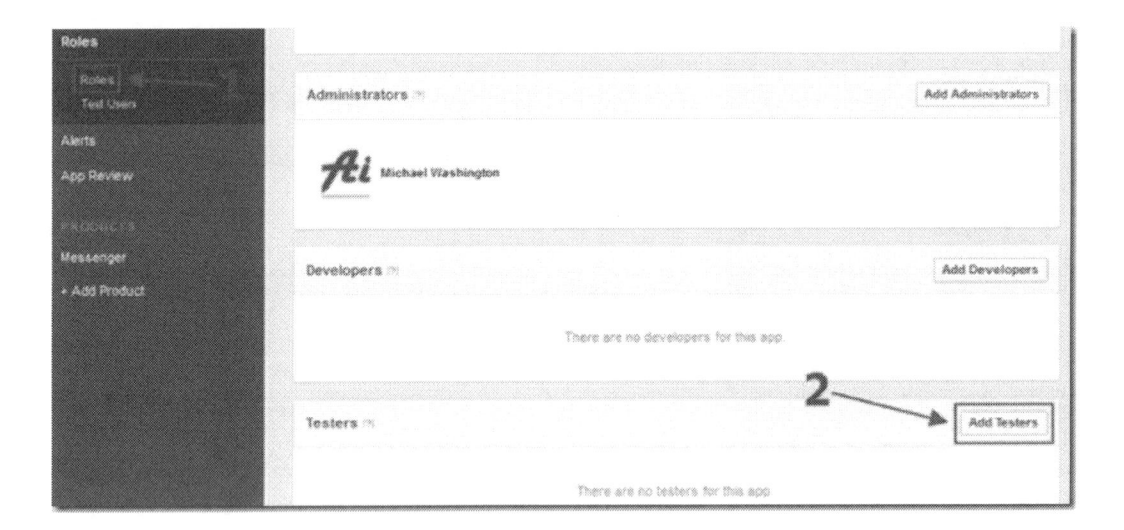

An Introduction to the Microsoft Bot Framework

To allow real **Facebook** users to test it, select **Roles** and then **Add Testers**.

Fill in the form that displays to allow access for the users.

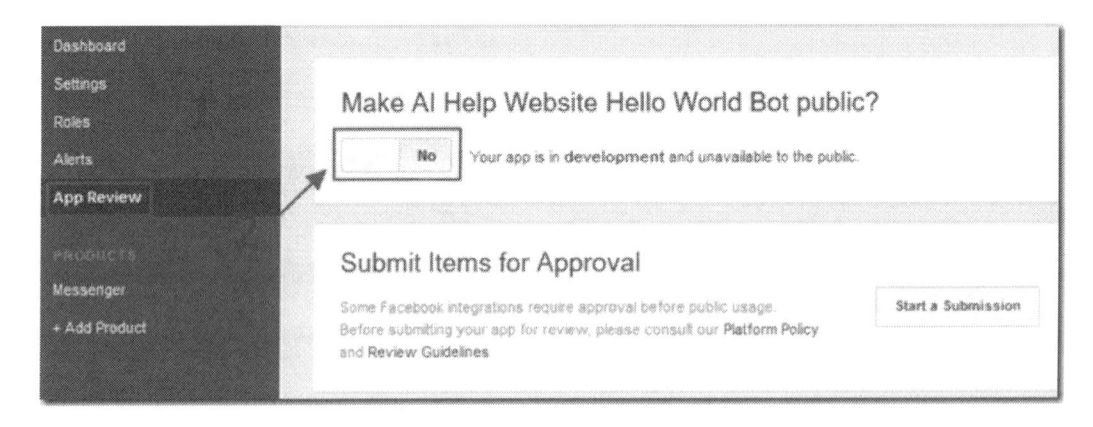

To make the **Bot** public, select **App Review**. Then click the slider to change it from **No** to **Yes**.

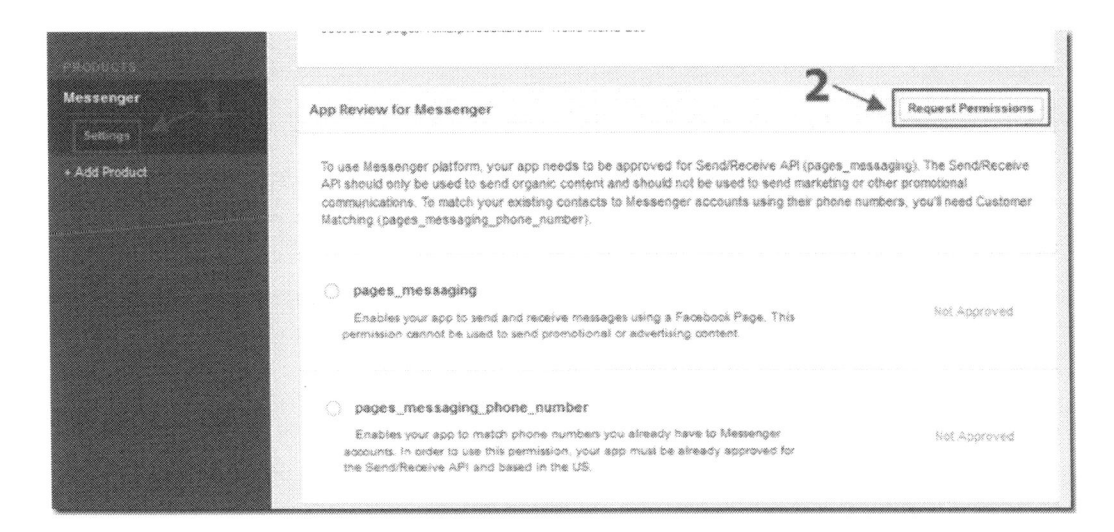

An Introduction to the Microsoft Bot Framework

To request the needed permissions, select **Settings** under **Messenger** then click the **Request Permissions** button.

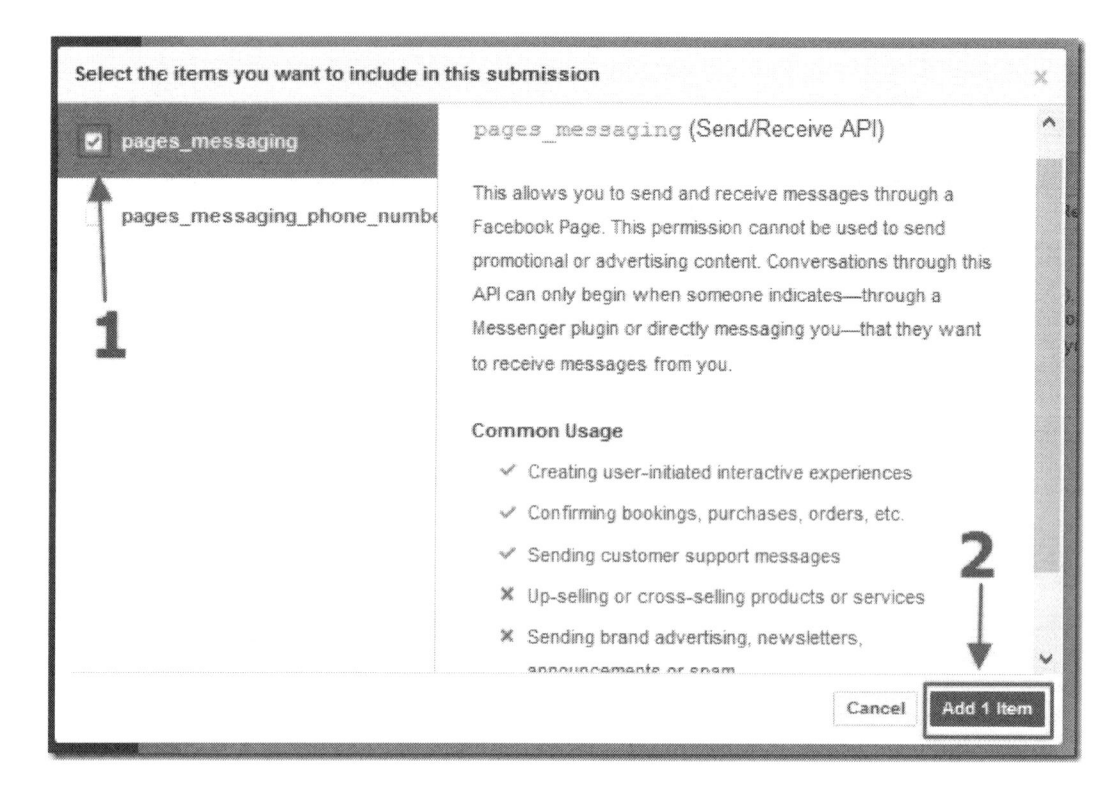

An Introduction to the Microsoft Bot Framework

Select **pages_messaging** and then click the **Add 1 Item** button.

See this page for more information on the App review process
https://developers.facebook.com/docs/messenger-platform/app-review

An Introduction to the Microsoft Bot Framework

About The Author

Michael Washington is an ASP.NET, C#, and Visual Basic programmer. He has extensive knowledge in process improvement, billing systems, and student information systems. He is a Microsoft MVP. He has a son, Zachary, and resides in Los Angeles with his wife, Valerie.

He has written several tutorials that are posted at http://AiHelpWebsite.com/Blog.

He is the author of six previous books:

- **Creating HTML 5 Websites and Cloud Business Apps Using LightSwitch In Visual Studio 2013-2015** (LightSwitchHelpWebsite.com)
- **Creating Web Pages Using the LightSwitch HTML Client In Visual Studio 2012** (LightSwitchHelpWebsite.com)
- **OData And Visual Studio LightSwitch** (LightSwitchHelpWebsite.com)
- **Creating Visual Studio LightSwitch Custom Controls (Beginner to Intermediate)** (LightSwitchHelpWebsite.com)
- **Building Websites with VB.NET and DotNetNuke 4** (Packt Publishing)
- **Building Websites with DotNetNuke 5** (Packt Publishing)

Printed in Great Britain
by Amazon